NATIONAL
GEOGRAPHIC

ATLAS

of

BEER

A server fills glasses with
kölsch in a traditional
bar in Cologne, Germany.

NATIONAL GEOGRAPHIC

ATLAS of BEER

a globe-trotting journey through the world of beer

NANCY HOALST-PULLEN & MARK W. PATTERSON
Foreword & Tasting Tips by Garrett Oliver

NATIONAL GEOGRAPHIC
WASHINGTON, D.C.

Beer drinkers gather at Grogan's Castle Lounge in Dublin, Ireland.

CONTENTS

THE WORLD OF BEER **6**
FOREWORD by Garrett Oliver **8**
AUTHORS' NOTE by Nancy Hoalst-Pullen & Mark W. Patterson **10**
ABOUT THIS BOOK **12**
INTRODUCTION **14**

THE WORLD
= of =
BEER

While beer is found in
nearly every country, the
countries highlighted here
were selected for inclusion
in this book based on their
beer history, culture,
and geography, and in
consultation with brewers
on six continents.

Alaska
(U.S.)

Canada

United States

NORTH
AMERICA
(pp. 138-185)

Hawai'i
(U.S.)

Mexico

Belize

Caribbean

PACIFIC

OCEAN

Costa Rica

Panama

Venezuela

Colombia

Ecuador

Peru

Brazil

French Polynesia
(France)

Tahiti

AUSTRALIA
AND OCEANIA
(pp. 248-271)

SOUTH
AMERICA
(pp. 186-213)

Argentina

Chile

ATLANTIC

OCEAN

United
Kingdom

Ireland

EUROPE
(pp. 26-137)

France

Spain

ARCTIC OCEAN

Norway
Sweden
Finland

Russia

Netherlands — Estonia
Denmark

Germany Poland
Czechia (Czech Republic)
Austria

Italy

Belgium

ASIA
(pp. 214–247)

Japan

South
Korea

China

India

PACIFIC

OCEAN

Taiwan

AFRICA
(pp. 272–291)

Thailand Vietnam Philippines
Cambodia

INDIAN

OCEAN

Gabon

Democratic
Republic
of the
Congo

Tanzania

Angola

Papua
New
Guinea

AUSTRALIA
AND OCEANIA
(pp. 248–271)

Fiji

Namibia

New
Caledonia
(France)

South
Africa

Australia

Country, dependency,
or region in this atlas

New
Zealand

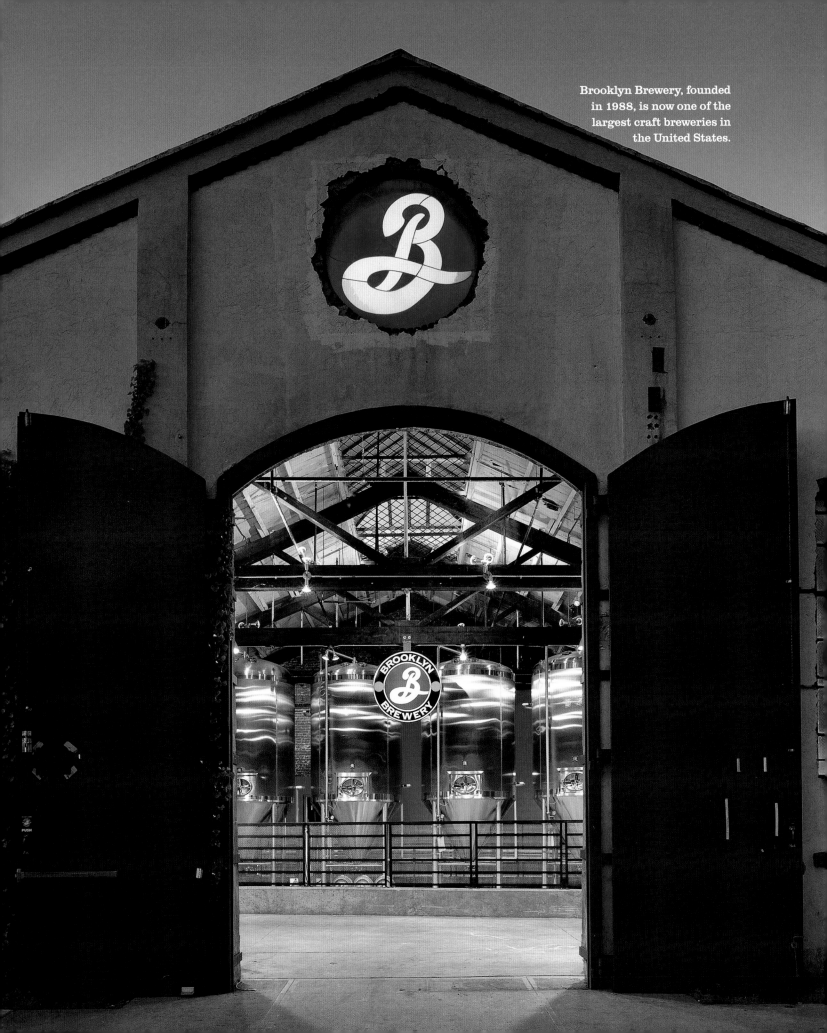

Brooklyn Brewery, founded in 1988, is now one of the largest craft breweries in the United States.

THE WORLD IN YOUR GLASS

GARRETT OLIVER
Brewmaster, Brooklyn Brewery

I didn't move to England for the beer. I moved for the music, because my best friend was moving there, and because *Lord of the Rings* and Monty Python were from there. But upon arriving in London in 1983, the beer was the first thing that struck me. It was amber, nearly brown, more flat than fizzy, and more warm than cold. Even now when I describe it, it doesn't sound very good. But I drank it, and my senses exploded into visions of flowers and hay, fruit and caramel, a swirling maelstrom of seemingly infinite subtleties. And in that moment, a small door opened. I stepped through, and on the other side was a better life.

Months later, in April 1984, I took a train down to Dover, boarded a ferry for France, and began a month-long trip across Europe. I drank bière de garde in France, lambic and Trappist beer in Belgium, weissbier and dunkel in West Germany, černé pivo in Czechoslovakia, Vienna lager in Vienna, and sharp, flinty pilsners in the mountains of Switzerland—each a talisman of its place and culture. When I finally got back to New York, I went to local bars and they offered . . . one type of beer. I knew that the United States could taste better than that. So I decided to brew my own, conjuring my experiences in Europe right there on my kitchen stovetop. Eventually beer wove a spell so powerful that I set aside my expensive film degree and became a brewmaster's apprentice. I have never looked back.

Three decades later, as the brewmaster of Brooklyn Brewery, I have been lucky enough to see the world while flying on a magic carpet of beer. I've drunk beer with a Bavarian prince in his castle; out of a communal tin bucket in a South African shantytown; at lunch amid Alsace's blooming hop fields; in a sugarcane field in Brazil; standing naked in the snow next to a frozen lake in Finland; and in front of a coal fire in Derbyshire, with mighty draft horses munching grass outside the door. People thank me for Brooklyn beer in all these places, not realizing that it was travel that gave *me* the gift of beer.

Beer is not just grains, hops, yeast, and water. Beer is love and friendship, technology and magic, identity and language, arguments and duels, music and fashion, conservatism and revolution, history and the future. In beer you can follow the rise of civilization, feel the character of nations, and witness the renaissance of our food culture. Because beer is not just a liquid. Beer is *people.* In these pages, you'll embark on an adventure with authors Nancy Hoalst-Pullen and Mark W. Patterson and meet the people and see the places that make the very best drink in the world. Follow the trails laid out here and you will surely come home with your own tales of grand beer-fueled travels and excellent new friends. ■

Garrett Oliver has been the brewmaster at Brooklyn Brewery since 1994. In 2015, Brooklyn was the 12th largest craft brewery in the United States by beer sales volume.

History, culture, and tastes around the world are responsible for a fascinating array of beer varieties.

WILL TRAVEL FOR BEER

NANCY HOALST-PULLEN, Ph.D. | MARK W. PATTERSON, Ph.D.

When do you become a beer person? Not just a beer lover, but someone who is passionate about understanding beer's many nuances: where it originated, how it's made, and why its many styles evolved the way they did. We realized we had become beer people on an early spring day at an Irish pub in San Francisco, during a break from a geography conference. As geographers, professors, and homebrewers, we found we weren't satisfied to sip our beers in contented silence. Instead, we pondered a medley of questions about the mysterious drink we held in our hands: Where did these ingredients come from? How did the water from a certain location affect the way the beer tastes? How did the environment, economics, politics, and culture influence this thing we're imbibing? These questions, along with some extensive traveling (we are geographers, after all), led us to produce our first beer book, *The Geography of Beer*, published in 2014.

The authors outside
Cafe Heffer in Amsterdam

Since then, we have returned again and again to the link between beer and geography: We've taught courses on it and taken students to Europe to learn about its many styles. The more we looked, the more we discovered that beer is going back to its roots—it is being brewed locally with regional ingredients, reflecting the history, culture, and environment of the place in which it's made. Nordic countries' farmhouse ales—*sahti* in Finland, *gotlandsdricka* in Sweden, and *hvidtøl* in Denmark—hark back to a time when all beer was made and consumed locally. Belgium's Trappist beers are steeped in the historic connection between brewing and the Catholic Church. Homebrews throughout Africa made with sorghum and millet are intimately connected to the landscape and the people who live there. We started to see how beer can shape history, influence culture, preserve tradition, and sometimes even resurrect it.

Our curiosity about how geography and beer interact led us to travel through six continents, 28 countries, and more than 160,000 miles (257,000 km) in 13 months. We visited more than 400 breweries and interviewed even more brewers, owners, general managers, and bartenders. We sampled more than 2,000 beers and witnessed how each country's craft beer movement is evolving. We traveled the world and immersed ourselves in beer history and culture. But this book is not our story; it's the story of how profoundly geography has influenced beer across different cultures, times, and places. It's the story of how the world of beer is becoming an ever clearer reflection of place. When we meet up to reminisce about our travels, it always comes with a toast: *For every wound, a balm. For every sorrow, cheer. For every storm, a calm. For every thirst, a beer.* ∎

ABOUT THIS BOOK

The *National Geographic Atlas of Beer* travels the world, exploring the link between taste and place. Organized geographically, this book includes all continents except Antarctica. Each chapter focuses on one continent, which is then divided into countries and regions. Each chapter explores how beer styles originated, what ingredients define them, and how each country's beer has evolved over time. More than 100 reference maps appear throughout the book. Entertaining sidebars provide beer-tasting tips, intriguing cultural anecdotes, and places to visit for the best beer experiences. Here's a look at some of the key features in the book:

CONTINENT INTRODUCTION

Appearing at the beginning of each chapter, these introductions provide an overview of a continent's beer history and culture, exploring a continent's beer stories—its geography, its signature ingredients, and its contemporary beer scene.

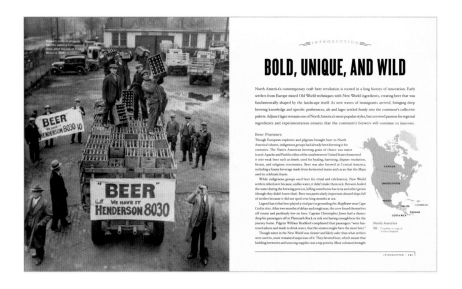

BREWLINE AND BEER FESTIVALS

"Brewline" marks notable dates in each continent's beer history. "Celebrations" sidebars, compiled from interviews with more than 400 brewers, note some of the continent's best beer festivals, and pop-up facts offer quirky details and trivia about beer in each place

BEER GUIDE
This feature highlights places to visit for authentic beer experiences, which have been compiled based on interviews with local brewers and industry insiders. A map highlights these venues and locates all of a country's breweries. The number next to each venue is not a ranking; it's there to indicate where to find it on the map.

LOCAL BREWS
Countries with extensive beer geographies are explored by region. In sidebars called "On Tap With Garrett Oliver," Brooklyn Brewery brewmaster Garrett Oliver highlights native beer styles or locally brewed craft beers. "Local Flavor" sidebars delve into local beer culture and brewing practices.

WHAT'S BREWING
Each chapter concludes by highlighting several up-and-coming beer countries within each continent, including facts about how much beer is being consumed and brewed, as well as the average cost of a bottle of beer in each country.

BEER MATTERS

HOW BEER HAS SHAPED OUR WORLD

With only four main ingredients—grains, water, hops, and yeast—beer might seem simple, but its history and geography are surprisingly complex. It's a drink that fueled workers as they built the great pyramids, bequeathed power to kings and nobles, bolstered soldiers during war, and sustained sailors in the age of exploration. Its vast cornucopia of styles has informed agriculture, economics, politics, and culture across six continents, and in turn has been shaped by them.

An early-20th-century
bar scene

Archaeological evidence suggests that beer was made as early as 7000 B.C. in China. Though grains were cultivated for bread, there is evidence to suggest that beer may have been a big part of what drove people to domesticate them. Beer is tied to human history, woven through so many of our important stories.

Beer has informed our art, dietary habits, explorations, and social rituals—it's even helped spark revolution. The Sumerians of ancient Mesopotamia produced the poem "A Hymn to Ninkasi," written nearly 4,000 years ago and dedicated to the goddess of beer. In the Middle Ages (A.D. 500–1500), beer in Europe was healthier and safer to drink than water. That's why royalty, nobility, and religious leaders fought for control of it: Whoever controlled beer production held a great deal of power. Beer sustained 15th- to 17th-century explorers as they pushed the boundaries of the known world. Part of the reason the *Mayflower* dropped off pilgrims at Plymouth Rock in 1620 instead of their intended destination was because the sailors were afraid of running out of beer. Beer money was critical in financing the Dutch Revolt (1568–1648), which led to the breakup of the Low Countries and the ultimate formation of Belgium. In this age of exploration and beyond, economics and warfare caused brewers to flee countries such as France and Austria to settle in countries such as Belgium and the United States. They applied their brewing knowledge to their new environments, shaping both culture and the beer styles we love today.

Beer's story is ultimately a story of geography: The crops grown in a certain place and the water used to brew it; how technology and human migration changed and influenced it; and how politics shaped its production and consumption. This book is about the evolution of beer, the adoption of styles, the importance of local traditions, and the exploration of new ones. Geography examines how people interact with their environment, looking for spatial similarities and differences. How did Bavaria's purity law of 1516 make its beer unique from what was being brewed outside its borders? Why didn't lager take off in Belgium in the same way it did in Germany? How did a beer style from Austria become the defining lager in Mexico? How have American hops influenced the world's beer styles? How did beer go from being a local product to one that is mass-produced and controlled by a powerful few?

Today, the world's four largest beer corporations control nearly half the world's beer market by volume and almost three-quarters by sales. The most consumed style, pale lager, originated in Bavaria (Germany) and Bohemia (Czechia), but its evolution has been a global one. These macrobreweries have made the world's beer scene nearly homogenous, engineering much of the local geography out of beer. That homogenization has allowed craft brewers—professional and amateur alike—to succeed at making interesting styles for beer drinkers seeking something different. What defines a craft brewery varies from country to country, but they are microbreweries that produce a relatively low volume of beer and make several styles. Craft brewers aren't afraid to experiment, and they continue to produce a dizzying array of styles that are redefining what beer is and can be.

The world's beerscape changes across time and space, continents and countries, and each place has its own story to tell. The aim of this book is to highlight these stories: the ingredients that make beer what it is; the styles that have survived industrialization, wars, prohibition, globalization, and changing tastes; the people who have shaped beer history; the places where beer is so ingrained that it defines a nation; and the places where beer is so new that brewers are making it up as they go along.

There will no doubt be debate over the countries, regions, breweries, beer festivals, and beer styles chosen for inclusion herein. Truth be told, it was an arduous, hotly debated task, and not everyone will be satisfied with our selections. We appreciate the brewers who helped guide our understanding of how beer has been, and continues to be, a thread in the fabric of life in these countries. We invite you to join us as we crisscross the globe in pursuit of understanding the ever evolving world of beer. ■

BEER TERROIR
HOW GEOGRAPHY SHAPES TASTE

Fields of barley and wheat adorn the landscape in Whitman County in Washington State, U.S.A.

The French word *terroir* translates to "earth" or "soil," but its meaning is more complicated. Terroir is about looking at taste from an agricultural point of view, defined by how environmental conditions—soil, precipitation, temperature, sunshine—influence the character of food and drink. In essence, terroir is about acknowledging that place is something you can taste. Though terroir is most often ascribed to wine, a beer's character can be greatly shaped by its four main ingredients: grains, hops, water, and yeast. The quality and character of these ingredients changes from place to place, and the conditions under which they are grown and found creates unique and discernible flavors that can make each beer unique.

Grains

Cereal grains—the edible seeds of grasses—are influenced widely by those who malt them (a process by which grains are germinated in order to develop the enzymes required to convert the starch within them to sugar). They also pick up different flavors based on where they are grown. Of the primary grains used in brewing—barley, wheat, and rye—barley is by far the most common. It dates back to the ancient Fertile Crescent around 8000 B.C., in what is now the Middle East, and some historians think that the desire for beer is what drove its cultivation. Barley is used as a base malt to provide proteins, minerals, and fermentable sugars; as a specialty malt to impart color, aroma, and flavor profiles; and as unmalted barley to provide beer with a thick, foamy head (think Guinness).

Domesticated at the same time as barley, wheat originates from the warm, moist eastern Mediterranean. Malted or unmalted, and usually combined with barley, wheat's proteins give beer a fuller mouthfeel and body, as well as a thicker and longer-lasting foam head.

Rye provides the crisp, slightly spicy character most commonly found in northern Europe's styles: bready, mint-flavored *kvass* from eastern Europe, juniper-laced *sahti* from Finland, and spicy, medieval *roggenbier* from Germany.

Secondary grains such as oats, maize (corn), rice, millet, and sorghum tend to play an important supporting role in a beer's grain bill—the grains and additional ingredients (adjuncts) that form a beer's backbone. Considered a weed until the

Barley

Wheat

Rye

Primary Grains

Primary grain-producing regions
Barley, wheat, and rye are the primary grains included.

Oats

Maize

Rice

Millet

Sorghum

start of the Bronze Age (2400–800 B.C.), oats were one of the last cereal grains to be domesticated. Though bitter as a primary grain, they add a smooth, rich texture as adjunct malt. Their use in stouts gained popularity in Scotland during the 1890s, touted for their supposed medicinal properties.

Maize, a highly fermentable grain, was first domesticated in Mexico and eventually migrated into South America, where it is used to make *chicha*. Rice is popular in Asia's light, clean lagers, as it imparts little taste. Maize and rice have both found their way into American-style lagers, where they help combat the haze and stability issues created by some U.S.-grown barley.

Millet and sorghum, both popular in Africa, are gluten free, prompting an increasing number of brewers around the world to try them in place of barley and wheat.

Hops

Hops are the female flowers (cones) of the hop plant, filled with alpha acids and essential oils that give beer aroma, flavor, and bitterness. Hops grown in the United States tend to be rank and dank, with big flavor notes of citrus and pine. But grow those same hops in England and the result will likely be more delicate

Secondary Grains

▨ Secondary grain-producing regions
Oats, maize, rice, millet, and sorghum are the secondary grains included.

ARCTIC OCEAN

NORTH AMERICA

ASIA

EUROPE

ATLANTIC OCEAN

PACIFIC OCEAN

PACIFIC OCEAN

AFRICA

OCEANIA

SOUTH AMERICA

INDIAN OCEAN

OCEANIA

AUSTRALIA

and muted. Old World varieties (deemed "noble hops") from Germany and Czechia (the Czech Republic), along with England's classic Golding and Fuggle hops, tend to be relatively low in bitterness and high in aroma, whereas American hops tend to be higher in both.

Water and Yeast

Prior to advances in chemistry and water treatment, water quality was determined solely by geographic location. Soft, low-mineral water is favored for creating the clean, crisp profile of lager, while hard, mineral-laden water improves the flavors of ale and dark beer. Water can influence a lot in brewing: the flavor of a beer's wort, the perceived bitterness of hops, and the fullness of malt.

Before yeast was first observed in 1680 and fermentation was officially understood in 1857, this living fungus found its way into beer spontaneously—from the natural environment—imparting the biggest taste profile of all. Sour beer, lambic, wild ale, and Flanders red all flaunt yeast and bacteria derived solely from what is in the air or wood around them. When it comes to a beer's terroir, water and yeast are the ultimate proof that geography matters. ▪

Hop vine with cones

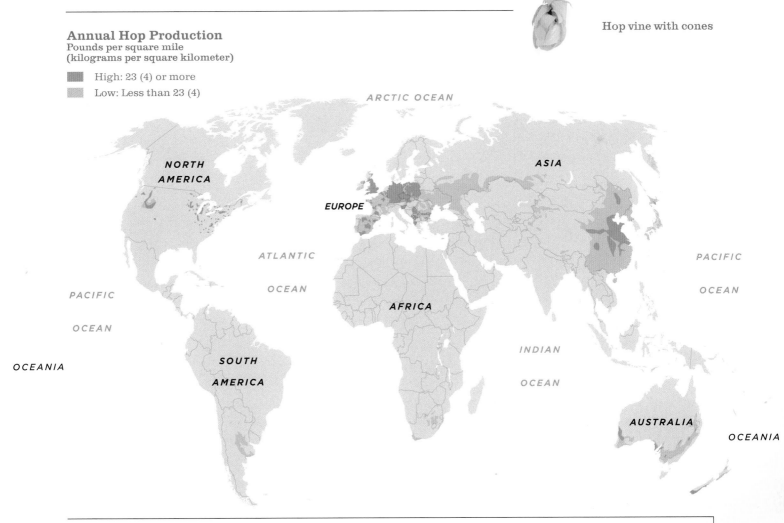

Annual Hop Production
Pounds per square mile
(kilograms per square kilometer)

▮ High: 23 (4) or more
▮ Low: Less than 23 (4)

ARCTIC OCEAN

NORTH AMERICA

ASIA

EUROPE

ATLANTIC OCEAN

PACIFIC OCEAN

PACIFIC OCEAN

OCEAN

AFRICA

PACIFIC OCEAN

OCEANIA

SOUTH AMERICA

INDIAN OCEAN

AUSTRALIA

OCEANIA

BEER CULTURE

AN EVER EVOLVING LANDSCAPE

Beer isn't only for the masses. The governments of countries such as Germany often serve beer to visiting dignitaries.

Beer has long been woven into the fabric of societies around the world. It has determined social status, reinforced religious rites and rituals, promoted community cohesion, and established cultural traditions and values. Beer has been a social lubricant, a medium for celebration, a medical prescription, and a catalyst for social reform. In some places, it is a living liquid heritage that defines a community, region, or nation.

On average, each person on Earth consumes almost 7 gallons (26 L) of beer a year. This average is a bit skewed, as beer isn't popular everywhere, but beer is the alcoholic drink of choice in most of North America, northern South America, western Europe, southern Africa, and Oceania. European countries have some of the world's highest consumption rates, with Czechia (the Czech Republic) leading the way at 38 gallons (144 L) per capita a year. It's no surprise that many of the countries with the highest consumption rate lie within the geographic "beer belt" between northern Europe and the United Kingdom, where conditions are ideal for growing barley and hops, and beer is historically the popular drink of choice. Consumption also has a lot to do with population size: The United States, Brazil, Russia, India, and China collectively make up nearly 15 percent of the global beer market. Beer consumption is projected to rise over the next few years, due in part to the increasing number of beer drinkers drawn to the ever expanding styles craft breweries provide.

Unlike consumption, beer production has declined. Macrobreweries making ubiquitous lagers have experienced the biggest hit, in part because of the global rise in craft brewing and an increasing shift back to local brewing. Consumers typically drink less craft beer in a sitting, but they pay more for it. The willingness to pay more for craft beer, called premiumization, has seen craft beer's global market share rise steadily since 2009.

Macrobreweries have deep pockets and big brand power, and their pervasive pale lagers aren't in danger of disappearing. These brewing giants are driving consolidation in the industry, buying up popular, well-established craft breweries and bringing them into the fold. But that hasn't stopped craft brewers from continuing to make a big impression. With a return to place-based beer, they are popularizing hyperlocal brands, bringing back long-forgotten styles, and creating

Annual Beer Consumption
Gallons per capita
(liters per capita)

- Greater than 16 (61)
- 7.8–16 (30–61)
- 2.6–7.7 (10–29)
- Less than 2.6 (10)
- Data not available

beers that defy categorization. In many countries, the number of small breweries is growing—most Americans now live within 10 miles (16 km) of a craft brewery. Beer is increasingly being brewed just around the corner, creating a local beer culture brimming with breweries, brewpubs, bars, and specialty stores.

Beer Types and Styles

Beer types can be divided in many ways and called by many names. When beer is classified based on its manner of fermentation, there are three main types: warm, top-fermenting (ale); cool, bottom-fermenting (lager); and wild, spontaneously fermenting (lambic and wild ale). But it's really the yeast used in the fermentation that defines its type: *Saccharomyces cerevisiae* is used for ale, *Saccharomyces pastorianus* is used for lager, and a multitude of wild yeasts, including *Brettanomyces,* are used to make lambic and wild ale.

Styles tend to fall under one of these beer-type umbrellas, but they are always being created and re-created. So is there a set universal number of recognized beer styles? Well, no. But are style designations helpful in recognizing, categorizing, and replicating colors, tastes, and characteristics, and appreciating a beer's origins and traditions? Most certainly.

Annual Beer Production
Millions of U.S. beer barrels per year
(millions of hectoliters per year)

 Greater than 5.1 (6)
1.9–5.1 (2.2–6)
0.6–1.8 (0.7–2.1)
Less than 0.6 (0.7)
Data not available

The Geographic Origins of Major Beer Styles

Beer styles come from all over the world, but the majority originated
in Belgium, Germany, the United Kingdom, and the United States.

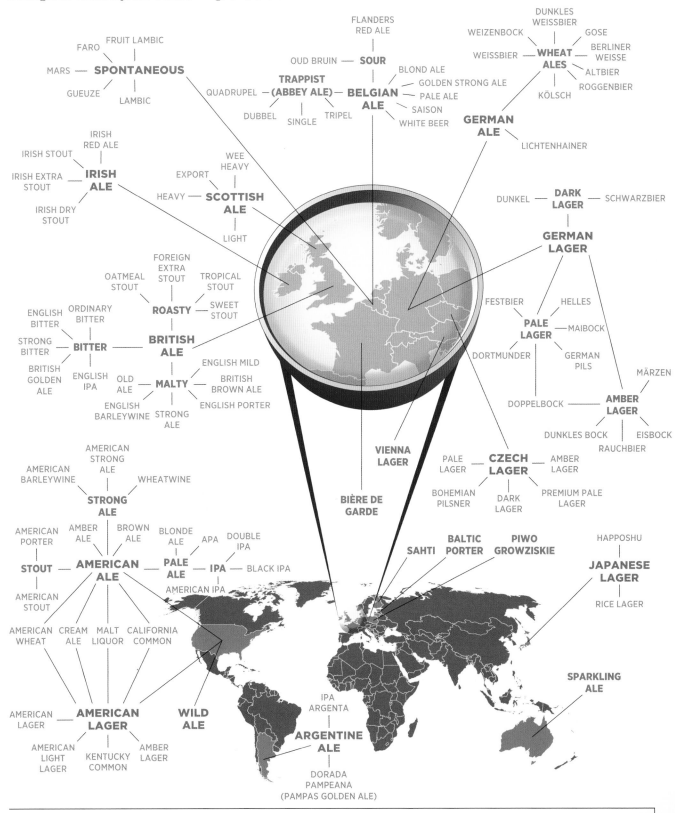

Pouring the Perfect Pint

Contrary to beer folklore (or just beer snobbery), canned beer can be just as good as its bottled counterpart. But regardless of how your beer is packaged, most styles are meant to be drunk from a glass. Pouring beer into a glass opens up its aromas—one of the elements brewers work hard to create. Follow these general serving tips to enjoy any beer in its optimal form.

CHECK YOUR TEMPERATURE.

Beer styles don't always have to be served ice cold. In fact, most shouldn't be. Temperature is key to enjoying any given beer style, so follow these three general rules of thumb: First, a beer's serving temperature should increase as its alcohol by volume (ABV) increases. Second, darker beer generally should be served at warmer temperatures. Third, beer that has little to no yeast flavor, like clean, crisp-tasting lagers, should be served cold. Beer should never be served in a frosted glass: The intense cold just dilutes its flavor.

NOT ALL BEER FOAMS ALIKE.

Having a head (foam) on top of your beer isn't always bad. In fact, it is preferred for certain beer styles. Some styles have large heads because they are unfiltered,

The Brewing Process

While the brewing process has many subtle variations and doesn't always involve big machines like these, this series of steps is generally what turns grains, hops, water, and yeast into the drink we love.

   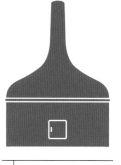 

1
Milling

Malted grains (grains that have been steeped in water and allowed to germinate, maximizing their starch content) are milled in a grain mill, crushing the seeds to expose their centers.

2
Mashing

The milled grains (grist) are soaked in a mash tun's hot-water bath, activating enzymes that transform starches and proteins into fermentable sugars. This sugar water is called wort.

3
Lautering

The wort is separated from the spent grains in a lauter tun. Sparging then commences: a process of rinsing the spent grains to extract as much sugar from them as possible.

4
Boiling

The wort is boiled in a kettle, usually for around an hour. Hops are added at various stages—at the beginning of the boil for bitterness, and later on for flavor and aroma.

5
Whirlpooling

Hopped wort is sent to a whirlpool, which separates out hop fragments and any remaining protein strains.

like wheat ales—the result of residual yeast, hops, and proteins. Foam, which is around 20 percent beer mixed with gas, can get rid of carbon dioxide that imparts a bitter taste. It can also produce subtle changes in the texture of beer that cannot be achieved in the brewing process. If you plan to drink a cask-conditioned ale, or one from a barrel rather than a keg or bottle, expect very little head (if any) and a mouthfeel that's a bit flat.

The pattern beer foam makes on the side of a glass is called **lacing**. It is usually a sign of a clean glass and good-quality ingredients.

GLASSWARE MATTERS.

Proper glassware reveals a beer's character and accentuates its color, aroma, and taste. While some bars use a pint glass regardless of the style they're serving, this certainly isn't the case everywhere. In Belgium, every brand of beer has its own glassware, designed to enhance the drinking experience. The glassware is so important that it's sometimes created before the beer itself (see page 40).

BUBBLES CAN MEAN YOUR GLASS IS DIRTY.

Don't be put off if bubbles rise up in a center column in your beer. That's just carbon dioxide escaping, which is completely normal. But gas bubbles that stick to the sides of your glass? Well, that's a sign that the glass is dirty. A dirty glass can kill a beer's head, which contributes to the beer's flavor and texture. ■

6 |
Chilling
The wort is quickly cooled using a heat exchanger until its temperature is low enough that yeast can be introduced. The quicker the process, the less likely beer is to oxidize and produce off flavors.

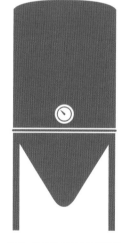

7 |
Fermenting
Wort is transferred to a fermentation tank and yeast is added. The yeast eats the sugars, creating two main by-products: alcohol and carbon dioxide.

8 |
Filtering (optional)
Any remaining particles—grains, hops, or yeast—are removed using a filter. Some brewers choose to skip this step and leave their beer cloudy. Filtering can happen before, during, or after step 9.

9 |
Conditioning
When the majority of sugars have been converted to alcohol, the beer is transferred to a brite tank or barrels. The yeast settles, the beer gains clarity, and off-flavors are reduced.

10 |
Packaging
Beer is poured into bottles, cans, casks, or kegs. Many beers are then carbonated, before being labeled and sent out into the world.

Beer is an integral part of cultures across Europe, especially in Belgium, where sidewalk cafés dot the streets of Ghent.

CHAPTER
1

EUROPE

Before mechanization, hop pickers wore stilts to reach the tallest hop vines during harvest time.

AN EPIC BREWING HISTORY

In Europe, beer is a reflection of place. Beer's terroir is irrevocably shaped by the geography of where it is brewed: the cereal grains and hop varieties brewers have access to, the mineral levels in the water supply, the wild yeast and microbiota floating in the air. And in turn, it is shaped by how brewers deal with these conditions and ingredients—the seasonality of when a beer is brewed, the temperatures used during fermentation, and even the rules (or lack thereof) about what constitutes a beer. Without the distinct differences and idiosyncrasies developed and parsed over time, Europe's beer scene would not be as eclectic, revered, or replicated as it is today.

Europe's Beer Belt

Europe is where many of the world's favorite beer styles emerged, proliferated, and evolved. Many came out of the European "beer belt": an area situated between northern Europe and the United Kingdom where beer has traditionally been the most popular beverage. This region grew up between the warmer grape-growing wine regions of southern Europe and the colder climates of northern Europe, where distilled grain alcohols (predominantly vodka) prevailed. England, Belgium, and Germany easily define the beer belt, though other countries within it have made noteworthy contributions (think farmhouse ales such as Finland's *sahti*, Sweden's *gotlandsdricka*, and Norway's seasonal *juleøl*).

Grain cultivation began in northern Europe during the Neolithic period (circa 7000–3000 B.C.), some 6,000 years ago. People learned how to raise livestock and grow cereal grains, and they developed tools for grinding and processing these grains, including an understanding of how to ferment them. By the fourth century B.C., when the Greeks conquered Egypt, beer was common throughout much of Europe. The Greeks (and, later, the Romans) viewed beer as inferior to wine, but when Roman legions found themselves occupying hostile, wine-barren regions like Hispania and Britain, they built breweries to ensure soldiers wouldn't have to go

Europe

Country in this chapter

7,367
The total number of breweries in Europe

without. Throughout the rule of the Western Roman Empire (31 B.C.–A.D. 476), the Celts, Gauls, and Germanic tribes preferred some version of beer over wine.

The demise of the wine-loving Roman Empire caused an interesting transition in terms of who brewed beer in the Middle Ages (A.D. 500–1500). The rise in power of the Roman Catholic Church moved much of the brewing knowledge and process behind monastery walls, when previously most beer had been brewed at home by women. But not all holy beer was created equal. More often than not, the monks kept higher-alcohol beer for their own consumption, giving the lower-alcohol brews to weary travelers, pilgrims, and paupers. Monastic beer was often sold to raise money for the church, to pay taxes, and to obtain goods, labor, or other services. Whoever controlled beer controlled a powerful economic tool.

As the merchant class rose during the High Middle Ages (A.D. 1000–1300) and European royalty untangled itself from the church, medieval beer was once again made at home. But dense housing in urban centers posed a problem for

celebrations Europe's Best Beer Festivals

Barcelona Beer Festival | **BARCELONA** | SPAIN | Catalonia's largest beer festival offers visitors more than 300 craft beers, most from Spain's burgeoning scene. Go to "meet the brewer" sessions and enjoy delicious Spanish tapas. *March*

Czech Beer Festival | **PRAGUE** | CZECHIA | Come to this festival in the capital of the country with the world's highest beer consumption per capita and sample more than 70 Czech beers of various styles. *May*

Great British Beer Festival | **LONDON** | ENGLAND | Called the "world's largest pub" with good reason, this five-day event, organized by the Campaign for Real Ale, hosts some 66,000 people and features more than 900 types of beer. *August*

Belgian Beer Weekend | **BRUSSELS** | BELGIUM | A beer festival held in the grandest of settings: Brussels's La Grand-Place. Sip one of the many Belgian beers served amid the pomp and circumstance, including offerings from all six of Belgium's Trappist monasteries (see page 38). *September*

Oktoberfest | **MUNICH** | GERMANY | Technically, Oktoberfest is not a beer fest, but rather a celebration of Bavarian culture in which beer has always played a major part (see page 54). Beer festivals don't get any bigger than this. *September/October*

EurHop! Roma Beer Festival | **ROME** | ITALY | This festival is one of the largest craft beer celebrations in Italy. There is plenty of Italian cuisine to enjoy while sipping a sampling of the festival's 250 beers. *October*

A server carries an armful of beer at Oktoberfest.

brewers: Fires used in the brewing process often turned into deadly infernos. Communal breweries formed in response to this danger, turning brewing into a professional business. It wasn't long until brewers formed ale-brewing guilds to teach the trade, impose regulations and taxes, gain political influence, and open taverns. "Purity laws" cropped up as early as 1156 in Germany, defining exactly what was and was not a beer.

A Profitable Trade Good

During the Middle Ages, Europe's various seafaring empires—the Vikings (8th–11th century), and the German Hansa, Dutch, and British from the 11th century on—started trading and exploring, and they took their ales with them. Beer was essential for these sailors because it provided a reliable source of

Historical Alcohol Belts of Europe

- Beer
- Beer and Vodka
- Beer and Wine
- Vodka
- Vodka and Wine
- Wine

sustenance on long voyages and also because it was a valuable export good that contributed greatly to their wealth. Hopped beer brewed with hardy wheat and barley proved especially well suited to sea travel. Hamburg, Germany, proved a good supplier of these ingredients, which turned the city into the center of the Hanseatic League: an economic alliance of maritime merchants that controlled trade in Europe from the 12th to 16th century and made beer and brewing a widely profitable business.

Beer continued to influence the economy and people's tastes beyond the Middle Ages. In the Netherlands, Amsterdam's skilled brewing industry led the region into its golden age (circa 1600–1690), bringing hopped beer to Britain and, later, to colonial America. As the British Empire grew, the India pale ale (IPA) emerged—first documented in 1829 and destined for soldiers and expats in India (see page 70). In England, the mass-produced style known as London porter brought forth industrial-scale brewing innovations, but it fell out of favor in the 19th century because of the heavy taxation on grains and hops. Industrialization and immigration sent German brewers and German-style lager across the globe. Lager became—and remains—the world's most popular type of beer.

Geography, culture, politics, and history all played a role in creating modern-day

brewline Historic Moments in Beer

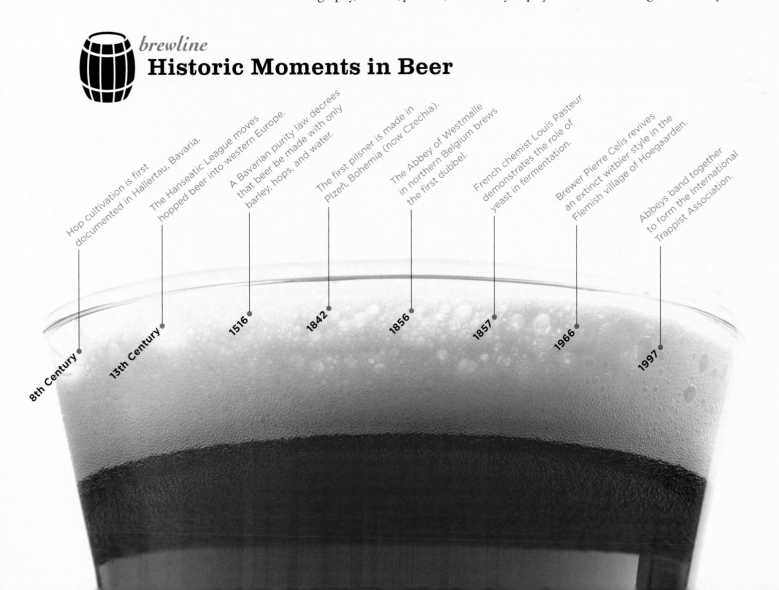

Hop cultivation is first documented in Hallertau, Bavaria.
8th Century

The Hanseatic League moves hopped beer into western Europe.
13th Century

A Bavarian purity law decrees that beer be made with only barley, hops, and water.
1516

The first pilsner is made in Plzeň, Bohemia (now Czechia).
1842

The Abbey of Westmalle in northern Belgium brews the first dubbel.
1856

French chemist Louis Pasteur demonstrates the role of yeast in fermentation.
1857

Brewer Pierre Celis revives an extinct witbier style in the Flemish village of Hoegaarden.
1966

Abbeys band together to form the International Trappist Association.
1997

regional preferences for certain types of beer: dark, sessionable (lower alcohol) stout and porter in Ireland; mild pale ale in the United Kingdom; pale lager in Czechia (the Czech Republic) and southeastern Germany; and saison and sour ale in Belgium. They also have turned Europe into a veritable patchwork of beer tastes with distinct geographic boundaries in which certain styles dominate.

At the end of a long work week, workers in London's financial district often head for pubs like the Trading House to unwind over a pint.

Global Reach, Local Focus

Today, the beer scene in Europe is dichotomous. As of 2015, the world's three largest beer companies—AB InBev, Heineken International, and Carlsberg Group—all headquartered in Europe, collectively control nearly 50 percent of the global market. But there is also a resurgence of local styles and breweries celebrating Europe's provincial beer scenes and flavors. Brewers are introducing local adjuncts and reviving native styles, bringing back indigenous flavors that had fallen by the wayside.

The globalization of commodities can be looked at in two ways as well. It has enabled the rise of the global brewing titans, which tend to brew the terroir out of beer. But it has also expanded the reach of Europe's beer and beer culture, influencing beer fans and aspiring brewers on many distant shores. The world's beer lovers are exploring Europe's many flavors, discovering the joys of almost limitless choices.

At Brasserie Nüetnigenough in Brussels, pairing Belgian beers with local cuisine is an art.

BELGIUM

EUROPE'S BEER CAPITAL

Sometimes the richest treasures come in the smallest packages. Such is the case with the Kingdom of Belgium, nestled between France, Germany, the Netherlands, and the English Channel. Though only around the size of Maryland in the United States, it produces more than 400 beer styles—far more than anywhere else, and many of these defy categorization.

How did such a small country become so important in the world of brewing? Beer has long been ingrained in the region's culture, in large part because of its geography. Belgium's beer history started more than 2,000 years ago, when the region was home to the Gauls. Romans are often credited with bringing beer to northern Europe in 55 B.C., but similar, more potent Gallic brews were already being made there. When Emperor Julius Caesar came conquering in 58 B.C., he was surprised that the people he called the "Belgae" consumed such large quantities of this strong drink. Given that the region was perfect for growing barley and too cold to grow grapes, it makes sense that beer was the Gallic drink of choice.

Brewing Influences

Latin and Germanic influences intermingled in the region that would come to be called Belgium, allowing brewers over the centuries to absorb the best of both. The Romans brought winemaking, the influence of which can still be seen in many of Belgium's popular beer styles, while the Germanic tribes brought brewing techniques and ingredients that forever shaped Belgium's beer.

AT A GLANCE
Featured Locations

🛢 Brewery
★ Capital
● City
PAJOTTENLAND Part of province
WEST FLANDERS Province
FLANDERS Region

The region's brewers continued to absorb ingredients and techniques introduced by its revolving door of European conquerors, but they largely resisted the styles and purity laws of neighboring Bavaria (now Germany). Though Bavaria's 1516 beer purity law (see page 53) decreed that only barley, water, and hops could be used in brewing in that country, Belgian brewers continued to experiment with the herbs, spices, and other adjuncts introduced by European powers. Everything from coffee and mustard to an assortment of fruits have found their way into Belgian brewing.

The scientific and technological innovations of the industrial revolution (1750–1900) heralded the discovery and isolation of yeast strains. This prompted

Above: Though Belgium is famous for its beer, Brussels has only a handful of breweries, including Brasserie En Stoemelings.

Right: Delirium Café in Brussels holds the world record for the most beers available to patrons: more than 2,500.

European brewers to select and brew with specific strains, but some of Belgium's brewers chose to stick with local yeast and spontaneous fermentation (see page 46), welcoming the sourness created by bacteria and yeast. Such choices kept Belgian beer unique, and incredibly region specific, creating styles that were—and remain—distinctly Belgian.

Keeping It Belgian

Belgium is home to a plethora of native beer styles, and it's also home to the world's most prolific beer producer. Industry giant AB InBev is headquartered in the city of Leuven, with one of its most popular beer brands, Stella Artois, based nearby.

Speakeasy

Three Ways to Say "Cheers!"

Primary Languages

◼ Dutch and French
◼ Dutch
◼ French
◼ German

If you want a pint in Flanders, where they speak Belgian Dutch, ask for **een pintje** (pronounced ayn PINCH-ya), or order by making a fist then putting out your pinkie finger. Cheers by saying **"Op uw gezondheid"** (op oow guh-zohnd'-HAYT) or **"Santé!"** (SAN-tey).

If you are in Brussels or Wallonia, where most Belgians speak French, go to the **brasserie** (BRA-sir-REE), or pub, and ask for a beer by saying **"Une bière"** (oon BEE-yair), then cheers with **"Santé!"**

In the German-speaking East Cantons, raise your **bier** at the **brauerei** (BROW-er-ee) and toast by saying **"Prost!"**

TRAPPIST BEERS

A LOOK BEHIND THE ABBEY WALLS

The story of Trappist beer begins in 1098, with a group of monks from the Benedictine abbey of Molesme in what is now eastern France. These monks wanted to pursue ideals of earlier times: a strict adherence to the original teachings of Saint Benedict, an effective balance between prayer and work, a detachment from worldly affairs, and communal-style living more in line with that of the early Christian apostles. The monks moved to a monastery near Cîteaux, France, to pursue this life of hard work and poverty. Their ethos caught on, and the Cistercian Order spread across Europe.

The early Cistercian abbeys focused on manual labor, many supporting themselves by growing crops and brewing ale. By 1664, study and learning had come to dominate the monks' days, prompting the monks at the Abbey La Grande Trappe in Normandy, France, to pursue reforms meant to return—once again—to a simpler way of life. They changed the name of their order to Trappists and brewed beer to support themselves.

This happy brewing era hit troubled times in the 1780s, when Holy Roman Emperor Joseph II implemented reforms that closed monasteries and limited the role of religious orders. A decade later, the French Revolution and the subsequent rule of Napoleon forced monks to flee northern France, with many Trappist monks resettling in Belgium, which now has six Trappist monasteries that all brew and sell beer.

The Trappist monks' commitment to hard work and study led them to refine the brewing process over the centuries. They figured out they could get different strengths of beer by running water through a mash more than once, keeping the first and strongest runoff for themselves while giving the later ones to the poor who sought refuge within their walls. Monk brewers likely marked their *cervisia duplex* (Latin for "double ale") with an XX on the cask, with weaker *simplex* beer marked with a single X. Trappist styles can be quite high in alcohol content, including the pale yellow single or blond (4.8 to 6 percent ABV); the brown, boozy dubbel (6 to 9 percent); and the even stronger quadrupel (above 10 percent). The golden tripel (8 to 10 percent), created in the 1930s and given its official name in 1956, was designed by a

Monks have been brewing at Chimay since 1862.

Abbaye Notre-Dame d'Orval is one of six abbeys in Belgium that produce official Trappist ale.

brewer for the Abbey of Westmalle when pale beer was all the rage.

The six remaining Trappist monasteries are often less well known than the breweries they house: Achel (Saint Benedictus-Abbey), Chimay (Abbaye Notre-Dame de Scourmont), Orval (Abbaye Notre-Dame d'Orval), Rochefort (Abbey of Notre-Dame de Saint-Rémy), Westvleteren (Saint-Sixtus Abbey of Westvleteren), and Westmalle (Abbey of Westmalle). None of the monasteries are open to the public, which lends Trappist beer a certain mystique. For instance, Saint-Sixtus Abbey produces just over 4,000 barrels of beer each year, consumers need appointments to stop in and purchase beer at the brewery, and they are only allowed to purchase two cases per visit. It's no wonder that a bottle of Westvleteren 12, a quadrupel often rated one of the top five beers in the world, fetches $20 or more on the open market.

Unlike other styles, Trappist beer cannot be brewed outside Trappist breweries, and Trappist monks must be involved in the brewing process—in fact, Trappist beer is protected. In 1985, a court in Belgium ruled that the term "Trappist" was a protected name and a recognized designation of origin. The ruling eventually led to the creation of the International Trappist Association (ITA) and its Authentic Trappist Product (ATP) label. Only sanctioned Trappist monasteries can use the term "Trappist" when marketing their goods. ■

But even while this industry giant fills the world's shelves with lager, the love for Belgium's regional beer styles is alive and well. In 2016, UNESCO formally recognized the integral role of beer and brewing in Belgium's social and culinary life, showcasing its importance as a tangible part of the nation's identity.

Belgian Signature Beer Styles

While Belgian beer is in a category all its own, it does have a few major recognized styles, all of which have been shaped by their region of origin.

1 | ABBEY ALE

Historically abbey ale was brewed by monks, and Trappist ale still is (see page 38). Types of abbey ale, all quite strong, include the rich and malty dubbel; the complex, golden tripel; and the boozy, dark, fruit-flavored quadrupel. In these top-fermented brews, yeast and fermentable sugars get added during bottling, resulting in a taste that can actually improve over time.

local flavor
The Perfect Glass

While beer is served at varying temperatures (cold, chilled, cellar, room) to bring out its best characteristics, the glassware it's served in is what matters most in Belgium. Pouring beer into a glass opens up its flavors and aromas, helps retain its head, and makes drinking it a more eventful experience. Belgians believe so fervently in the importance of glassware that cafés often use a brewery's own distinctive glasses, which are made to highlight the color, aroma, and taste of each beer the brewery produces. Some Belgian breweries engineer their glassware even before they create the beer that goes into it. As a result, many Belgian cafés and pubs stock hundreds, if not thousands, of glasses. If bartenders do not have the proper glassware for a particular beer, they will often ask the customer if a different glass is acceptable, or if they would rather choose another beer.

| Strong Dark Ale (Goblet) | Strong Ale (Tulip) | Flanders Red (Tulip) | Dubbel (Flute) | Lambic (Flute) | White Beer (Weizen) | Tripel (Goblet) | Saison (Tulip) | Oud Bruin (Snifter) |

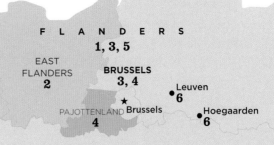

2 | FLEMISH SOUR

Revered for its complex and fruity winelike taste, this "mixed fermentation" style uses a combination of top-fermenting brewer's yeast, *Saccharomyces cerevisiae*, and a cocktail of various wild yeasts and bacteria. Flanders red ale, indigenous to West Flanders, is aged in oak casks and is generally more sour than the *oud bruin* (Flanders brown) style from East Flanders.

3 | GOLDEN STRONG

The unifying characteristic of most Belgian beer is Belgian yeast strains, with their distinctive notes of fruit, spice, and even bubblegum. Enter the Belgian golden strong—and the emblematic Duvel (a warped form of the Flemish word for "devil")—a crisp, highly carbonated, and surprisingly boozy ale style that originates from a Scotch ale's single yeast strain.

4 | LAMBIC

This winelike sour beer is spontaneously fermented by unique Belgian microbiota found in and around Brussels and Pajottenland. It can be aged for years in port wine or sherry barrels. Varieties include straight lambics, which are unblended and lightly carbonated; gueuze, made from blending young and old lambics; faro, sweetened with darkened candy sugar; and various fruit lambics like *kriek* (cherry) and *framboise* (raspberry). Most taste a bit dry, sour, and funky.

5 | SAISON

Arguably one the most individualistic and interpretive beer styles, this seasonal farmhouse-ale style originated in agrarian French-speaking Wallonia and some agricultural regions of Flanders. Light in color, low in alcohol, and high in carbonation, these provisional beers were brewed for working-class villagers, farmers, and seasonal *saisonniers* (farmhands).

6 | WHITE BEER

White beer (called *witbier* in Flemish and *bière blanche* in French) is a wheat-style ale from the farming region east of Brussels, created by Hoegaarden's monks around 1445. After its near extinction following World War II, the style was revived in Hoegaarden by milkman turned brewer Pierre Celis in 1966. Although the style was historically sour, today's tart contemporary can be spiced with coriander and bitter orange peel, a nod to the plants medieval brewers used to flavor beer and thwart spoilage.

Origins of Beer Styles

- ▓ Part of province
- ▓ Province within region
- ▒ Region
- ★ Capital
- ● City
- **1** Featured beer style

BEER GUIDE

WHERE BEER LOVERS GO

A trip to Belgium would not be complete without experiencing a tasting at a Belgian brewery or café. Out of the many beer experiences on offer, Belgian brewers and beer industry experts recommend a visit to these destinations.

1 | Brasserie Cantillon

Brussels

One of the country's most famous lambic breweries, Cantillon feels like a living museum. It's a labyrinth of weathered boards, antiquated equipment, and dimly lit surroundings—all at various levels of unkempt—that create ideal conditions for the production of its sought-after lambic and gueuze.

2 | Brouwerij De Halve Maan

Bruges

Founded in 1564, De Halve Maan is the only remaining brewery within Bruges's walls and is still producing beer after nearly 500 years. With a one-of-a-kind pipeline completed in 2016, beer flows under the medieval streets and buildings of Bruges, from the historic brewery to its bottling plant some two miles (three kilometers) away. Be sure to climb to the brewery's rooftop for picturesque city views.

3 | Brouwerij Rodenbach

Roeselare

This brewery, which started producing beer in 1821, makes Rodenbach Grand Cru, which defines the Flanders red ale style. Stop by for a tour—Rudy, the longtime brewmaster, may even be there to answer questions.

4 | Poperinge

Flanders

Poperinge is Belgium's agricultural hops heartland. Visit a Belgian hop farm to see how hops are harvested, or visit the Hopmuseum Poperinge and learn about the local history of hops. The Poperinge Bierfestival, in October, features more than 25 breweries.

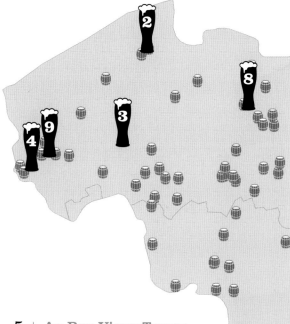

5 | Au Bon Vieux Temps

Brussels

The entrance to this café, located near La Grand-Place, is ornate but small—walking too fast could mean missing it! The bar is filled with old wooden tables and counters as well as beautiful stained-glass windows. It offers the prized and hard-to-get Trappist ale Westvleteren 12.

6 | Brouwerij Stella Artois

Leuven

Even if mass-produced lager isn't your thing, a trip to Stella Artois is worth making. The brewery documents the beer's rich history, and the tour shows off the inner workings of a large modern brewery. After the tour, stop by the bar and learn how to properly pour and drink a Stella Artois.

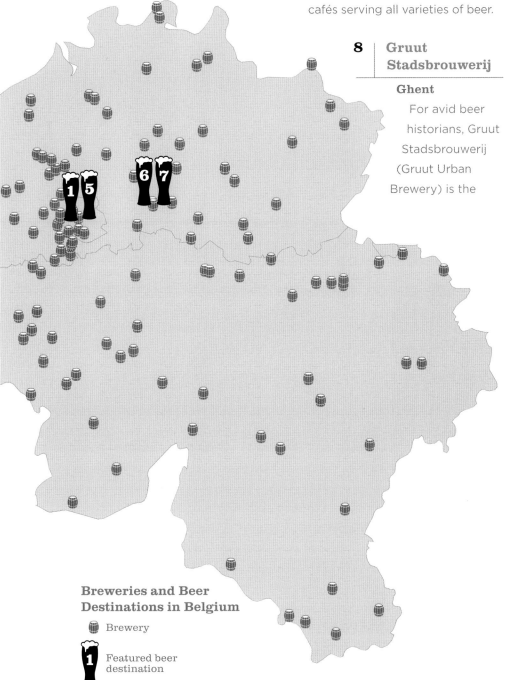

Breweries and Beer Destinations in Belgium

🛢 Brewery

 Featured beer destination

7 | Oude Markt

Leuven

Originally built in 1150, Leuven's Oude Markt (Old Market) claims to be the world's longest bar. Don't make the mistake of looking for a bar here—the town's rectangular center *is* the bar, with nearly 40 cafés serving all varieties of beer.

8 | Gruut Stadsbrouwerij

Ghent

For avid beer historians, Gruut Stadsbrouwerij (Gruut Urban Brewery) is the place to visit. It brews beer using a medieval assortment of herbs like gruit (see page 72). Take a stroll to the riverfront to see the Bierhaus; St. Michael, the church built with money from the local brewers' guild; and Café t'Galgenhuis, the city's smallest pub.

9 | Sint-Sixtusabdij Westvleteren

Westvleteren

A pilgrimage to the brewery at Sint-Sixtusabdij Westvleteren (Saint-Sixtus Abbey of West-vletern), one of Belgium's six Trappist breweries (see page 38), will take you to the home of some of Belgium's most coveted libations. Unlike the other five breweries, Westvleteren does not distribute its beer. Visitors wanting to buy the famous West-vleteren 12 will need to make reservations and provide the brewery with their license plate number. Just make sure that plate hasn't visited in the past 60 days.

Photos

1 *Owner and brewer Jean van Roy pours a lambic at Brasserie Cantillon.*
9 *The Westvleteren Brewery produces the famous Westvleteren 12 quadrupel.*

For years, brewers relied on the Ghent canal to transport their wares. Today, you can cruise the canal on a beer tour.

LOCAL BREWS
FLANDERS
TRUE TO ITS ROOTS

Sour beer is a polarizing drink. Some love it, some hate it, and some just hope that their palates can acclimate to its complex, mouth-puckering taste. This conversation-starting beverage is what defines Flanders, the northern region of Belgium, whose anachronistic brewing traditions were shaped, above all, by a desire to keep fermentation wild.

Before Louis Pasteur definitively determined the role of yeast in alcoholic fermentation in 1857, all beer was either spontaneously fermented (see page 46) or inoculated with yeast from a previous batch. The science behind this process was not yet understood, meaning that beer was left to the wild mercy of whatever touched each new batch, be it a bit of old beer, a prized stirring stick, or whatever was in the air itself. Flanders's assortment of red and brown ales was dark and sour, thanks to bacteria such as *Lactobacillus* and *Pediococcus*, and yeast such as *Brettanomyces*, which they were exposed to as they aged in wooden barrels. To the Flemish, this was how beer was supposed to taste—a little sour, a little musty, even a little "off," but with a sweet malt character and a large dose of complexity.

As scientific advances unveiled the mysteries of yeast and fermentation, brewers in neighboring countries started to clean up, control, and manipulate what got into their beer. Bavarians (now Germans) and Bohemians (now Czechs) used this knowledge to produce lager, which became a popular type. More brewers adopted the use of propagated yeast, but the Flemish and English chose to continue to age and blend beer from various vintages. This practice continues today in Flanders, resulting in ales that are low in carbonation, sour in taste, dark in appearance, and as unique as they come.

But not all Flemish ales are sour. Flanders is on the western border of the "wheat beer belt" and has used poorly modified malts—unmalted wheat with little sign of germination—to make light-colored, hazy, sweet-flavored beer. Historic styles include the strong amber known as *peeterman*, darkened by the use of chalk, and the slightly sweet *bière de diest*. Many of these styles have fallen out of favor, but Hoegaarden's witbier was revived in a rather noteworthy way.

Monks from Hoegaarden and bordering Flanders and Wallonia developed a beer recipe made with wheat around 1445. Dutch trade with the Caribbean colony of Curaçao brought in orange peel and coriander, which made the beer more popular—so much so that Hoegaarden had 36 breweries by the early 18th century. The last of these breweries closed in the 1950s but was revived by Pierre Celis in 1966. After he fiddled with the recipe in his hayloft, the style became so popular that InterBrew (now AB InBev) bought his brewery in 1989. Today, the Hoegaarden brand is to witbier what Guinness is to Irish stout.

Nearly 60 percent of all modern-day Belgian breweries are located in Flemish-speaking Flanders. Even AB InBev, the world's largest brewing conglomerate, has its headquarters here, in the town of Leuven. As interest in its styles grows, Flanders continues to inspire and challenge people's palettes with beer that tastes like that of nowhere else.

local flavor Mixed Fermentation

Mixed fermentation combines traditional high-temperature fermentation practices and the spontaneous fermentation techniques synonymous with sour styles. The combination of yeast and bacteria gives beer a fruity, sour taste, but timing is important too. For example, blends of ale yeast *Saccharomyces cerevisiae*, lactic bacteria *Lactobacillus*, and the wild yeast *Brettanomyces* are mixed during fermentation and again in wooden vats, then allowed to mature for a number of months. The microorganisms hanging out in the wood impart fruitier flavors, and even some acidification, producing a more refined taste. Master blenders then combine older beer with new beer using their signature, secret methods, resulting in beer that embodies the nuances and creativity of its creators.

on tap with Garrett Oliver

Flanders Red Ale

Acidity was once a big part of beer's flavor, and the sour beers of Flanders have retained an almost winelike taste that is expressive of these traditions. These beers are akin to lambics, but they are not spontaneously fermented. Instead, yeast and souring bacteria are intentionally added to the wort, resulting in a complex style often referred to as "the burgundy of Belgium."

ABV 4.5-6.5% | **IBU** 10-22

Aroma Fruity, complex, and vinous; black cherry, plum, often slightly acetic

Appearance Vibrant reddish-brown, garnet

Flavor Fruity and moderately tart, with toasty caramel and vanilla notes

Mouthfeel Medium-bodied and finely effervescent, sometimes showing tannin

Presentation White wine, tulip, or sherry glass

Food Pairings Stew, game meat, hard cheese

Classic to Try Rodenbach Grand Cru

LOCAL BREWS
PAJOTTENLAND

HOME OF LAMBIC AND GUEUZE

Pajottenland, full of picturesque farmland and rolling green hills, is located southwest of Brussels, between the Zenne and Dender Rivers. Nestled between Flanders to the north and Wallonia to the south, the region is famous for its lambic, brewed with wild bacteria found nowhere else on Earth.

Two millennia ago the area was one of Europe's major crossroads, occupied at different times by the Celts, the Franks, the Romans, the Austrians, the Dutch, and the French. Though the Romans controlled lands encompassing all of modern-day Belgium, they discovered that this region made the most consistent beer.

This regularly excellent beer was produced by way of spontaneous fermentation. The region's signature styles relied on ambient wild yeasts like *Brettanomyces bruxellensis* and *Brettanomyces lambicus*, alongside a

local flavor
Spontaneous Fermentation

Lambic is spontaneously fermented—not top-fermented like ale or bottom-fermented like lager—and so is in a brewing class all its own. Spontaneous fermentation in lambic occurs when the wort, made from pale malt and 30 to 40 percent unmalted wheat, is exposed to native yeasts and airborne bacteria. These natural microflorae shape lambic's flavor characteristics and alcohol content, so breweries that make it are generally not fully sterilized—in stark contrast to the majority of modern-day facilities.

Traditionally, lambic is inoculated with yeasts and microbes naturally by way of a big open fermenter called a coolship *(koelschip)*. Fresh, hot wort placed in the coolship cools overnight, allowing wild yeast to get in. This process customarily occurs from October to May, when temperatures can cool the wort down to 68°F (20°C) overnight. In short, here's how to make lambic: Expose the wort to the elements, let it condition in wooden casks, then raise a glass and toast to your good fortune.

Wort in Brasserie Cantillon's coolship is exposed to the air.

The airborne microbiota in Pajottenland are unique to the region, contributing to lambic beers produced nowhere else.

dozen or so other microbes, to produce their singular flavors. But the unpredictability of airborne bacteria meant that these styles weren't easy to make. Lambic has to be brewed in the spring and autumn to avoid undesirable bacteria. Having the "wrong" sort of warm-weather bacterial guests show up in a barrel of lambic threatens to spoil the fermentation process, leading to off-flavors. When these beers are brewed well, Pajottenland's microbial terroir generates the tastes and smells of a barnyard, a horse blanket, well-worn leather, fruit, and a general mustiness.

Pajottenland's combination of airborne bacteria and wild yeast helped produce two of the world's oldest styles: lambic and gueuze. Gueuze is created when aged lambic is blended with a younger batch, causing it to enter into secondary fermentation. The process transforms sour, flat, and fairly hazy lambic into dry, bright, sparkling gueuze.

No one knows for certain how the name lambic came to be. Regional folklore suggests it was derived from one of four Belgian villages: Lembeek, Borchtlombeek, Onze-Lieve-Vrouw-Lombeek, or Sint-Katelijne-Lombeek. Some attribute the name to the term *alambic*, a French name for a still that was used by peasants to distill alcohols like wine into spirits such as brandy. Regardless of its name's etymology, lambic and its blended cousin gueuze are protected by the European Union as "traditional specialties guaranteed," a designation that defines its methods of production. While brewers argue this designation ignores that the region's wild yeasts and microbes are what makes a lambic, it maintains the authenticity of these styles for future generations of devotees.

on tap with Garrett Oliver

Lambic

Among the oldest and most complex beer types in the world, lambic ferments without the addition of any laboratory yeasts.

ABV 5-7% | **IBU** 0-10

Aroma Earthy and complex, with an "animal funk"; often shows apples and citrus fruits

Appearance Full gold, sometimes with a slight haze; sturdy white foam

Flavor Distinctly tart, but good examples are well balanced and married; bitterness is very low, and honey notes are common

Mouthfeel Brisk, light, and highly carbonated, with a champagnelike bead

Presentation Champagne flute, sherry glass, or tulip glass

Food Pairings Salad, seafood, goat cheese

Classic to Try Cantillon Gueuze

LOCAL BREWS
WALLONIA

WHERE ANYTHING GOES

Farmers along the Semois River in southern Belgium first produced the saison beer style.

Most modern beer styles are made year-round and available whenever we want them, but that wasn't always the case. Beer was highly seasonal before refrigeration and global access to ingredients, and certain seasons yielded unique and particular styles. This is especially true amid the rolling hills and hedgerows of Wallonia in southern Belgium, whose signature style, saison, has an origin story that's as seasonal as they come.

Whereas many of Belgium's traditional styles were born from monasteries, noble estates, or brewhouses, the saison has its rustic roots in the French Wallonian countryside of the 1700s. This so-called farmhouse ale began as a pale ale brewed by farmers and laborers in the winter to quench their thirst as they worked in the summer. It was often safer to drink than water, and the lower alcohol content made it an important fuel on any working farm. Its name (French for "season") stems from its seasonal limitations: Prior to refrigeration, beer had to be brewed during the cooler months to prevent bad batches, which occur when fermentation temperatures are too warm. It was also important to get the beer's strength right: too strong and it could hinder workers' productivity, too weak and it might spoil in storage.

Each farmhouse had its own recipe, so interpretations on the style depended on who was brewing it. The grain bills used varied widely. Some included wheat (Wallonia is part of the wheat beer belt), dark Vienna malt, rye, and oats, while others included a combination of grains. Different combinations of earthy, herbal hops—such as England's Kent Goldings or Germany's Hallertau—and a heaping of various herbs and spices added to the taste and complexity of the beer. Most farmers had their own house yeast, which no doubt imparted its own unique flavors and aromas. And there was always the potential for some wild yeast strains to sneak into the wort, as in styles such as the Flanders sour and Pajottenland lambic. With so much variation, it's a wonder that modern-day saison is collectively categorized as its own style.

A server presents Belgian beers, including saison, at a local cafe.

Today's saison breweries have overwhelmingly resisted the call of large-scale brewing. Brewers in Wallonia are using higher hopping rates to carve out a niche, differentiating themselves from the less hoppy, sour styles of Flanders and the maltier, less spicy bière de garde from France. While many of today's saisons differ from those of the past, they still encompass their provincial roots and "anything goes" brewing style. With its difficult-to-categorize saisons and three Trappist breweries (see page 38), Wallonia enjoys a beerscape with very few limitations and as many exciting beers as there are breweries producing them.

local flavor
Reclaiming Grisette

This centuries-old, relatively obscure Belgian farmhouse ale is making a comeback. Grisette is traditionally brewed around the Scheldt and Dender River areas, which were important centers in the industrial revolution. While saison remained the drink of choice for the Wallonian farmer, grisette emerged as the beer style of choice for the coal and stone miners who found it was dry and refreshing after a long day at work. It was typically a low-alcohol, light-bodied pale wheat ale that lacked the lactic acid and aging more common in a saison. Young women, known as grisettes (from the French word for gray, the color of the stones being mined), provided trays of it to tired miners at the end of their shift. Grisette faded along with Belgium's mining, but the beer is seeing a resurgence, largely because U.S. brewers are creating modern interpretations.

on tap with Garrett Oliver
Saison

Saison probably once showed acidity and wild yeast character, but it was reborn in the 1920s as a perfect blend of modern pilsner-like directness and classically spicy yeast flavors.

ABV Varies, with most 6-8% | **IBU** 20-35

Aroma Spicy, peppery, lemony, fruity, and sometimes hoppy

Appearance Deep gold to full orange, typically with some haze

Flavor Very dry, snappy, refreshing, and moderately bitter

Mouthfeel Light to medium body, with exuberant effervescence

Presentation White wine, tulip, or highball glass

Food Pairings Shrimp, salmon, ham, goat cheese—versatile

Classic to Try Saison Dupont

Munich's Hofbräuhaus has been brewing and serving beer for more than 400 years.

GERMANY

THE EPICENTER OF TRADITION

Beer has long been tied to wealth and power in Germany. Those who brewed it had a bountiful revenue stream; those who controlled its sale controlled much of the German world. Clergy, lords, and kings have all used brewing to gain power, but beer has also always been a drink of the German people.

The rise and fall of pre-20th-century Germany intertwines with the history of its beer. After the Roman Empire fell in A.D. 476, Germanic tribes granted the right for every home to brew beer, a task which usually fell to women. Then feudalism came along in the Early Middle Ages (500–1000), with power-hungry lords eager to take land and brewing rights from peasants. Charlemagne, Holy Roman Emperor and ruler of the Frankish Empire, required all estates to have a brewery. But the massive conversion of tribal societies to Christianity between the sixth and ninth centuries expanded the power of the Catholic Church, and the large-scale production of beer outside the home shifted to monasteries. The church's bishops and monks took charge of land rights, social services, taxes, and commerce—including the production of beer.

The dawn of the second millennium saw more than 500 monasteries brewing beer in Germany, 300 of them located in Bavaria. But feudal lords began to take back that power, opening their own commercial *hofbräuhauses* (court brewhouses). While the church and lords grappled for power, the rising merchant class—predominantly in northern Europe, including northern modern-day Germany—was getting wealthy through trade, commerce, and industry. Within a few centuries, these enterprising merchants were making high-quality beer and selling it along their established trade routes, turning beer into a hugely profitable commodity.

AT A GLANCE
Featured Locations

🛢	Brewery
★	Capital
•	City
HALLERTAU	Region
BAVARIA	State

First Came Ale

Lager is arguably the most prolific German beer type, but that wasn't always the case. For much of its history, Germany has been a land of ales, both top-fermenting and without hops. But that changed in the late 15th and early 16th centuries with the introduction of the bottom-fermenting *Saccharomyces pastorianus*, a hybrid of two yeast strains.

Environment, luck, and politics drew geographic lines between Germany's top-fermenting and bottom-fermenting regions. By 1553, brewers believed that cold lagering yielded a purer beer. The law dictated that beer could no longer be brewed during the Bavarian summer, which is when top-fermenting yeast is most active. No such restrictions existed for bottom-fermenting yeast, which is most active in winter's cooler months. Hence southern Germany evolved into a lager culture while the north remained an ale culture.

As ales reigned in northern Germany, the port cities of Hamburg, Bremen, and Lübeck became the centers of an expanding beer trade. By the 1520s Hamburg had more than 500 breweries, collectively brewing 25 million liters (213,000 U.S. barrels) of beer and employing nearly half of the city's residents. A century later, the 30 Years' War (1618–1648) put an end to this glorious beer scene. The country was partitioned into 370 semiautonomous states, each with its own laws regarding

Beer cafés such as Biergarten am Muffatwerk in Munich are common in most German cities.

beer's production, sale, and taxation. Germany wouldn't be unified again until 120 years later.

By the time of unification under Otto von Bismarck in the mid-19th century, the second industrial revolution was well under way. Two things arose as brewing science advanced and fermentation became better understood: beer's quality control improved and the cost of brewing came down. Refrigeration meant lager could be brewed anywhere, anytime, and brewers were no longer completely beholden to their region's climate when it came to what kinds of beer they made. With the exceptions of the Rhine River Valley and places brewing wheat beer, the lagerization of Germany was full steam ahead.

Beer, Power, and Purity

Both treasured and criticized, a series of German purity laws, collectively known as the Reinheitsgebot, have shaped the history of the nation's beer. In 1516, Duke Wilhelm IV of Bavaria instituted a purity law called the Substitutionsverbot (substitution prohibition), stating that beer was to be made exclusively with barley, water, and hops. It was meant as a health measure at a time when beer quality was inconsistent; breweries could be unsanitary places, with brewers using ingredients such as bark, roots, and potentially hallucinogenic fungi. Many scholars, however, argue that the law was really about money, as it kept wheat available and inexpensive for bakers. It made beer more affordable, but it penalized brewers who didn't toe the law's well-defined lines.

The law applied only to brewers in Bavaria—where lager was born. In other parts of Germany, brewers were using wheat, spices, and fruit to brew beer. Problems arose with Germany's unification in 1871—how could the law be applied to brewers outside Bavaria who were using adjuncts? It was rewritten with separate rules for lager and ale and enacted in 1906, and yeast was added into the list of sanctioned ingredients. The law was rewritten again after World War I to impose tight restrictions on lager and fewer on ale. This revised version of the law came to be known as the Reinheitsgebot, which it is still called today.

For 500 years, the Reinheitsgebot simultaneously protected Bavarian (and German) brewers and stifled their creativity. Foreign breweries using adjuncts and selling their beer in Germany were not allowed to call their beer "beer," which protected the domestic industry. But in 1987, a European court ruled that Germany had to broaden its interpretation of the term "beer" to include imported beer that didn't follow the Reinheitsgebot, which brought a wave of new offerings to German consumers.

Many Germans approve of the law, but some brewers are opting to innovate instead of adhering to the rules required to have their product labeled as "beer." Others still swear by the Reinheitsgebot; they say it keeps the beer at a high and uncompromising standard. Even so, the German beer industry is facing pressures to broaden its brewing horizons.

Speakeasy

How to Order Beer in Germany

Unlike in the United States, where beer is ordered by naming the brewery, in Germany, beer is typically ordered by style designation. Each beer comes in a glass specifically created to complement its style. Say **"Einen halben Liter___, bitte"** (IHN-en HALB-en LEE-tah ___, BIT-teh): "A half liter of ___, please." Fill in the blank with a beer style:

dunkel (DOON-kel)—dark
gose (GO-zah)—salty sour wheat ale from Leipzig
altbier (AHLT-beer)—bitter ale from the Düsseldorf region
weissbier (VICE-beer)—wheat beer
pilsner (pilss)—pilsner

———————

If you'd like the same beer again, point to your glass and say, **"Noch ein Bier bitte"** (nokh IHN beer BIT-teh): "Another beer, please."

———————

Most beer halls have shared seating, so don't be surprised if strangers sit down beside you. Raise your glass and toast them with **"Prost!"** which means "Cheers!"

OKTOBERFEST

A CELEBRATION OF BAVARIAN CULTURE

Most weddings feature certain celebratory staples—things like vows, cake, and dancing. Not many include horse racing or invitations extended to an entire city. Such was the case at the wedding of Ludwig and Therese, who would go on to become King Ludwig I of Bavaria and Crown Princess Therese in October 1810. Little did they know that their nuptials would create the world's most famous beer festival.

A second festival was held in October 1811 in honor of this famous wedding. It featured horse racing and an agricultural show aimed at increasing Bavaria's output. The event became an annual tradition, though it was canceled in 1813 because of a war against Napoleon and in 1854 because of a cholera outbreak. In 1818, a carousel and swings were added, as were beer stands, which—not surprisingly—turned out to be quite popular. Other additions in the early years were tree climbing, sack races, eating contests, and goose chases. By 1819 the citizens of Munich had taken on the duty of organizing the event, which was lengthened to two weeks and moved to mid-September to take advantage of warmer weather.

The first parade of breweries took place in 1887, highlighted by horses pulling kegs of beer and musicians playing while patrons enjoyed their beverages. The beer style consumed at the festival was chiefly märzen (see page 57), a darker beer traditionally brewed in March and allowed to age over summer so that it was ready to drink in time for Oktoberfest. By 1896, the beer stands were replaced by large beer tents and beer halls sponsored by local breweries. Beer drinking had become such a popular feature that nearly 31,700 gallons (120,000 L) of beer were consumed at the festival's 100th anniversary, in 1910. Several pavilions were constructed that year, capable of seating more than 10,000 people. Oktoberfest was canceled only for major events such as World Wars I and II. In 1938, it was temporarily renamed Grossdeutsches Volksfest (German Empire Folk Festival) by the Nazi government. The now traditional opening event—Munich's mayor tapping the first keg—dates back to 1950.

With so much entertainment by way of the opening parade, competitions, rides, and games, the horse races were retired in 1960. The sack races and goose chases are gone, too, cleared away to make room for roughly seven million visitors who make this the world's largest beer festival. Today, six brewers make the aptly named Oktoberfestbier for the eager masses.

Oktoberfest is celebrated in thousands of places across the globe, with beer consumption measured in millions of gallons. But Bavarians would argue that Oktoberfest is not a beer fest at all; it's really a celebration of Bavarian culture, of which beer is an important part. ■

To celebrate Oktoberfest, patrons often don traditional Bavarian peasant clothing: a *dirndl* for women and *lederhosen* for men.

The use of **stein lids** became German law in the late 1300s, following the bubonic plague, as a means of reducing disease by keeping flies out of beer.

Expanding Tradition

German beer is big business. Of the more than $56 billion the beer industry contributed to the European economy in 2015, Germany generated almost $12 billion. Around half of Germany's 1,400 breweries are considered microbreweries, but they produce less than one percent of the total output. German craft beer drinkers are seeking hoppier U.S.-style ale over maltier German-style lager, but traditional beer styles will always have a place in Germany's beer halls. These halls will just be more crowded with options.

German Signature Beer Styles

Germany is home to two to five dozen beer styles, depending on how you define the term. Each style is characteristic of its region of origin.

1 | ALTBIER

This copper-colored wheat ale originates from Düsseldorf and the surrounding Rhineland. Although altbier is cool-fermented and cool-conditioned, like lager, it's actually an ale—its name means "old beer," reminding consumers that ale was the first beer on the German scene. It has a creamy head, a medium body, and a dry finish.

2 | BERLINER WEISSE

Its name, which means "white from Berlin," has the legal protection of a controlled-designation-of-origin product: To be called a Berliner weisse, this beer style has to be made in Berlin. Brewed with roughly 30 percent wheat, it is mildly sour, and it has a low alcohol content and a light effervescence, which make it a good summer drink. Berliner weisse is often sweetened with syrup made from raspberries, lemons, or woodruff (see page 62).

3 | DOPPELBOCK

Bavaria's doppelbock (double bock) has a fitting name, given that this is one of Germany's highest ABV beers, ranging from 7 to 13 percent. Some varieties of doppelbock can be quite malty and have almost no bitterness. It originated in the 1700s as a lager version of the strong ale brewed in monasteries. Copious amounts of this "liquid bread" were consumed during religious fasting seasons.

4 | DUNKEL

A dark lager hailing from Bavaria, dunkel is an all-barley beer. It started out dark because kilning techniques often left the malt a bit scorched. Dunkel was the first beer subject to the purity law in 1516 (see page 53) and thus is widely considered the precursor to most German lagers. It has little bitterness, a lot of maltiness, and an occasional hint of vanilla or nutty flavors, with an ABV typically ranging from 4.5 to 5.6 percent.

5 | HELLES

Hell is the German word for "pale" or "bright" and the nickname of this straw-blonde beer. Helles is a malt-forward, mildly sweet, low-bitterness lager invented in Munich by Spaten Brewery in 1894 as a competitor to the popular but foreign Bohemian pilsner. While higher alcohol and specialty versions exist, the original style is fairly quaffable at 5 percent ABV.

6 | KÖLSCH

This pale-colored, low-malt, low-bitterness ale is made with top-fermenting yeast but lagered for a month or more. It originated in Cologne, a city off the Rhine and 24 miles (39 km) upstream from Düsseldorf. Named after the city's dialect, the style enjoys the legal protection of a controlled designation of origin: A kölsch can only be called a kölsch if it was brewed in Cologne. It is served in a narrow, tall glass called a *stange* (meaning "pole" or "stick").

7 | MÄRZEN

This amber lager takes its name from the German word for March, signifying the time of year it was brewed. Märzen was made with a higher ABV (5 to 6.5 percent) and more hops than a typical Bavarian lager to prevent the beer from spoiling while it lagered through the summer months. It was first introduced to the world at the 1872 Oktoberfest and now is the main beer served at Oktoberfest in Munich (see page 54).

8 | RAUCHBIER

The name of this barley-based lager means "smoke beer," which comes from the smoky flavor the malt picks up in the kiln during the drying process. The style hails from the Bamberg region in Franconia, where a handful of breweries still produce it. This meaty, amber-copper beer typically has a creamy head and an ABV ranging from 4.8 to 6 percent.

9 | WEISSBIER

A variety of ale, weissbier (white beer) is also known as weizenbier (wheat beer) or weisse; those outside Germany may know it as hefeweizen (yeast wheat). Its name comes from the pale wheat in its grain bill, which often constitutes 50 to 70 percent of the grain. Its distinct flavor comes from the yeast and wheat, but it may also contain notes of clove, banana, or bubblegum. Weissbier is typically unfiltered, but there is a filtered version called kristallweizen (crystal wheat) as well as a dark version known as dunkelweizen (dark wheat).

Origins of Beer Styles

- Featured state
- Non-subject state
- ★ Capital
- ● City
- **1** Featured beer style

BEER GUIDE
WHERE BEER LOVERS GO

These recommendations from German brewers offer a guided tour of the country's many regional beer experiences.

1 | Hofbräuhaus
Munich

Stop by and enjoy a *mass* (signs will say *maß*) of beer at one of Munich's most popular tourist stops, which has been around since the late 1500s. It's always crowded, but with a live polka band and giant *laugenbrezel* (traditional German pretzel), it is well worth a visit.

2 | Haxenhaus zum Rheingarten
Cologne

This 13th-century pub just steps from the Rhine used to cater to sailors and dockworkers by providing food, drink, and lodging. Today's visitors can visit the traditional *wirtshaus* (inn) and still find all three. It serves only Gaffel Kölsch in seven-fluid-ounce (207-mL) pours, but you can drink as many as you want (within reason). Try it with the pub's culinary specialty: pig knuckles.

3 | Bayerische Staatsbrauerei Weihenstephan
Freising

On a sprawling estate on top of Weihenstephan Hill, the world's oldest operating brewery was founded in 1040 by Benedictine monks. It's also where Duke Wilhelm IV of Bavaria issued the Bavarian purity law of 1516. Take a guided tour through the historic campus, then head to the *biergarten* to try beer produced on-site.

4 | Neue Promenade
Berlin

This pedestrian-friendly promenade comes alive at night, when an assortment of street musicians and performers entertain for tips. The ambience here is perfect for sitting outside at one of several beer cafés, including Weihenstephaner Berlin.

5 | Gröninger Privatbrauerei
Hamburg

Located at the site of Hamburg's old brewing quarter during the Middle Ages, this modern-day brewery lays claim to being the first wheat brewery in Hamburg. Grill up some sausage at the table while enjoying its specialties: the Gröninger Pils and Hanseaten Weisse.

Breweries and Beer Destinations in Germany

🛢 Brewery

1 Featured beer destination

6 | Gosenschenke Ohne Bedenken

Leipzig

A visit to this pub is a must to learn about the interesting history of the beer style gose, which is enjoying a revival. First made in the town of Goslar around A.D. 1000, this style became popular in Leipzig by the 1800s but went extinct in 1966. Sit in the top-rated beer garden and enjoy locally brewed gose, especially perfect for summer drinking.

7 | Red Beer in Deep Cellars

Nuremberg

This tour goes under the city into caves hewn from sandstone, where citizens stored their beer going back to 1380, and gives insight into local history and the importance of beer to the city of Nuremberg. Bring a jacket, because it's only 50°F (10°C) in the caves. Luckily, there's a beer tasting after the tour at the Hausbrauerei Altstadthof to warm things up.

Photos

1 Live oompah music is part of the Hofbräuhaus experience. **3** Visitors can tour the facilities at the Bayerische Staatsbrauerei Weihenstephan (Weihenstephan Brewery). **4** Berlin's Hackescher Markt, on Neue Promenade, is filled with beer cafés.

LOCAL BREWS
BAVARIA
BEER HEAVEN

The picturesque Bavarian Alps provide the backdrop to a region with a rich beer history.

Look for a brewery that has not been influenced by Bavaria's beer culture, laws, techniques, and styles, and you're bound to come up empty-handed. Bavaria's geography seems tailor-made for producing beer: Its rolling farmlands grow wheat and barley; the Hallertau area hosts the world's largest contiguous hop-growing region; and aquifers offer the soft water needed to create its famous beer styles. To the south, the mighty Alps provided the perfect place to dig out caves for storing lager before the advent of refrigeration. With its geography primed for brewing, it's no wonder that beer has long been a huge part of Bavarian culture.

Bavarian brewers, undeterred by the purity law of 1516 (see page 53), which mandated that the only acceptable ingredients in brewing were barley, hops, and water, created many different lager styles, among them helles,

kellerbier, märzen, bockbier, schwarzbier, and rauchbier. They range in color from pale gold to black, and in flavor from clean and crisp to intensely smoky. There is even a Bavarian pilsner: a lighter, drier, crisper version of its Czech counterpart. This region was also the birthplace of a wheat-based ale called weissbier—or hefeweizen, as it is often called in the United States. The purity law contained a loophole that allowed for the production of wheat beer, as the ruling Duke of Wittlesbach had a penchant for it.

Hops have played a major role in this beerscape, with a history stretching back to the eighth century. Bavaria's Hallertau region, 45 miles (70 km) north of Munich, is the world's largest hop growing region. It produces approximately one-third of the world's hops and 90 percent of Germany's.

Bavaria also gave the world a summertime beer-drinking staple: the *biergarten* (beer garden). When lagers first became popular, brewers found they needed a cool place to store them, especially after Duke Albrecht V followed up Wilhelm's purity law by forbidding the production of beer in summer. They would dig large caverns, then line them with large blocks of ice so the beer wouldn't spoil during summer. Above them, the spreading branches of chestnut trees provided added protection against the sun's damaging heat, and a pretty place to drink beer in the shade. These gardens became popular picnic areas, as selling food was banned in beer gardens to protect taverns and inns from losing customers.

Bavaria has played an important role in German and European beer culture—so much so that the European Union dubbed it a protected geographical indication, meaning that only beer brewed in Bavaria is permitted to be labeled as Bavarian beer. This designation protects Bavaria's brewing legacy, preserving a drink that lies at the heart of German culture.

local flavor

The Beer Behind the Zoigl Star

Zoigl is a hazy, copper-colored, malty beer that most people have never heard of. That's because it's only brewed in communal brewhouses in five towns in the Oberpfalz region of eastern Bavaria: Eslarn, Falkenberg, Mitterteich, Neuhaus, and Windischeschenbach. The term *zoigl* is derived from the German word *zeichen*, meaning "sign" or "symbol." The six-sided zoigl star brewers hang above their doors is similar in appearance to the Star of David. Brewers in the Middle Ages (A.D. 500–1500) used this star to represent the three elements of water, earth, and fire and the three ingredients of water, grains, and hops.

Zoigl's wort is made at a communal brewhouse, then delivered to private cellars in a brewer's home and allowed to ferment. After two weeks, the fermented beer is transferred to storage tanks and allowed to condition. When it's ready to drink, the beer is tapped directly from the lagering

A zoigl star marks fresh beer.

tank. One of the brewers hangs a six-sided star outside his house to indicate he is currently selling the beer in his private rooms. Once the beer in that cellar is gone, the next brewer taps his tank and begins to sell his share, and the star is passed on to him. The beer varies from batch to batch and town to town, as each brewer has his own secret recipe. To sample zoigl, check the local newspaper to see which house currently has the star up on its door.

LOCAL BREWS
BERLIN

MIXING OLD AND NEW

Germany's capital city is an eclectic blend of past and present. Nearly 80 percent of the city was leveled in World War II, but Berlin rebuilt itself by constructing modernist buildings on the ashes of traditional ones. When the Berlin Wall was erected in 1961, West Berlin continued to thrive while East Berlin did not—a dichotomy that runs through Berlin's beer history as well.

local flavor
Mixing It Up

Germans have invented two beer cocktails that are gaining traction outside Germany. The first is made with Berliner weisse mixed with a shot of syrup and called *Berliner weisse mit schuss* (Berliner weisse with a shot). Berliners order their weisse by color: *rot* (red) from raspberry syrup, *grün* (green) from woodruff syrup, or *gelb* (yellow) from lemon syrup.

The second cocktail, called *radler,* was born on a fine Saturday in June 1922, when about 13,000 cyclists from Munich descended on an inn in the small town of Deisenhofen. They were drinking their way through the inn's beer, so the innkeeper mixed it with lemon soda. The innkeeper called it *radler-mass,* German for "cyclist's liter." Radlers are now created around the world using all sorts of beer styles and sodas. Red Hare Brewing Company in Georgia (U.S.) makes SPF 50/50: a blend of IPA and grapefruit soda.

If there is one beer style for which Berlin is known, it's Berliner weisse: a pale, sour, low-alcohol wheat-and-barley-based beer. Recipes call for the bacterium *Lactobacillus* to sour the beer, while others also use the yeast *Brettanomyces* for a funkier taste. Historians are divided as to whether the style originated in Berlin or was brought to the area by French Protestants fleeing persecution in the late 1600s. Regardless, hundreds of Berlin's breweries were producing it by the 1800s and the city had become one of Europe's leading cities for beer. The light effervescence of this great summer drink is why experts think Napoleon and his occupying troops in 1809 called it the "champagne of the north."

Berliner weisse's popularity was waning by the time the 20th century came around, as Bavarian lager was taking over. The Berlin Wall had a major impact on brewing here, too, as brewers in West Berlin had access to the best equipment and ingredients, whereas the same could not be said for those in the communist East. Therefore, West Berlin's beer quality was superior to the East's.

The fall of the Berlin Wall in 1989 meant that people, and beer, could flow freely between the two Berlins. Breweries in the former East Berlin were either closed, modernized, or acquired by breweries in the former West Berlin. The result was consolidation and unification. But Berlin's beer industry soon faced pressure from another source: craft beer.

Bier-Company was one of the earliest craft breweries in Berlin, founded in 1995. Its brewers were tired of

Escehnbräu, a basement brewpub in Berlin's Wedding district, serves up new specialty beers monthly.

traditional German beer styles, so they decided to brew beer that fell outside the bounds of the purity law—much to the chagrin of the German Brewing Association. Their brewery grew, albeit slowly, and a few employees struck out on their own to establish Brauhaus Südstern and Brewbaker in 2001. These breweries pushed the beer envelope with their nontraditional styles. Other craft breweries such as BRLO (Slavic for "Berlin") and Schoppe Bräu continue to expand Berlin's craft beer horizons with their own takes on various beer styles.

The rise in popularity of German craft beer became quite evident in 2012, when Germany imported more hops from the United States than the number of German hops they exported to the U.S. German craft beer recipes often call for U.S. hops, as they are typically more flavorful and aromatic than local varieties. This desire for bold craft beer may have to do with Berlin's large number of international residents, which makes its population more inclined to accept craft beer. No matter the reason, craft beer has claimed a prominent place alongside the more traditional offerings in Berlin's beerscape.

on tap with Garrett Oliver

Berliner Wiesse

One of the progenitors of the modern trend back toward tartness, this style once filled more than 100 breweries in the city of Berlin. Today, it is in the vanguard of a return to acidity in modern craft beers and is a popular choice in American brewpubs.

ABV 2.8–3.5% | **IBU** 4–8

Aroma Pasta-like (wheaty) with lemony, yogurt notes

Appearance Very pale straw with a dense white foam

Flavor Cleanly tart, dry, lemony, with underlying wheat (taking on additional flavors if syrups are added)

Mouthfeel Crisp, light, dry, juicy

Presentation Goblet, chalice, or white wine glass

Food Pairings Seafood, salad, feta and goat cheese, ceviche, veal sausage

Craft to Try Brewbaker Berliner Weisse

NORTH RHINE-WESTPHALIA

DRINKS BY THE WATER

Two popular German ales, kölsch and altbier, originated in the Rhine River Valley.

The Rhine River meanders through the hills of North Rhine–Westphalia, adorned with castles and fortresses that stand testament to the importance of this waterway in centuries past. Beer in Germany's North Rhineland has long been dominated by two riverside cities: Düsseldorf and Cologne. No purity law ever banned summer brewing here, creating a beer scene distinct from those of many other places in Germany. Each city and surrounding region produced its own unique style of beer in spite of being only about 25 miles (40 km) apart—specifically altbier and kölsch, two of Germany's ale styles.

Düsseldorf is home to altbier, which remains essentially the same as it was 800 years ago: copper in color, medium bodied, and slightly malty with a dry finish. Altbier dates to the 13th century, when nearly every house in what is now called Altstadt (Old Town) brewed its own. It makes up about 2 to 3 percent of the German market share as a whole, but is closer to 50 percent in Düsseldorf.

Upstream is the city of Cologne, where a brewing industry thrived through the Middle Ages (A.D. 500–1500), when gruit was still a popular ingredient in beer (see page 72). In 1396, roughly two dozen German breweries created a guild to provide a unified voice over brewing matters. Meanwhile, farther north, an increasingly popular beer called *keutebier* was being made with wheat, barley, and hops. It eventually made its way to Cologne, and keutebier brewers gained admittance to the guild in 1471. They pushed to outlaw gruit, as keutebier was brewed using hops. Gradually, wheat was also eliminated from keutebier. With the advent of refrigeration in the late 1800s, brewers in Cologne and Düsseldorf started cold-conditioning their ales to ensure they were smooth. The result in Cologne was the style known as kölsch.

Kölsch is a subtle ale that's lightly colored, moderately carbonated, and with little maltiness and a hint of hoppiness. Only breweries that are part of the Kölsch Konvention can legally call their beer kölsch.

(see page 72)

on tap with Garrett Oliver
Kölsch

Originally brewed as a warm-fermented rival style to Bohemia's then-new golden pilsner, kölsch has become a favorite among craft brewers around the world, particularly in the United States.

ABV 4.5–5.2% | **IBU** 18–25

Aroma Subtle fruitiness with floral overlay

Appearance Bright pale gold with fluffy white foam

Flavor Soft, brisk, and lightly bready, with honeyed notes

Mouthfeel Light to medium body, crisp, with robust carbonation

Presentation Stange or highball glass

Food Pairings Sandwiches, ham, shellfish, sausage—versatile

Classic to Try Reissdorf Kölsch

local flavor
Carrying Tradition

Go to any kölsch bar in Cologne or any pub serving altbier in Düsseldorf and soak in a rich beer-serving tradition that's hard to find elsewhere. Watch a *köbe* (waiter) roll a wooden barrel out into the serving area, hoist it onto the bar, and bang in a tap with a *zappes* (tapper). They tap their beer using gravity instead of carbon dioxide. Köbes in blue aprons then load up a special metal tray, called a *kranz* (crown). This tray wasn't always made of metal; it used to be made of wood. Prior to the industrial revolution, ships bringing goods into the port of Cologne had to be loaded and unloaded manually. Ship captains would often hire local laborers, who gathered at the breweries in hopes of being hired. The more industrious laborers would write their names on a wooden kranz to advertise their services. As the köbe went from table to table, captains would see these handwritten ads and perhaps be more likely to hire those laborers. The Haxenhaus zum Rheingarten in Cologne still serves its kölsch on a wooden kranz.

Today, köbes deliver kölsch in a narrow glass called a *stange*, from the German word for "stick." The cylindrical stange is made to hold made to hold 200 milliliters (about 7 oz), a smaller pour meant to keep the beer from getting warm in a hurry. Köbes in Dusseldorf use similar glasses for serving altbier, but in two different sizes. As patrons finish a beer, the köbe quickly replaces their empty stange with a new one unless a coaster has been placed over the top of the glass. It's on the coaster that the köbe tallies the bill, marking it up with a pencil every time he brings a fresh glass. Those who refuse to cover their glass with a coaster are likely to turn into *bierleichen* (beer zombies) by the end of the night.

Public houses are nearly as iconic to England as Big Ben, and they are a cornerstone of English culture.

UNITED KINGDOM

REAL ALES OF PROMISE

This collection of islands has many iconic sights: England's rolling green hills bisected by hedgerows; Scotland's rocky outcrops exposed to wind and rain; Northern Ireland's Giant's Causeway; the glowing beacon of London's Big Ben. The defining sound in all of these places may well be that of laughter emanating from a neighborhood pub, where patrons discuss the day's events as they sip unfiltered, unpasteurized, nearly room-temperature beer. The popularity and availability of traditional styles has waxed and waned, but the influence of the United Kingdom on the world of beer has never wavered.

Beer was being brewed in the U.K. even before the Romans invaded in 55 B.C. Wooden tablets from the first century A.D. show Roman troops purchasing beer, and old wax writings feature beer barons and deliveries as a common part of Londinium (London) life. After the Romans withdrew in the fifth century, Roman *tabernae* (shops) were turned into taverns that sold local ales.

When invaders from Normandy (northern France) defeated the English and seized the throne in 1066, the Anglo-Norman way of life meant that every village had an ale-making guild house. Styles included "mild ales" that were fresh and perhaps sweet, "bright ales" that were aged and likely sour, "Welsh ales" likely made from wheat and honey, and new, old, sour, pure, and twice-brewed ales, among others. Ales were tailor-made for important moments: "bride ales" for weddings and "scot ales" for raising money for the lord of the manor.

Beer production increased again during the Hundred Years' War (1337–1453) between France and England. Soldiers received a daily ration of eight pints of beer, a demand that led brewing to expand beyond homes and monasteries and into factories. In the mid-1400s, all British beer was called "ale" and made with water, grains, gruit (see page 70), and yeast. When hops from the Netherlands were introduced in the late 15th century, brews made with hops became known as "beer." By the 1700s, all English beer was made using hops (see page 150).

AT A GLANCE
Featured Locations

🛢	Brewery
★	Capital
●	City
WALES	Country or province
WILTSHIRE	County
IRELAND	Non-subject country

Growing and Changing

By the turn of the 20th century, 6,500 breweries existed in the United Kingdom, owned by more than 1,400 companies. By the early 1970s, these numbers had dwindled to 177 breweries owned by 96 companies. Industry consolidation was the primary cause. Unlike those in the United States, which also experienced a lot of consolidation, many breweries in the U.K. owned pubs that distributed their beer. These "tied houses" were only allowed to sell the owning brewery's beer, cutting off potential competition. By the late 1960s, the six largest breweries in the U.K. were called the Big Six; by the 1980s, they produced 75 percent of domestic beer and owned 75 percent of U.K. pubs.

In the 1960s and '70s, brewers also stopped producing many traditional styles. These styles needed to be cask-conditioned—fermented in the casks they're served in—because they didn't keep for long periods and required a watchful eye to make sure they didn't spoil. Switching to brewery-conditioned (kegged) beer meant ending the fermentation process through pasteurization, and thus killing the live bacteria and yeast that would continue to age and flavor beer.

Consolidation continued to shape the industry, turning the Big Six into the Big Four. These companies owned fewer pubs than they used to—an outcome of the Beer Orders of 1989, which set limits on how many pubs a brewery could own—but their hold on local pubs remained strong. A staple of British culture, the neighborhood pub is now most likely part of a large conglomerate such as Enterprise Inns or Punch Taverns. The Beer Orders were rescinded in 2003, but the beer scene had made a permanent shift that limited consumers' choices, leaving them with brewery-conditioned beer without a distinctive local flavor.

Embracing Tradition

While consolidation certainly played a part in the United Kingdom's evolving beerscape, organizations such as the Campaign for Real Ale (CAMRA) in the 1970s were instrumental in bringing flavor and tradition back into beer. Formed as a response to what the four founders saw as little choice and blandness in the beer market, CAMRA advocated for "real ale": traditional styles that are cask-conditioned in the traditional way, allowing them to continue to ferment and mature in barrels. The carbonation in real ale isn't forced, as it is in many commercial brews. Instead, it is a by-product of the fermentation process. The public embraced CAMRA's goal of bringing back these traditional practices, and its membership has grown from 30,000 in 1991 to more than 180,000 today. But its advocacy for cask ale leaves out craft brewers, whose beer is often pasteurized or filtered, or requires carbon dioxide to be served from a keg. Even so, the craft beer scene in the U.K. is growing. Overall, beer drinkers are more concerned with flavor and variety than they are with production and dispensation processes, making craft beer a competitive choice.

The U.K. boasts more than 1,400 breweries, one of the world's highest figures in terms of breweries per capita. The tax on beer may be responsible, as it doubles for breweries producing more than around 3,100 U.K. barrels

While there isn't a pub on every corner in the U.K., there are nearly 50,000 of them throughout the country.

ENGLAND'S IPA

MYTHS, TRUTHS, AND LEGENDS

The legendary story of the India pale ale (IPA) starts with the founding of the East India Company (EIC). This private trading company was the main shipper of goods between England and India in the 1600s. It frequently carried beer for British military and expats in India, as well as for thirsty sailors on the four- to six-month voyage there.

Some historians say that pale ales—any beer that was lighter in color than the common, darker beer of the time—were first brewed in England and transported to India in the late 1670s. A variety called October beer (so called because of when it was typically brewed) was matured for 18 months or more. Maturing it in barrels on the open sea for six months resulted in a similar, winelike beer that became popular among the English gentry in India. It helped that it

was light and refreshing—perfect in India's warm weather. Beer was often rejected on arrival because of spoilage, but hopped beer was rejected less, leading brewers to conclude that hops had some preservative effect. EIC captains procured much of their beer from Old Bow Brewery, just east of London and near the mouth of the Thames.

Despite myths to the contrary, Old Bow did not invent the IPA. The term didn't exist yet, so most of these pale ales were referred to instead as India ale, pale India ale, pale export India ale, or even just pale ale prepared for India. Old Bow's owner, George Hodgson, did popularize it, and his brewery became synonymous with good beer for decades. Part of Hodgson's success boils down to his geographic advantage, as his brewery's location made it easier

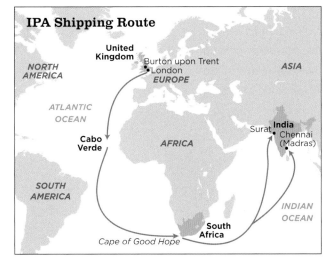

IPAs were a staple in far-flung British colonies like India (left) and Australia (right) in the 19th century.

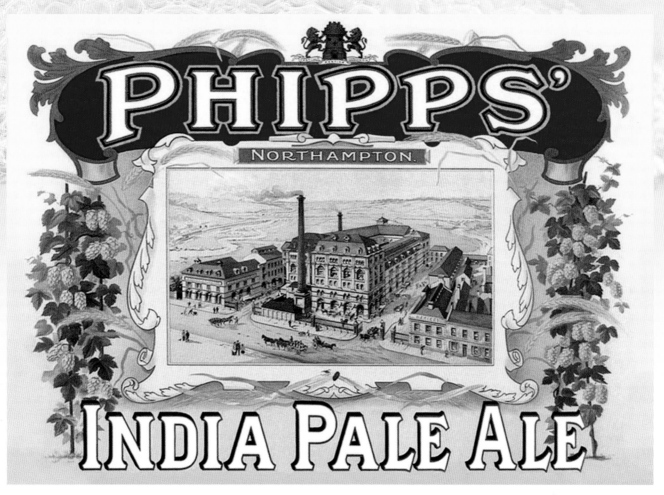

Phipps Northampton Brewery Company in England began producing IPA in 1880.

to load beer onto ships docked at port. Hodgson sweetened the deal by extending an 18-month credit to EIC captains. By 1821 Frederick Hodgson, George's son, and Thomas Drane had decided to cut the EIC out of the profits entirely and ship the beer themselves. They set up a retail infrastructure in India that bypassed local retailers, which did not sit well with EIC captains. In 1822, these captains convinced a brewer named Samuel Allsopp from Burton upon Trent, a small town just northeast of Birmingham, to provide them with beer for export to the subcontinent. Allsopp replicated the Old Bow pale ale and, as luck would have it, the beer was a little lighter, more bitter, and more effervescent than Hodgson's. Allsopp may not have known it, but his location meant that he had harder water (and thus

higher quantities of minerals such as calcium and magnesium) to brew with, which made for a far better pale ale. A year later, Allsopp sent the first shipment of his pale to India, where it met with huge success. Before long, other brewers set up shop in Burton, and eventually their beer dominated the beer scene half a world away.

There is debate over the origin of the term "India pale ale," as neither Hodgson nor Allsopp used it. Historical documents show it appearing in England in the early 1830s as well as in Australia, where Hodgson's beer was shipped. Regardless of who coined the term, today's craft beer enthusiasts know it well. American craft brewers revived the IPA in the 1970s (see page 150), and this bold style is now one of the craft world's favorites. ∎

(4,300 U.S. barrels/5,000 hL), leaving brewers with little incentive to grow beyond the 3,100-barrel threshold. One of the results is a high number of small breweries and more than 1,100 varieties of beer to enjoy.

U.K. Signature Beer Styles

Pales and porters, milds and bitters—a deeper look into these styles will cast U.K. beers in a new light.

1 | BRITISH GOLDEN ALE

This relatively new style was created in 1986 as English brewers looked for something to compete with the lagers that were starting to find an audience in the U.K. Its aroma and flavor are moderately hoppy, and there is little maltiness in this beer with a low ABV of 3.8 to 5 percent. Some English brewers are now replacing English hops with American ones, which impart a slight citrusy flavor.

2 | ENGLISH BARLEYWINE

The name of this rich, malty style comes from its high ABV, which approaches that of wine. English-brewed versions have a hint of hoppiness to balance the malt and alcohol, but American-brewed versions are more assertive in their hoppiness. Some varieties are aged in wine or port barrels and thus take on a bit of those flavors.

3 | ENGLISH BITTER

Though not considered especially bitter today, this style used to push the

local flavor
For the Love of Gruit

Gruit defined European brewing long before hops were the apple of every brewer's eye. Apart from a few monks here and there, everyone prior to the ninth century used this herbal precursor to hops. Ales were seasoned with this varying mixture of herbs, such as yarrow, sweet gale, and marsh rosemary, along with dozens of other flavorings such as cinnamon, heather, and juniper. Even hops were used—just not alone. Gruit was said to have medicinal properties, but it was also mildly narcotic, psychotropic, and perhaps an aphrodisiac. Bitter, sagelike yarrow was even known to cause madness. Money-hungry kings, nobles, and the Catholic Church sought control of its distribution because of the revenue it brought in.

When it came to trade and navigation, brewers found that hopped beer lasted far longer than gruit ale, giving the former a distinct economic advantage (see page 150). In 1268, King Louis IX of France decreed that only malt and hops could be used to make beer. Centuries later, in 1516, Bavaria's purity law (see page 53) decreed that hops—not gruit—were one of three acceptable ingredients in brewing. Hops became the taxed ingredient, and gruit's star status began to fade.

The U.K. held on to its gruit-loving ways until the 18th century, but even there hops eventually made gruit obsolete (see page 76). Modern-day brewers are getting interested in gruit, and unique herbal mixtures are bringing back the flavors of ales past.

bitterness envelope. Back in 19th-century Britain, bitter was hoppier than the popular mild of the time, and likely Britain's first aromatically hopped beer. The waters in Burton upon Trent helped create a copper-colored, malt-forward beer that became a quintessential cask-conditioned ale. Classified loosely by increasing strength, bitters are called ordinary (standard), best (special, premium), and extra special bitter, or ESB.

4 | ENGLISH INDIA PALE ALE (IPA)

First brewed in 18th-century London and then in Burton upon Trent, the English IPA was one of many beer styles sent to expats and soldiers in India (see page 70). This hop-forward style succumbed to mass-produced lager in the 1970s, only to be revived when the U.S. craft revolution reinvented it (see page 150). This golden- to amber-colored beer is far maltier and less hoppy than its American cousin.

5 | ENGLISH MILD

Originally a term meant to indicate a beer's freshness, the mild has evolved into its own style. Early versions were strong and cheap, while later interpretations had ABVs of 3 to 4.5 percent. This popular draft style tends to be amber to brown with a caramel maltiness. Brown ale—a sweeter, darker version of the mild—is also common, but it's usually bottled rather than on draft.

6 | ENGLISH PORTER

This style likely evolved from the brown ale popularized by laborers in London. The world's first mass-produced style is a light to dark brown beer, well liked for its caramel-chocolate maltiness, creamy texture, and moderate ABV of 4 to 5.5 percent. Though it disappeared in the 1970s, English porter is making a comeback.

7 | IMPERIAL STOUT

The origin of this style traces back to the early 1700s when English porters were brewed to be sold overseas. It was so favored by Tsar Peter the Great and the Russian imperial court that the style is often referred to as Russian imperial stout (see page 129). This big stout with a gravity of 8 to 12 percent ABV has been revived by the craft beer movement in both England and the United States.

8 | WEE HEAVY

The name means "small strong" because this beer is served in smaller portions, given its high ABV (6.5 to 10 percent). These Scottish ales can be amber to brown in color and is quite malty, sometimes with a slight smoke or nut flavor.

Origins of Beer Styles

- Featured country
- Featured region
- Non-subject country or province
- ★ Capital
- ● City
- **1** Featured beer style

BEER GUIDE

WHERE BEER LOVERS GO

Gone are the days when beer drinkers in the U.K. had few options. Today it boasts an evolving beerscape that celebrates its brewing traditions alongside a bubbling craft beer scene.

1 | Griffin Brewery

London, England

This brewery in Chiswick has been producing Fuller's beer since the late 1820s and is the last of London's family-owned breweries. Griffin offers a must-do tour of the facility, which delves into the company's history and, of course, encourages visitors to taste its beer, such as London Pride.

2 | The Horse and Groom

Bourton on the Hill, England

Voted Pub of the Year by *The Good Pub Guide*, The Horse and

Groom is a one-stop shop when it comes to trying local brews. It features local real ales from several breweries.

3 | Mumbles Brewery

Swansea, Wales

A relative newcomer to the U.K. beer scene, the brewery produces five different ales and a few seasonal beers. A must-try is the Oystermouth Stout, made with

oysters to give it the "slightest hint of the sea."

4 | Sheffield Ale Trail

Sheffield, England

The U.K. claims to have no definitive beer capital, but Sheffield begs to differ. The "real ale capital of the world" offers an ale trail that winds past both modern pubs and traditional establishments, taking those who wander down it to some of the country's best places to enjoy a pint.

5 | Hilden Brewery

Lisburn, Northern Ireland

Established in 1981, this is the oldest independent brewery in Northern Ireland. Try one or more of its 11 draft beers in the taproom, or take a tour and learn about its history.

6 | Wadworth Brewery

Wiltshire, England

Located near Bath, this brewery makes beer for all 240 of its pubs, some of which provide accommodation. Make sure to take the tour, see the Shire horses, and climb the brewery tower.

7 | Orkney Brewery

Orkney Islands, Scotland

The remoteness of this island north of Scotland is part of its charm. Visit this former Victorian schoolhouse turned brewery, which offers tours where visitors learn about, and then taste, the terroir in its beer.

8 | Ye Olde Trip to Jerusalem

Nottingham, England

The country's oldest inn dates back to 1189, when the inn was a rest point for those en route from England to Jerusalem. Be sure to tour the cellars carved out of sandstone and the famous pregnancy chair, rumored to increase the fertility of the women who sit in it.

Photos

1 Fuller's London Pride is the flagship beer of Griffin Brewery. **2** The Horse and Groom pub dates back to 1580. **3** Mumbles Pier is a landmark in the village of Mumbles, in Swansea. **5** Beer kegs await transport from Hilden Brewery. **6** Shire horses help deliver beer from Wadworth Brewery.

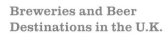

Breweries and Beer Destinations in the U.K.

🍺 Brewery

🍺 Featured beer destination

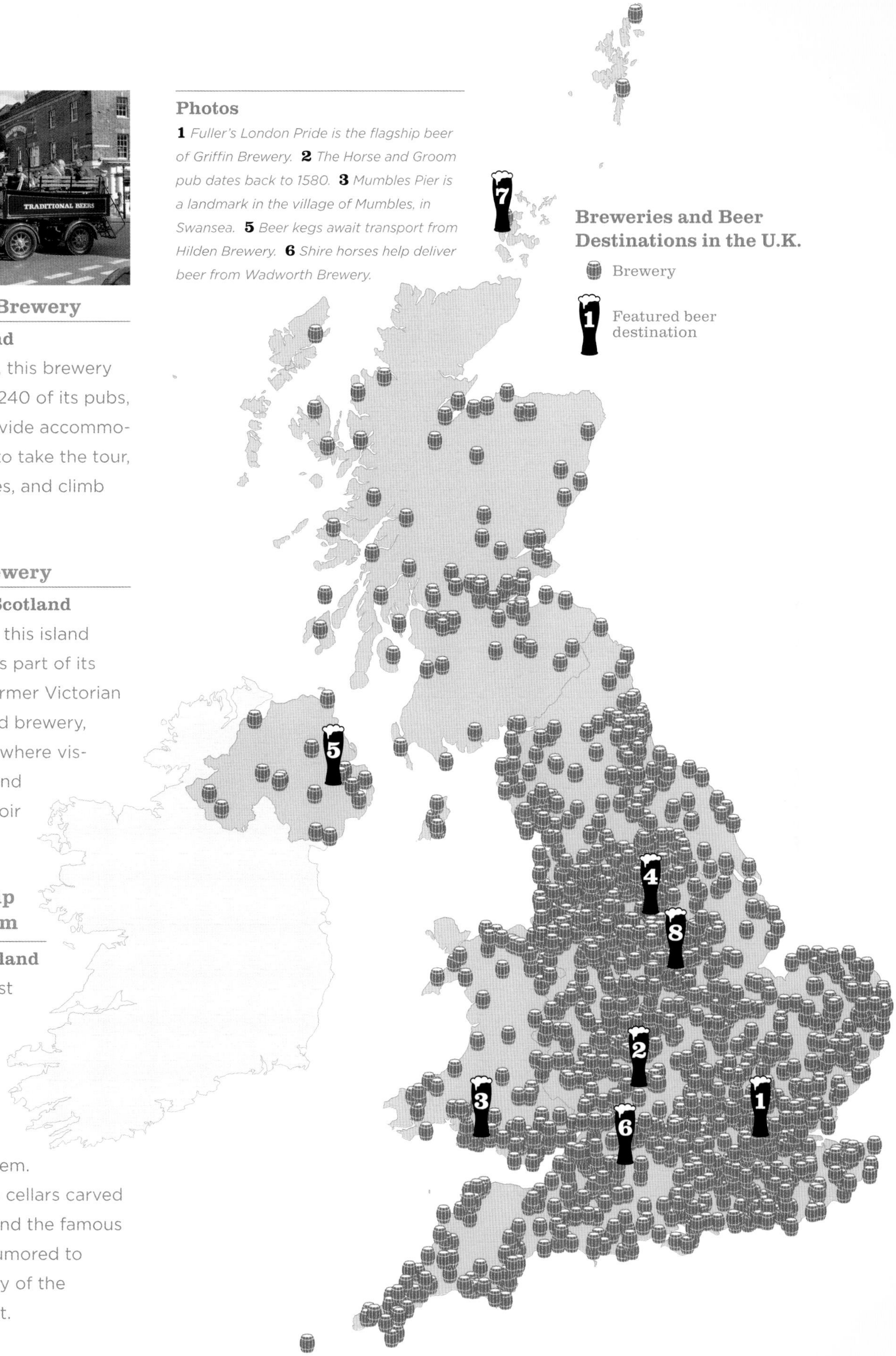

LOCAL BREWS
ENGLAND
KEEPING IT REAL

It was once said that the sun never set on the British Empire. The same could have been said of the empire's beer, which was an everyday part of its subjects' way of life. In the Middle Ages (A.D. 500–1500), beer was one of Britain's most common and healthful drinks, brewed by monks and in people's homes. In fact, the British Isles are part of Europe's beer belt: an area where, historically, beer has long been the alcohol of choice. This preference is in part due to environmental conditions well suited to growing grains such as wheat and barley. Ale was considered a naval necessity as the British Empire expanded in the 15th century—so much so that Henry VII built a naval brewery in Portsmouth in 1492.

Hops made their way here from the Low Countries around the 15th century. Before then, brewers used gruit, a mix of various herbs and spices (see page 72). Even after hops arrived, the English were hesitant to give up gruit. When Henry VIII invaded Picardy—coincidentally, the first place to document hops in beer in A.D. 822—his captain complained that they had no choice but to drink hopped beer when the troops ran out of ale. In the 15th

The Mortal Man is a traditional English inn located in the Lake District and home to a small pub.

and 16th centuries, the English fought to preserve the distinction between "ale" and "beer." Ale was malted and made with gruit, whereas the newer beer was made with hops. But a British law change in 1710 pushed gruit out, cementing hops in England's beer scene.

By the 18th century, gin had become a popular drink and was seen as a destructive one. The Beer House Act of 1830, which loosened restrictions on brewers and the sale of beer, was put in place to help people switch from spirits to what was seen as a safer and healthier beverage. Stout and porter were popular beer styles in the 18th and 19th centuries, particularly in London. But then hopped pale ale and eventually IPA worked their way into the mix alongside milder ales, pushing out dark malted beer and influencing the bitter styles of today.

Lager didn't make its way into the rotation until the mid-20th century, marking a real departure from traditional English ale. England had long made top-fermented beer, whereas lager was bottom-fermented at lower temperatures. As has happened in most of the world, lager has come to dominate much of England's beer market, and almost all of it is now brewed by big conglomerates.

The 1970s was a low point for the English beer scene: few breweries, few owners, and not much choice. Organizations such as the Campaign for Real Ale (CAMRA) grew out of the frustration over these diminishing choices and were quite successful at bringing real ale—cask-conditioned traditional styles—back to the forefront. But CAMRA's success and goals didn't support much of what modern craft breweries were doing: innovating in unconventional ways.

The number of pubs in England is declining and alcohol consumption is falling, but the number of microbreweries began to rise in 2002 when the government gave tax breaks to breweries producing less than 5,000 hectoliters (132,086 gallons) annually, approximately 3,055 U.K. barrels. In England, there is no agreed-upon definition of what a "craft brewery" or "craft beer" actually is, which makes record keeping difficult, but the Society of Independent Brewers reports the English craft beer sector has grown by 15 percent by volume every year since 2013. Moreover, 80 percent of the beer consumed in England is also brewed there.

local flavor
The London Beer Flood

A pub in London called the Holborn Whippet brews an anniversary ale to commemorate an unthinkable accident that unfolded in October 1814, when one of the iron rings around Horse Shoe Brewery's huge wooden fermentation tank snapped. The tank ruptured, releasing 3,500 barrels' worth of brown porter ale. This wave of beer ruptured several more tanks and slammed into one of the brewery's walls. The result was a 320,000-gallon (12,000-hL) torrent of runaway beer. Eyewitness reports say that the resulting wave, 15 feet (5 m) high, slammed into the nearby slum of St. Giles Rookery, killing at least eight people. A jury later cleared the brewery owners of any wrongdoing and awarded them a refund for the excise tax the brewery had paid for the beer.

The Horse Shoe Brewery in 1830, 16 years after the London Beer Flood

LOCAL BREWS
SCOTLAND

BETTER WITH AGE

Rocky mountains, lush glens, picturesque lochs, and embattled coasts all contribute to Scotland's dramatic geography, which has had a major impact on its alcohol. Scotch whisky is likely the first thing that comes to mind when thinking about alcohol in Scotland, so it may come as a surprise to learn that more beer is consumed here than Scotch.

Scotland's beer history, like Europe's, features monasteries at the center of brewing during the Middle Ages (500–1500) and women as the primary brewers for some centuries after that. Unlike elsewhere in Europe, Scotland didn't have hops. Scotland's climate was too cold to grow them, so brewers used heather, myrtle, and broom to bitter beer. Scottish brewers' climate and soils

did bless them with an abundance of barley, wheat, and oats. Since the Scottish climate required yeast that could ferment at colder temperatures, and ale yeast didn't fully ferment quickly, it was common for beer to be lagered in cellars. Thus many Scottish ales showcase the characteristics that come with being aged: They are mellow and smooth, with a full malty taste and a fairly dry finish. Over the centuries, these conditions—along with the region's water—made Scottish beer a force to be reckoned with.

By the mid-19th century, Edinburgh had become one of the brewing centers of the world. While its success was in part due to the accessibility of grain and, later, hops, it was the water from the aquifer beneath the city that made it thrive. A geologic fault provided soft water

local flavor
Scotland's Shilling-Strength Beer

The shilling became a monetary relic when Britain went to decimal currency in 1971, but Scottish shilling-strength beer lives on. In the early 20th century, the beer industry entered the "shilling era," when a beer's name was based on a barrel's invoice price. Originally brought in for taxation, this convention later became an indicator of an ale's style and strength. Low-alcohol beer, known as table and harvest beer, was priced the lowest, between 28 and 36 shillings per barrel. Light and mild ales were a bit higher, at 42 and 48 shillings per barrel, and

pale ales were 54 shillings per barrel. Export and imperial ales invoiced at 70 and 80 shillings, and strong ales at 90 to 160 shillings, depending on the ABV. Because strong ale, with an ABV of 6 to 10 percent, had more alcohol, it was sold in smaller volumes: usually one-third of an English pint. The term "wee heavy" was coined to reflect the style's small volume and to denote its higher alcohol content. Wee heavy is now one of the more commonly produced Scottish-style beers in the United States, forged from this uniquely Scottish tradition.

Scotland's iconic Eilean Donan Castle was built in the 13th century. It is managed by the MacRae family, who have brewed an ale named after the castle.

at certain depths and hard water at others. The soft water had fewer minerals, making it ideal for brewing ales like porter, whereas the hard water was great for making pale ale. This diverse and excellent water allowed Edinburgh's brewers to produce a cornucopia of styles made distinct by local ingredients and Scotland's cold conditions. At the city's brewing peak in 1840, it had 280 breweries. Many were consolidated toward the end of the 19th century, and by the end of World War I that number had fallen to just 11.

In a world where consolidation is the norm, Scotland's beer industry swelled from 11 breweries in 1970 to 93 breweries in 2015. Microbreweries such as BrewDog are revitalizing the beer market: Started in 2007, its pubs have spread to a dozen countries. And though lager-producing conglomerates control 60 percent of the market, dozens of smaller breweries are producing outstanding real ale and craft beer. Scottish preferences are shifting as drinkers discover more choices and demand more variety at their local pubs.

on tap with Garrett Oliver

Scottish Heavy

Northern climes and traditional ties to Europe led Scotland to less hoppy beer with strong continental influences. Scottish brewing techniques and fermentation temperatures bear a greater resemblance to German traditions than to English ones.

ABV 4-6% | **IBU** 12-30

Aroma Malty, bready, slightly fruity, with butterscotch notes

Appearance Pale copper to dark brown

Flavor Distinctly malt-forward with caramel notes and restrained fruit; actual Scottish ales are never peat-smoked

Mouthfeel Medium-bodied, with relatively low carbonation and a full malty richness

Presentation British pint glass

Food Pairings Roasted meat, game, steak, burger

Classic to Try Belhaven Scottish Ale

Prague's Old Town Square is the site of many cultural celebrations, and has beer cafés catering to locals and tourists alike.

CZECHIA

COMING FULL CIRCLE

The rise, fall, and ultimate triumph of Czech brewing mirrors the story of its oldest brewery, Prague's Břevnov Monastery. Records show that Benedictine monks produced beer here as early as A.D. 993. Over the centuries, it was destroyed and rebuilt, seized and liberated, closed and reopened, but ultimately returned to its brewing tradition. Such is the long, resilient history of brewing in Czechia (the Czech Republic).

Nestled between Austria, Germany, Poland, and Slovakia, Czechia has low-lying mountains at its borders that give way to lower, flatter farmlands that resemble a patchwork quilt. Grains and hops flourish here, which is part of what makes this country a leading player in the global beer scene. Hops were used in brewing here as early as 1088—several centuries before the practice caught on in most European countries. Bohemian hops, especially those from the Saaz region, were considered to be of particularly high quality—enough so that they fetched great prices from buyers in neighboring Bavaria (Germany). Emperor Charles IV—who ruled Bohemia during the 14th century and made brewing legal for everyone—expanded the production and limited the export of hops to ensure that domestic brewers had enough. The church and the wealthy controlled much of that market, which gave them power.

AT A GLANCE
Featured Locations

- 🛢 Brewery
- ★ Capital
- ● City
- **BAVARIA** German state
- BOHEMIA Historic region

Beverage of Privilege

In the centuries before Charles IV's rule, monks were responsible for most of the region's brewing. Pope Innocent IV removed a ban on nonmonastic brewing in

Bohemia that had been in place around for 250 years. In larger towns, burghers and nobles often obtained the rights to brew and sell beer. In many cases, this right also included the Mílové Právo (Mile Right), which essentially gave the burghers a monopoly on beer production and sales for a radius of one Czech mile (about 4.6 miles, or 7.4 km). The Mile Right applied only to cities and towns (and the rural areas covered within the Right), leaving residents in the countryside free to brew. But it also led to a decline in beer quality, as breweries that fell within the Right had no competition. Breweries sprang up in many towns that were previously brewery-less, including Svitavy (1256), České Budějovice (1265), and Plzeň (1290). Most produced *bilé pivo* (white beer), a cloudy wheat beer, and *staré pivo* (old beer), a bottom-fermented beer that kept for longer periods. Beer scholars debate whether bilé pivo was taken from Bohemia to neighboring Bavaria in the 15th century, where it evolved into the modern-day weissbier style, or vice versa. Moreover, some beer historians contend that lagering may have started in Bohemia and then was introduced to Bavaria.

Then came the Hussite Wars (1419–1434), when many breweries were destroyed. The 30 Years' War in the first half of the 1600s was also hard on Czech brewing, as the population fell by 30 percent. Before these wars, most breweries were making ales—but that shifted when lagering was introduced.

Rise, Fall, Triumph

While Czechia's pilsner is probably its best-known style, lager was king here when brewing picked up speed again. During the 1860s, the number of breweries producing lager increased from just over 100 to more than 800, due largely to the popularity of pilsner. As this popularity spread, wheat-based beer all but disappeared.

Though breweries were either nationalized or closed after World War II, beer

local flavor
What's in Plzeň's Water?

Though beer drinkers tend to overlook its importance, water quality can have a big impact on a beer's terroir. Such was the case with pilsner, first brewed in the town of Plzeň with the local soft water that helped create its distinctive taste. You cannot make a Czech pilsner using water from another part of the world and expect it to taste the same; that's because the number and type of ions (calcium, sodium, magnesium, etc.) in water change depending on where in the world it's from. "Hard" water has a high mineral content that brings out the bitterness in

hops, making it great for hoppy beer styles. "Soft" water, which has a lower mineral content, can subdue the bitterness of hops. Plzeň's water measures in at 10 parts per million (ppm) for calcium, 3 ppm for magnesium, and 3 ppm for bicarbonate. The result? A light, crisp Czech pilsner that continues to thrill beer drinkers today. It's highly unlikely that Josef Groll, who created pilsner in 1842, knew anything about Plzeň's water-quality profile (see page 87). Czech pilsner, like many traditional beer styles, is a glorious example of serendipity.

remained inexpensive. Unfortunately, the government invested little in these breweries and many fell into a state of disrepair. Those breweries that stayed open usually produced only two styles: a dark lager and a light lager.

When the Velvet Revolution dispatched the communist government in 1989, the Czech brewing industry had a lot of catching up to do. At the start of the 21st century, only 60 breweries were still standing. Then brewpubs opened, experimenting with styles such as native wheat beer—a style they resurrected after 150 years of dormancy. By 2015, the number of breweries had increased to 250.

Resurrecting Choice

Czechia leads the world when it comes to beer consumption, and 98 percent of that beer is domestic pilsner. It ranks near the middle of the European pack in terms of beer imports from Europe and near the bottom when it comes to international beer imports, which goes to show that Czech beer drinkers are very loyal to domestic lager. Pilsner Urquell (Plzeňský Prazdroj) and Budweiser (Budejovický Budvar) are the most consumed beers in the country.

This loyalty doesn't reflect preference as much as a country of price-sensitive lager drinkers. Generations of Czechs were spoiled by cheap beer prices, which is part of the reason why Czech craft brewers say that ale is having a hard time catching on. Even so, the Czech beer scene is becoming increasingly diverse. Prague alone has more than 20 breweries and many specialty beer bars offering selections from around the world and close to home.

Czech pilsners are the drink of choice at the Czech Beer Festival, the largest festival of its kind in the country.

BEER GUIDE

WHERE BEER LOVERS GO

See how much Czechia has contributed to the world's beer scene at these intriguing spots recommended by Czech beer-scene insiders.

1 | Plzeňský Prazdroj

Plzeň

This brewery, which makes the famous Pilsner Urquell, is a 90-minute train ride from Prague. Tour the state-of-the-art bottling plant and an underground labyrinth where the famous beer is lagered, and taste Pilsner Urquell right out of a fermentation barrel. It doesn't get any fresher than that.

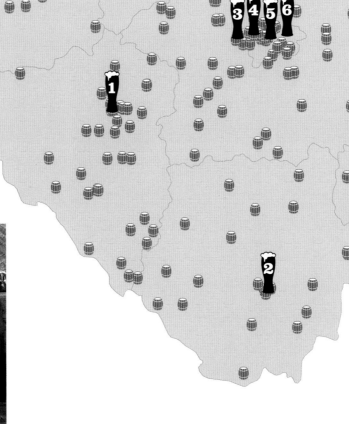

Breweries and Beer Destinations in Czechia

 Brewery

Featured beer destination

2 | Budějovický Budvar
České Budějovice

If you think Budweiser is all-American, think again. This

brewery is home to the original Budweiser, and fiercely proud of the beer it produces. With its light, floral aroma and slightly grassy taste, the Czech original is nothing like the U.S. version.

3 | Prague Beer Museum
Prague

If a museum trip sounds sedate, never fear—this museum is far from typical. It houses a collection of the best beer in Czechia, all of which can be sampled. With good food, live music, and more than 30 beers on tap, museumgoing doesn't sound so stuffy.

4 | Bernard Pivní Lázně/ Beer Spa
Prague

Imagine soaking in a warm, soothing bath. Now imagine the water has yeast and fine Czech hops in it (no barley, though). Imagine drinking a great Czech pilsner while you soak away your cares, then enjoying a massage and an unlimited supply of unpasteurized Bernard beer. You aren't dreaming; you're at a beer spa.

5 | U Fleků
Prague

Operating since 1499, this brewery produces one style, a dark lager, that is only sold on-site. Spend time in the amazing beer garden in the center of the building, as well as the eight ornately decorated halls, perfect for any get-together.

6 | Pivovarský Dům
Prague

One of a handful of craft breweries in Prague, this is a great place to go when you need a reprieve from pilsner. At Pivovarský Dům, variety is the spice of life. Try the coffee beer, sour-cherry beer, nettle beer, banana beer . . . the list goes on.

Photos

1 *Barrels of Pilsner Urquell are stored in a network of underground caves.* **2** *An original Budweiser is poured at Budějovický Budvar.* **4** *Enjoy a beer and a bath at the Beer Spa Bernard in Prague.* **5** *Live music is part of the tradition at U Fleků's beer garden.*

LOCAL BREWS
PLZEŇ & PRAGUE

BREWING UP UNIQUE STYLES

THE CITY THAT INVENTED PILSNER
Located about 60 miles (100 km) southwest of Prague, the Bohemian city of Plzeň and its surroundings have profoundly shaped the world of beer. It's the birthplace of the wildly popular pilsner and the home of Plzeňský Prazdroj (Pilsner Urquell), the brewery that first produced it. Pilsner was first brewed in the 1830s, when Plzeň was inundated with low-quality lagers. Some of the town's burghers decided to build their own brewery and commissioned Martin Stelzer, a local architect, to design it. Stelzer visited breweries in Bavaria to learn about what it took to build one. Josef Groll (see page 87) was hired as the brewer, and he was the one who created the style. But Plzeň's water is what made pilsner so popular (see page 82). Most tourists travel to Plzeň to check out the Pilsner Urquell brewery, but it's far from the only beer being brewed here. There is also Gambrinus, a beer brand named after a mythical king of Flanders whose brewing abilities are the stuff of legend.

Plzeň's rich and remarkable beer history is documented at the local beer museum. It's also a stop along a regional beer trail, which includes breweries such as Dobřanská Pivo in nearby Dobřany. Plzeň is also close to Rokycany, home to the microbrewery U Stočesů, which brews several different takes on pilsner. Žatec, north of Plzeň, is the area where the famed Saaz hops used to make pilsner are grown. Ninety percent of these hops are used in Czechia, thanks largely to the export restrictions Emperor Charles IV put in place some seven centuries earlier. Pull up a chair and taste how those hops have shaped the region's styles.

BUILDING ON TRADITION Prague is known for many things, including its bridges, its baroque architecture, and its beer. Though Prague's beer history has largely been overshadowed by Plzeň's, the city has around 30 small breweries, giving Pražané (the Czech word for Prague's residents) plenty of choice. In *The Beer Guide to Prague*, noted beer writer Evan Rail calls Prague the best beer city in Europe, as it has numerous breweries, brewpubs, bottle shops, and specialty beer bars.

Czech pilsner still dominates, but Prague's breweries are working to expand Czech beer lovers' palates by introducing them to other styles. Even

Modern sculptures adorn Plzeň's Square of the Republic, once the largest square in Europe.

some of Prague's oldest breweries are shifting away from the classic pilsner. Every major brewery in the region now produces a traditional black lager, bringing back what was once a popular indigenous style. Perhaps the best known brewery in Prague is U Fleků, which has been in operation since 1499. The brewery is famous both for its longevity and its lone beer, a dark lager called Flekovský Ležák 13. The beautiful Břevnov Monastery, the first friary in Bohemia and one of the earliest Czech breweries, reopened in 2012 after a 120-year brewing hiatus. Visitors can try a Czech lager, a dark lager, a wheat beer, an imperial lager, and an abbey IPA—not quite an English IPA or an American IPA, but something all its own.

local flavor
The Birth of Pilsner

Pilsner is the world's top-selling beer style, claiming nearly 90 percent of the market. So where did this celebrated style come from? Its story opens in 1839, when Plzeň, because of its proximity to Bavaria, became inundated with the dark Bavarian-style lager. To fight back against the flood of imports, the town's burghers decided to build their own brewery and produce a local lager. While legends about the invention of pilsner abound, the more historically accurate story leads to a Bavarian brewer named Josef Groll who was hired to brew beer in Plzeň's new brewery around 1840. He wanted to produce a high-quality beer that no one in Plzeň (or anywhere else, for that matter) had tried before. He labored in secret until 1842, when the beer was ready. Then he rolled a barrel into the town square and presented the townsfolk with a pale gold lager. Initially they were taken aback, as they were used to all beer being dark. But as soon as they tried it, they knew that Groll was on to something. He eventually returned to his native Bavaria, where he continued brewing pilsner. The brewery where Groll worked was eventually named Plzeňský Prazdroj. Today we know it as Pilsner Urquell, which means "from the original source."

PLZEŇ
Pilsner

Pilsner was a golden sensation when it arrived on the scene in the mid-1800s. Its clarity and pale hue vanquished all other traditional beers in its path, and established it as the beer of the future.

ABV 4.5–5.2% | **IBU** 30–45

Aroma Richly malty and bready, with floral, herbal hop notes; some examples are slightly buttery

Appearance Full to deep gold

Flavor Complex bready malts balanced by soft, insistent bitterness

Mouthfeel Medium-bodied, with high drinkability

Presentation Pilsner glass, often footed

Food Pairings Very versatile, from fried fish to burgers

Classic to Try Pilsner Urquell

PRAGUE
Czech Black Lager

While Prague has certainly taken up the basic pilsner style, its true beer is an older style of dark lager that is still popular today. Brewed by every major brewery in the region, this beer shows colors ranging from *tmavý* (dark) to *černý* (black). The best examples drink beautifully and invite lingering sessions in Prague's great beer halls.

ABV 4.7–5.2% | **IBU** 20–30

Aroma High-temperature caramel, dark bread, light coffee, and chocolate

Appearance Dark brown, nearly black, with reddish highlights

Flavor Structured, with dominant light roast and caramel; remains very drinkable

Mouthfeel Medium-bodied and balanced

Presentation Footed tumbler

Food Pairings Roasted or grilled meat and fowl, grilled vegetables—versatile

Classic to Try Staropramen Dark

Historically, Paris's Montmartre district was home to artists of all kinds. Today, it is a lively, bustling neighborhood filled with cafés.

FRANCE

JOIE DE VIVRE

France is undoubtedly a land of the vine, where wine is typically named after its region of origin (Bordeaux, Beaujolais, Champagne) rather than the grape from which it is made. Beer may not hold the revered position that wine does in French culture, but it certainly has a place in the country's illustrious history of alcoholic drinks.

Archaeological evidence uncovered in Provence indicates that beer was brewed in France as early as the Late Bronze Age (1700–1200 B.C.). Findings at Provence's Roquepertuse archaeological site indicate that barley was malted and kiln-dried during the Iron Age (1200–600 B.C.), suggesting a rather sophisticated knowledge of beermaking given the technology available at the time.

Fast-forward to the Early Middle Ages (A.D. 500–1000) when brewing was a household activity in France. The early ninth century also saw French monasteries start brewing their own beer, which gained them a monopoly that lasted until the 14th century and the Hundred Years' War (1337–1453) between France and England. By the late 1480s, Paris had enacted laws to oversee brewing in the city. A new guild created mandatory apprenticeships, policed over brewing disputes, and tasted all beer before it was sold.

When peace returned to France and monasteries began brewing again, the Benedictines and the Cistercians (an offshoot of the Benedictine order) were the primary religious brewers. It is from the Cistercians that a separate order evolved, starting in 1664, called the Trappists (see page 38). Leading up to the French

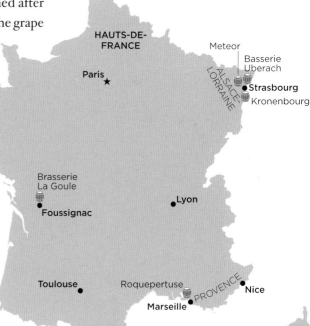

AT A GLANCE
Featured Locations

🛢	Brewery
★	Capital
●	City
PROVENCE	Historic province, or territory
HAUTS-DE-FRANCE	Region

Revolution (1789–1799), at least nine Trappist monasteries produced beer in France. Today, none are left. The French Revolution, and the subsequent battles led by Napoleon Bonaparte, forced many brewers and monks to flee for places like Belgium and the Netherlands, taking their brewing knowledge with them.

Boom and Bust

Technological advancements brought on by the industrial revolution were a double-edged sword for the brewing industry—they helped it grow, but they also made the field competitive. By 1910 France had nearly 3,000 breweries. World War I reduced this number to just over 900, and continued consolidation often left towns with only one brewery. By the end of World War II, the number had fallen to slightly more than 500. By 1975, only 23 breweries were operating in France.

A Quiet Revolution

France's artisanal (craft) beer movement started in the 1980s, led by brewers dissatisfied with beer that had little to no connection to the country's culture

local flavor
The Alchemy of Artisanal Beer

France had nearly 3,000 breweries at its brewing height in the late 1800s and early 1900s. The breweries were generally small, often producing beer for a single town, pub, or tavern. Brewers knew—though they didn't totally understand how or why—that using ingredients grown in different locations would produce different-tasting beer. This is the essence of terroir, which was slowly becoming understood in France's wine and beer industries.

The French often talk about terroir today in terms of wine. But wine is shaped by only one ingredient—grapes—whereas beer is shaped by grains, hops, water, and adjuncts. Terroir marks one of the biggest differences between today's macro- and microbreweries: Macrobreweries engineer terroir out of their beer to ensure that it tastes consistent across all markets, while craft brewers embrace the variation that comes with encouraging a taste of place. Like alchemists tinkering with raw materials to make gold, French craft brewers are trying ingredients from different locales to brew the perfect beer.

Jean-Philippe Mallé is the head brewer at O'Neil brewery in the heart of Saint-Germain-des-Prés, Paris.

and history. These early craft brewers faced an uphill battle against foreign imports, which soon became fixtures in the French beerscape. But in some areas in France, craft beer built up a promising base. Craft breweries returned to French tradition, using local ingredients to make beer that reflected the land in the same ways that wine did.

The rise of French artisanal brewing started in the countryside, where brewers had an intimate knowledge of the land. Terroir has always been an important part of French food and drink, and beer is no exception. Modern French craft brewers are also not afraid to borrow from other countries' brewing traditions, and to experiment with what they throw into the boil. Raspberries, blueberries, apricots, cherries, and other fruits often find their way into French craft beer. Brasserie Uberach in Alsace makes a beer called Juliette with roses, ginger, and peaches, and Brasserie La Goule in Foussignac makes La Goule Bois Bandé with *bois bandé* (erection wood), a tree spice from the Caribbean said to be an aphrodisiac.

France's craft beer terroir varies, but one thing rings consistently true of all French craft beer: It represents a departure from macrobrewery offerings. As France's beer scene grows, the fight for a more diverse beerscape is one revolution that French beer lovers will likely win.

Patrons enjoy local Parisian craft beer at Chez Prune, a bar and bistro along Canal Saint-Martin.

BEER GUIDE

WHERE BEER LOVERS GO

France's breweries are producing some outstanding beer. But don't take our word for it; check out these recommendations from French brewers.

1 | La Brasserie Artisanale de Nice

Nice

Ah, the French Riviera—people (and beer) full of beauty, wealth, and class. This brewery in the heart of Nice has a brewer, Olivier Cautain, who takes pride in using local ingredients. Try his Zytha, a crisp blonde ale made with chickpeas.

2 | Brasserie de la Goutte d'Or

Paris

This brewery's name translates to "The Golden Drop," named after the wine produced here during the Middle Ages. It is located in the working-class neighborhood that some call African Paris. While the brewery is small in size, its beers are a big hit. Adventurous souls should try the Go Men, a session ale made with wasabi.

3 | Pico'Mousse

Lyon

Learn about brewing craft beer at Pico'Mousse, then seize the chance to make your own. Decide what beer style to brew, then share the fruit of your labor a few weeks later when your beer is ready to drink.

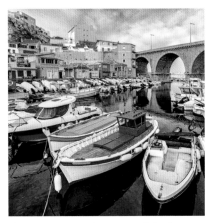

4 | Brasserie de la Plaine

Marseille

Located far from France's craft beer hot spots, this brewery is making a name for itself. The brewer, Salem Haji, has been called the Walter White of French microbrew. He makes such good beer that even local wine stores are carrying it. Try the Houblonnée (French for "hoppy"), an American-style IPA.

5 | Autour d'une Bière

Toulouse

This beer shop in southern France is far from Germany and Belgium, but it carries exceptional beer from both countries as well as local French brews.

Keep an eye out for something special for the *tégestophile* (someone who collects beer paraphernalia) in your life.

6 | Le Triangle

Paris

At this small microbrewery, restaurant, and beer bar, pairing beer with food is the name of the game. The chef and beer sommelier work together to create the best pairings. Try the Cèdre des Barbares (Cedar Barbarians), an IPA that's been aged in Spanish cedar barrels.

Photos

1 *Place Masséna in downtown Nice is home to the Fontaine du Soleil (Sun Fountain).*
3 *Visitors to Pico'Mousse craft their own beers from scratch, including hop choice.*
4 *Fishing boats dock in Vallon des Auffes harbor in Marseille.* **5** *Autour d'une Bière in Toulouse carries beers from across Europe.*

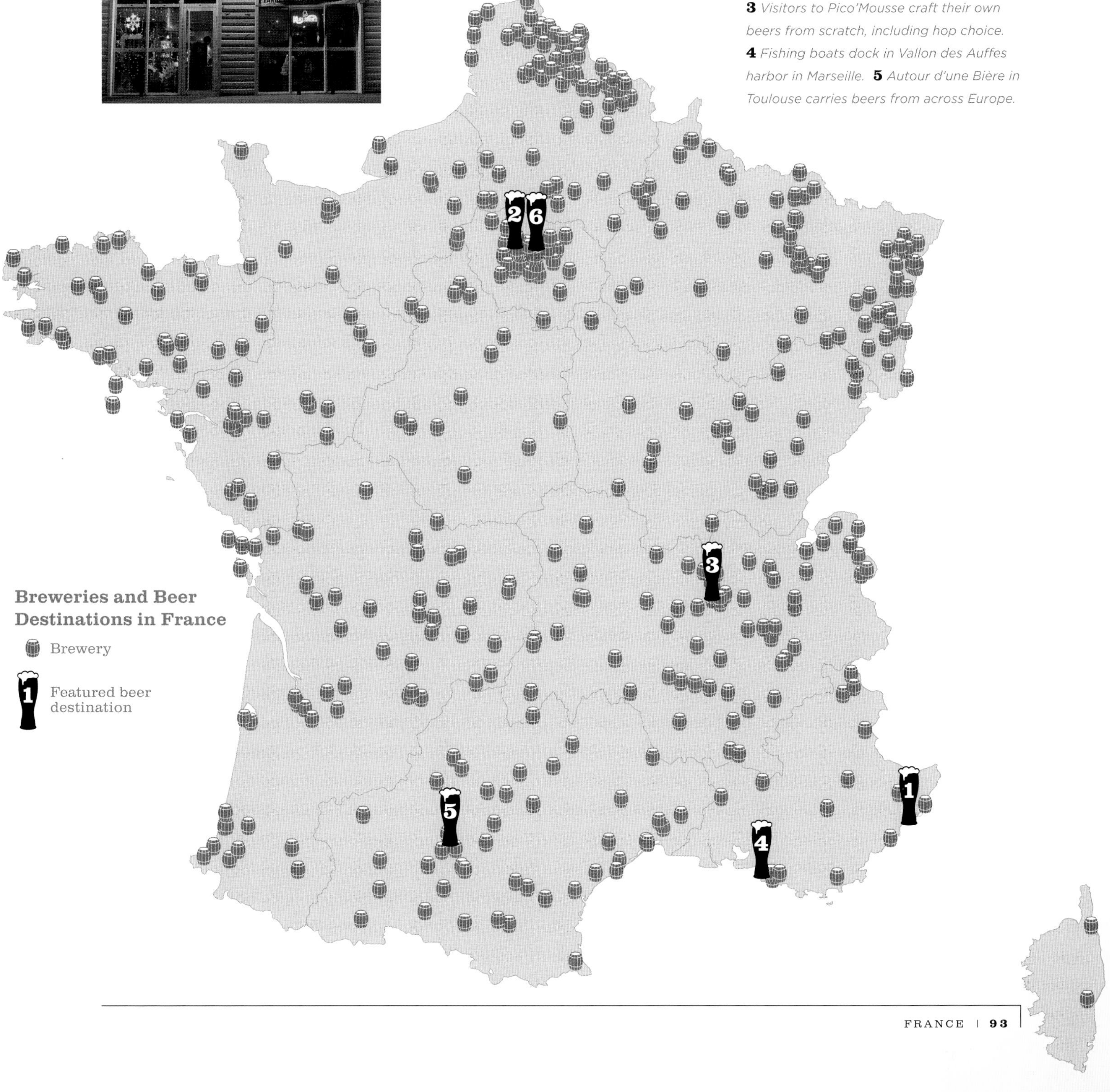

Breweries and Beer Destinations in France

🛢 Brewery

🍺 Featured beer destination

LOCAL BREWS
ALSACE-LORRAINE & HAUTS-DE-FRANCE

EVER FLOWING TAPS

BEERS APLENTY Alsace-Lorraine—in the northeastern part of France and bordering Belgium, Luxembourg, Germany, and Switzerland—produces more beer than anywhere else in the country. Brewer and maltster Arnoldus Cervisarius founded the region's first brewery that was neither monastery nor household in 1259. By the 1800s Strasbourg, a town on the Rhine River and abutting the German border, had more than 250 breweries. The region is home to France's largest breweries, including Kronenbourg and Meteor, whose lagers dominate the French beer market. Evidence of the region's close geographic and cultural connection with Germany shows through in the pilsner and other lager styles brewed here.

Two beer styles got their start in this region, both born from the movement from season to season. The *bière de Mars* (beer of March), also called *bière de printemps* (beer of spring), was traditionally brewed by farmers in late winter or early spring and was meant to be consumed right after fermentation. The second style is *bière de Noël* (Christmas beer). To make space to store the harvest, farmers would empty storage bins of grains left over from the previous year. These grains were used to produce the last brew of the season, typically in late October. More grains and hops were used and topped off with additional sugar and spices. The result was an amber to brown beer with spicy notes and a high alcohol level: in other words, holiday cheer in a glass.

BREW TO KEEP Hauts-de-France has more breweries than any other region in France. It borders Belgium, whose influence in the realm of styles,

---

Speakeasy

How to Order Beer in France

Once you arrive at the pub, order by saying **"Une bière, s'il vous plait"** (Oo-n BEE-yair, si voo play): "A beer, please." When toasting, say **"Santé"** (SAN-tey), which means "Good health."

───────

When ordering a **bière à la pression** (BEE-yair ah lah preh-syohN), or draft beer, you'll need to indicate which one you want. You can ask for it by name, or you can order it by style:
bière brune (BEE-yair broon)—stout
bière blonde (BEE-yair blond)—lager

bière blanche (BEE-yair blanch)— white beer
bière anglaise (BEE-yair AN-glez)—ale
le blé (LE blay)—wheat

───────

You'll also need to pick a serving size. The two most common are **une pinte** (OON peent), a pint, and **un demi** (un de-MEE), a half pint.

While the word **brasserie** (BRA-sir-REE) does mean "brewery," it is also used to denote a restaurant that does not necessarily make beer. Make sure to check the menu before asking for a **table** (TAH-ble), or table.

The architecture in Colmar, a town in Alsace, is heavily influenced by nearby Germany, much like its beer.

ALSACE-LORRAINE
Blonde Export Lager

Reflecting the tug-of-war between Germany and France that has shaped this region, Alsatian beer shows traditional Germanic roots with occasional French flair. It can be considered a stronger, more full-bodied variant of pilsner.

ABV 5.5% | **IBU** 20-25

Aroma Bready, malty, with a distinctly floral hop aroma

Appearance Bright full gold

Flavor Candied malts in a dryish frame with good hop aromatics

Mouthfeel Fairly full-bodied, but avoiding sweetness

Presentation Pilsner glass

Food Pairings Tarte flambée, choucroute, ham

Classic to Try Licorne Elsass

NORD-PAS-DE-CALAIS
Bière de Garde

Earthier, rounder, and sweeter than its Belgian cousin, the saison, the French farmhouse ale excels at the dinner table. Slightly musty flavors are fairly common, though opinion varies as to their desirability.

ABV 6-8.5% | **IBU** 20-28

Aroma Malty and biscuity, sometimes showing slight spiciness

Appearance Blonde through amber to brown, depending on type

Flavor Malty, smooth, and almost sweet, but drying into the finish

Mouthfeel Medium-bodied, with moderate carbonation

Presentation Tulip glass, chalice, or footed goblet

Food Pairings Roasted fowl, game meat, charcuterie, washed-rind cheese

Classic to Try Brasserie de Saint Sylvestre 3 Monts

ingredients, and seasonal brewing is apparent in every sip of Hauts-de-France beer. The craft beer industry has returned here with a vengeance, and there's now more than 40 microbreweries in the region. Geography has helped brewing thrive here, too, thanks to clean groundwater and soils and a climate conducive to growing barley, wheat, and hops. It doesn't hurt that the region is largely inhospitable for growing grapes, thus ruling it out as a wine region.

This brewing hotbed gave rise to France's native bière de garde. Often compared to its Belgian relative, the saison, bière de garde is typically richer, maltier, and not as tart. Historically, brewing was done here in the cooler months to keep the beer from spoiling, which meant no one was brewing in summer. The bière de garde style was developed to make sure beer was available to hardworking farmers during warmer months, so it was made with a higher ABV (6 to 8 percent) to keep it fresher for longer. Expect a mild, spicy taste with toasted or caramel notes and a slight acidity in this highly carbonated, amber-colored beer. Many brewers outside the region are making bière de garde, but those looking for a taste of this region's terroir will find it only in the brews of northern France.

Dingle, a small town in southwest Ireland, has a population of 1,500 but boasts nearly 40 pubs—most of which serve Guinness.

IRELAND

QUINTESSENTIAL PUB CULTURE

The Emerald Isle's famous pubs are everywhere: tucked among its green hills, its rural villages, and the thrumming streets of historic Dublin. These pubs are part of the island's living history; they've helped forge the national identity and continue to be an important part of Irish community. From the famous Irish stout to the lesser-known red ale, the Irish have long used brewing as a means of differentiating themselves from foreign powers across the Irish Sea.

Ireland has the oldest known pub in the world, dating back to A.D. 900 near the island's geographical center in the town of Athlone. But brewing beer in Ireland goes back even further, all the way to the Bronze Age (2400 to 800 B.C.). As in most of Europe, brewing in Ireland was done largely in monasteries. Ireland's patron saint, St. Patrick, assigned a priest named Mescan to the role of brewer in the fifth century A.D. Local cottage breweries, most of which were run by women, replaced monasteries as the dominant brewing center in the 1600s. These women, called alewives, were common throughout Ireland and most of Europe, particularly in medieval times. They often had cats around to catch the rodents that ate their grains. Many brewed outside, spending much time hunched over a cauldron. When the beer was ready to sell, they would tie barley stalks to the end of a long stake that looked like a broom. Thus alewives helped inspire our vision of witches and witchcraft. These early brewers didn't have readily available hops until the mid-18th century—Ireland's climate was not conducive to growing them—so they often used gentian root, which had a bittering effect.

Importation of English beer to Ireland grew steadily in the 18th century,

AT A GLANCE
Featured Locations

🛢 Brewery
★ Capital
● City
NORTHERN IRELAND   Non-subject country

It takes **119.5** seconds to pour the perfect pint of Guinness draft.

partially because the American colonies stopped buying it, but domestic Irish beer production still remained relatively constant. Not even the potato famine (1845–49) could keep Irish beer down: The population decreased by 20 to 25 percent, prompting Irish breweries to turn to the rest of the world to sell their beer.

Big Names in Brewing

Many of the country's most famous beers are named after the men who founded their respective breweries. In 1710 John Smithwick established Ireland's first large-scale commercial brewery in Kilkenny. Arthur Guinness set up his brewery in Dublin in 1759. The two Williams—Beamish and Crawford—founded theirs in Cork in 1792, while James Murphy started his Cork-based brewery in 1856. By the start of the 1800s, Ireland had nearly 100 local breweries.

Porter, including stout, was all the rage in 19th-century Dublin and London. Though we think of porter and stout as dark styles, early versions made with brown and amber malt varied quite a lot depending on where they were brewed. Then the deeply roasted black patent malt was introduced in 1817, which made porter much darker. It became so popular in Ireland that huge quantities were imported from England, but Dublin eventually brewed so much of it that the city exported more to London than it imported from there. The demand prompted Arthur Guinness to switch from brewing ales to brewing porter. His brewery soon became the largest not just in Ireland but also in all of Europe, exporting its stout across the globe. By the time World War II broke out, Guinness and Mountjoy were the only two breweries left in Dublin.

local flavor
Worldwide Love for the Irish Pub

The pub, short for "public house," was historically a place in Ireland where anyone could go to drink. Private houses required a membership, so pubs were favored by the working class. For many Irish, a visit to a local (the colloquial term for pub) is more than just an opportunity to enjoy a beer. It also offers a chance to socialize, discuss current events, and gossip. Great Irish writers such as James Joyce, William Butler Yeats, Oscar Wilde, and Samuel Beckett were regular pub visitors. Back in the mid-20th century, you could drink around the clock in Dublin—at a pub until it closed, then at a "bona fide" pub located the required distance outside of town to be officially for travelers, and then at an underground club or a "kip"

speakeasy, where the menu was predominantly spirits and a bit of hedonism. For those still up for it, the last port of call was an "early house," a pub that opened around 7 a.m. Early houses originally catered to fishmongers, milkmen, and market gardeners, but now are more often enjoyed by those coming off a night shift or waiting until the majority of pubs open around midmorning. Only about 15 of the 1,000 pubs in Dublin city and county are early houses.

The popularity of Irish pubs has led businesses like the Irish Pub Company to partner with beer conglomerates such as Diageo to build pubs across the globe. These days travelers can go almost anywhere in the world and enjoy the ambiance of an Irish-style pub.

The Rising Beer Tide

Since the end of World War II, consolidation, mergers, and acquisitions have made it difficult for craft breweries to enter the Irish market.

The craft beer movement sputtered in the early 1980s. Most pubs already had distribution agreements with larger breweries, which encouraged publicans (pub owners) not to sell craft beer. Though their first two breweries failed, Liam LaHart and Oliver Hughes succeeded in opening Ireland's first modern brewpub, Porterhouse Brewing Company, in 1996 in Dublin's Temple Bar neighborhood.

Craft beer accounts for less than 2 percent of today's Irish beer market, but that number is growing. Ireland has more than 60 craft breweries, up from 12 in 2008. In 2010 only 27 pubs offered craft beer, while today there are more than 650 serving it. To put things in perspective, Ireland has more than 7,500 pubs, with more than 1,000 in Dublin alone—so craft breweries have plenty of room to expand. While craft breweries are developing a domestic following, many are also cultivating an export market. With one in four Irish beers being shipped overseas, finding an Irish beer outside Ireland is easier than ever.

Nancy's Pub, a family-owned bar in County Donegal, is filled with antiques curated by the former owner, Margaret McHugh.

BEER GUIDE

WHERE BEER LOVERS GO

Irish brewers recommended these highlights of Ireland's beer scene. These destinations show there's more to Ireland than dark beer.

1 | Guinness Storehouse
Dublin

Make time for one of Dublin's most famous landmarks. Visit the museum in the storehouse to learn about the history of Ireland and Guinness. Learn to pour the perfect pint, then enjoy a dry Irish stout in the Gravity Bar, which is located on the seventh floor and has an exceptional 360-degree view of the city.

2 | Eight Degrees Brewing Company
Mitchelstown

This brewery in northern County Cork, run by an Aussie and a Kiwi, produces an amazing line of single-hop IPAs, one of which is a 2016 Dublin Cup award winner. The IPAs don't last long, so there is no telling what will be available on any given day.

3 | Oslo
Galway

Should you find yourself on Ireland's dramatic, windswept west coast, this bar is definitely worth a visit as it's the mother ship of Galway Bay Brewery. Try some or all of its five regular beer styles, including the award-winning Of

Foam and Fury, a double IPA. It offers limited-edition and seasonal bottled beers as well.

4 | Temple Bar Area
Dublin

Dozens of pubs and bars are located in this area, which extends over four blocks at Dublin's vibrant heart, where visitors celebrate one of Ireland's favorite pastimes: sharing a pint. Be sure to stop by the famous Temple Bar pub at the center of all the bustle.

5 | Metalman Brewing Company
Waterford

Crystal isn't the only treasure produced in Waterford. This brewery's pale ale and seasonal

beers, as well as unique standouts like their Equinox (a wheat lager) and Heatsink (a chili porter), are putting this brewery on Ireland's beer destination map.

6 | Franciscan Well Brewery

Cork

Founded in 1998 and built on the site of a 13th-century Franciscan monastery, this brewery makes chemical- and preservative-free beer that includes its bestsellers Rebel Red and Shandon Stout.

7 | Dublin Literary Pub Crawl

Dublin

Joyce, Shaw, Yeats, Wilde—Ireland's literary tradition is rich in masterful writers. This pub crawl stops in for refreshments at four different pubs, where actors recite the prose of famous Irish writers. This evening full of stories, history, and regional beer is truly one to savor.

Photos

1 *The Guinness Storehouse in Dublin is a top tourist spot.* **3** *The Oslo bar is the flagship pub of the Galway Bay Brewery.* **4** *Dublin's Temple Bar pub was established in 1840.* **5** *Lismore Castle is one of the sights in the scenic town of Waterford.*

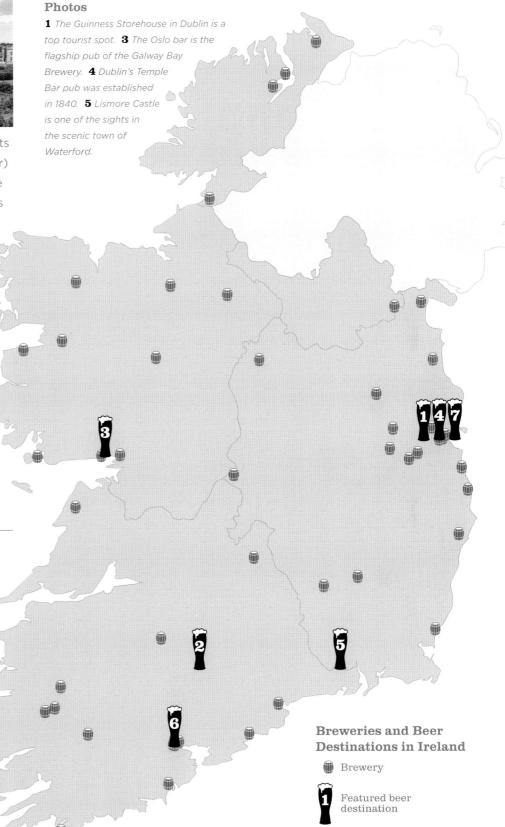

Breweries and Beer Destinations in Ireland

🍺 Brewery

🍺 Featured beer destination

LOCAL BREWS
DUBLIN & CORK
DARK AND STORMY

THE DARK BEER OF DUBLIN Ireland's political capital is also arguably its beer capital. The greater Dublin area contains 1.8 million people and 16 breweries: more than any other city in Ireland. Guinness is by far the city's largest beer producer, though its sales have been declining across the whole of Ireland. No need to worry about this Dublin icon, though: When Arthur Guinness took over St. James Gate Brewery in 1759, he signed a 9,000-year lease. But the Irish *are* drinking less than they used to, and their beer preferences are becoming more diverse. Ireland's contemporary beer drinkers enjoy a pint of stout, but it doesn't necessarily have to be a Guinness. Indeed, Irish craft breweries like Carlow and Porterhouse are producing stout to compete with

Guinness. And of course, pubs in Dublin serve many different brands of stout.

Dubliners today have more eclectic tastes, and craft breweries are stepping up to meet their diversifying palates. In fact, domestic craft beer sales in Dublin and Ireland have increased over the past five years. The IPA is becoming increasingly popular, and craft breweries are turning out their own versions.

Pubs and breweries are not the only places contributing to the craft beer scene. Dublin is home to several beer festivals, including the Irish Craft Beer Festival, the largest of its kind in Ireland. Guinness still reigns in Dublin, but there is much more to talk about here than Irish stout.

local flavor
How Guinness Got Into Records

Did you know that the record for the most 1-liter (34-oz) beer-filled steins carried by an individual is 24? Or that the largest number of beer bottles opened using a chain saw in one minute is also 24? Keeping track of such superlatives began in earnest in 1955 with the first edition of the *Guinness Book of Records*. Its roots go back to 1951, which is when Sir Hugh Beaver and his host went bird hunting. They got into an argument over which was Europe's fastest game bird: the golden plover or the red grouse. These gentlemen didn't have an Internet

database to check or a record book to reference, so their argument had to go unsettled. A few years later, Beaver commissioned two brothers, Norris and Ross McWhirter, to compile a book filled with such argument-settling superlatives. The book was published in 1955 and became an instant bestseller. Since the company Beaver worked for as a managing director provided him with the funding needed to hire the brothers, it had its name printed on the book's cover. Today we know it as the *Guinness World Records*.

Ha'Penny Bridge crosses the River Liffey in Dublin.

REBELS WITH A CAUSE In the beautiful southern city of Cork, craft brewery Franciscan Well is brewing beer on the site of a 13th-century monastery that, like so many of its time, produced beer. The city is also home to some of Ireland's historic names in brewing, the two most famous being Murphy's and Beamish & Crawford. Murphy's was founded in 1856, producing an Irish red ale and a stout meant to be a lighter, less bitter alternative to Guinness. Murphy's in-town rival, Beamish & Crawford, founded its brewery in 1792. It was very successful with porter—so much so that for several years Cork Porter Brewery was the largest in Ireland.

Cork got the nickname of Rebel City because it was home to Michael Collins, a leader in Ireland's independence movement in the early 1900s. The success of Cork's Irish red ales certainly reflects a spirit of rebellion here. In a country dominated by Irish stout, Irish red ale offers beer lovers a slightly sweet, lightly hopped alternative. Franciscan Well's Rebel Red is now the best-selling domestic craft beer in Ireland, and other breweries are introducing unique versions of Irish red ale.

on tap with Garrett Oliver

DUBLIN
Irish Stout

Perhaps no beer style is so emblematic of its home country as Irish stout, which is so intertwined with the culture that we might not be surprised if its image appeared on the national flag.

ABV 3.9–4.5% | **IBU** 35–45

Aroma Coffee, dark chocolate, with better examples showing light, resiny hops

Appearance Very dark brown to jet-black, with a trademark thick, tan foam

Flavor Dry and relatively bitter, with notes of coffee and dark chocolate

Mouthfeel Light, crisp, and dry with a roasted bite; thick foam adds creaminess

Presentation British pint glass

Food Pairings Roasted meat, ham, Stilton cheese, sausage

Craft to Try O'Hara's Irish Stout

CORK
Irish Red Ale

Beer enthusiasts will argue over whether this is truly a native style or something that sprang from an inventive (and probably American) marketing department. Regardless, many Irish craft brewers are perfectly happy to "nationalize" it and have made the style their own.

ABV 4.5–5.2% | **IBU** 18–25

Aroma Caramel malts, with a gentle hint of roast

Appearance Deep reddish amber

Flavor Slightly sweet, soft caramel flavors with bitterness in gentle balance

Mouthfeel Medium-bodied and round; very drinkable

Presentation British pint glass

Food Pairings Beef, pork, roasted meat, washed-rind cheese

Craft to Try Eight Degrees Brewing Company Sunburnt Irish Red Ale

Many of the quaint outdoor trattorias that Tuscany is known for are starting to serve craft beer in addition to wine.

ITALY

REDISCOVERING BEER

Whether it's the mountains and lakes in northern Italy, the tree-lined agricultural fields in Tuscany, or Sicily's iconic Mount Etna volcano, this country's landscape is nothing if not picturesque. Its terroir shines through its wine—a huge part of life here—but also shows up in its beer, shaping a scene that grows more exciting with time.

As far back as the seventh century B.C., the Phoenicians (from a region that now includes Israel, Syria, Lebanon, and Jordan) consumed and traded beer in Sicily. In the foothills of the Italian Alps to the north, traces of beer have been discovered in tombs dating back to the sixth century B.C. Beer probably wasn't introduced into Roman culture until Rome's first emperor, Augustus, defeated Cleopatra in 31 B.C. and Egypt became part of the Roman Empire. A century later, in A.D. 77, the Roman historian Pliny the Elder wrote about beer in his 37-volume *Naturalis Historia,* saying that the Celts who came from northwestern Europe and lived in what is now Italy must have had a basic understanding of the causes of fermentation, as their beer did not spoil as quickly as the beer made by Egyptians.

Beer pops up in Italy's history when Roman general Gnaeus Julius Agricola returned to Rome after conquering Britain in A.D. 85, bringing three brewers with him. It shows up again nearly 400 years later, when St. Benedict founded the order of Benedictine monks at Monte Cassino in central Italy. He understood the importance of beer as a source of nourishment, so monks were given a daily ration equivalent to nearly ten 12-ounce (355-mL) bottles; the beer wasn't quite so strong

AT A GLANCE
Featured Locations

🛢	Brewery
★	Capital
●	City
+	Peak
⌑	Point of interest
SICILY	Administrative region
NORTHERN ITALY	Cultural region
SAN MARINO	Non-subject country
ALPS	Physical feature

Peroni Nastro Azzuro (blue ribbon) was named after the 1933 prize awarded to the ship that could cross the Atlantic the **fastest.**

back then. As the Roman Empire faded, parts of northern Italy were incorporated into the German and Austrian Empires, where beer was a staple. Even so, little beer was consumed in Italy during the Middle Ages (A.D. 500–1500) and Renaissance (1300–1600).

Beer Among the Vines

The first commercial brewery with modern equipment in Italy opened in 1789, in Nizza Monferrato, about halfway between Turin and Genoa. By the time Risorgimento (the Italian unification) was complete in 1871, nearly 150 breweries were operating in Italy. By the turn of the century, the number had increased to 300 and included iconic labels Birra Peroni (1846) and Birra Moretti (1859).

While Italy is very much a wine country—it is the second largest producer of wine in the world—it does have an emerging beer market. Most people equate Peroni and Moretti's ever present lagers with Italian beer, but the craft beer revolution is introducing a new world of styles and flavors. The movement started in 1995 when the Italian government legalized homebrewing and reduced the red tape involved in operating a brewpub. At the time the beer scene was dominated by macrobreweries, which produced mostly lager such as pilsner. Italian craft brewers, unlike their vintner counterparts, had to make up new traditions as they went along.

Today Italy boasts nearly 600 microbreweries—the northern Piedmont region alone has more than 100. At Piedmont's Birrificio Le Baladin, opened in 1996, pioneering brewer Teo Musso (see page 111) makes beer that incorporates local adjuncts such as honey, fruit, and nuts. Italy's passion for food and drink explains why Musso's beer is so popular—he brews with food pairings in mind. Food pairing and the use of local adjuncts are hallmarks of the Italian craft beer scene.

Regional Flavors

What makes Italian craft beer special is that it tends to embody the geography of where it is produced. Brewers accentuate terroir by using local adjuncts and utilizing local equipment such as wine barrels. In the Piedmont region, brewers make their beer unique by incorporating the ingredients at hand: indigenous grains, local fruit such as peaches or blueberries, vegetables such as green peppers, and spices such as basil. Travel south to Tuscany in the heart of Italy's wine country, and you will find more than 60 thriving breweries. Given their locale, it makes sense that the region's brewers often use old wine barrels for aging their beer. The beer picks up flavors, tannins, bacteria, and yeast from the barrels, which results in wildly different and interesting tastes. Even farther south, around citrus-rich Naples, it isn't unusual to find beer with hints of orange or lemon.

Unlike with craft brewers in the United States, for whom big, bold craft beer tends to win the day, Italian brewers tend toward harmonious brews. So regardless of where you travel in Italy, drinking local craft beer promises to be a smooth and well-balanced experience.

Birrificio Lambrate in Milan has grown from producing 40 gallons (150 L) a day in 1996 to more than 1,000 gallons (4,000 L) a day currently.

How to Order Beer in Italy

With craft beer on the rise in Italy, you won't have to look far for good brew. When in doubt, ask, **"Dove posso ottenere birra?"** (DO-veh POS-soh o-ten-AIR-a beer-RAH)?: "Do you have beer?"

———————

You can order a draft beer simply by saying **"Gradirei una birra alla spina, per favore"** (grad-ee-RA-ee U-na beer-RAH AI-la SPI-na, PER fa-VOR-ay): "I would like a beer."

———————

If you know what beer style you're after, you can ask for one of these:

birra lager (BEE-ra la-GER)—lager
birra al malto (BEE-ra AL MAL-to)—stout
birra inglese scura (BEE-ra IN-glay-sa SCOO-ra)—brown ale

———————

When you raise your glass, don't forget to toast by saying **"Salute"** (sa-LOO-tay) or **"Cin-cin"** (chin-chin), which is the sound glasses make when you clink them together.

BEER GUIDE

WHERE BEER LOVERS GO

When it's time to take break from touring art and architecture, stop by these beer spots suggested by Italian brewers.

1 | Il Santo Bevitore

Venice

Italian for "the Holy Drinker" (named after the book *The Legend of the Holy Drinker* by Joseph Roth), this Venetian pub boasts one of the city's largest selections of local craft and imported beer. It is the place to go for beer in the City of Canals.

2 | Birrificio San Michele

Sant'Ambrogio Di Torino

This brewery, founded in 2010, offers beer that is unfiltered, unpasteurized, and full of flavor. Brewing here is an "opera of passion." In fact, its 13 different beer styles are each named after an opera or a character within one—Carmen pale ale and the Butterfly kölsch, for example.

3 | Orzo Bruno

Pisa

The Orzo Bruno (Brown Bear) taproom only serves beer brewed at Il Birrificio Artigiano in Bientina, which consists of four styles that are all unpasteurized and unfiltered. Be sure to try the Picca, which has ginger, black pepper, cinnamon, and vanilla adjuncts.

4 | Abazzia delle Tre Fontane

Rome

This monastery is the only one in Italy producing Trappist beer (see page 38). The monks brew one beer, a Belgian tripel, with

eucalyptus leaves, which give it a sweet aftertaste. They only make 850 to 1,700 U.S. barrels (1,000–2,000 hL) a year, meaning their solo offering is a rare delight.

5 | Birrificio Artigianale Karma

Alvignano

Located about an hour north of Naples, this brewery's beer features local adjuncts—chestnut honey, lemon, gentian root, and spices—that infuse each beer with unique and tasty flavors. Their popular Lemon Ale is made with lemons and coriander from the nearby Amalfi Coast.

6 | Luppolo l'Ottavo Nano

Palermo

This pub is Sicily's must-experience beer spot. Italian for "Hops

7 | Birra Cerqua

Bologna

This brewery was born when a group of friends decided to bring something new to their local beer scene. Opened in 2011, the brewery produces beers such as Lu.Bo, an IPA made from Italy's very small supply of locally grown hops.

Breweries and Beer Destinations in Italy

🍺 Brewery

🍺 Featured beer destination

the Eighth Dwarf," the pub carries a wide selection of draft and bottled craft beer from both domestic and foreign breweries. The pub's motto sums things up perfectly: "We all need to believe in something. I believe that soon I will have a beer."

Photos

1 *A scenic view of one of Venice's famous canals.* **4** *The Roman Forum is one of the city's iconic landmarks.* **5** *A brewer adds grains to the mash tun at Birrificio Artigianale Karma in Alvignano.* **7** *A visit to Birra Cerqua is the perfect end to a day in Bologna.*

LOCAL BREWS
NORTHERN ITALY & ROME
PERFECT PAIRINGS

Firenze (Florence) is the birthplace of the Renaissance and home to a growing craft beer community.

MARRYING BEER WITH FOOD Stretching from the French border to the border of Slovenia, Northern Italy is the birthplace of Italy's craft beer movement. It centers on a small town called Piozzo in the heart of Langhe wine country. That's where Teo Musso started Birrificio Le Baladin in 1996, shortly after government regulations made it easier for people to operate brewpubs. Musso followed Italian tradition by brewing his beer with food pairings in mind, prompting more aspiring brewers to do the same.

Other notable breweries in this region include Birrificio Torino in Torino, Birrificio Torrechiara (Panil) in Torrechiara, Birrificio Italiano in Limido Comasco, and Birrificio Lambrate in Milan. These breweries all produce outstanding beer using local adjuncts such as myrrh, ginger, pepper, and fruit. Some breweries add a twist by barrel-aging their beer or adding in *Brettanomyces* yeast to add funk. While these beers pair nicely with northern Italian cuisine, they are also wonderful to drink on their own. Brewers in this region continue to experiment, offering a selection that never stops surprising.

WHEN IN ROME Italy's craft beer movement is relatively young, but that didn't stop the *Beer Connoisseur* magazine from naming Rome as one of the world's top 20 cities for beer in 2015. The Eternal City's inclusion on this list stems largely from the proliferation of breweries, brewpubs, and taprooms that have sprung up to meet the population's demand. When it comes to craft beer consumption in Italy, Rome is the nation's undisputed leader.

Rome's enthusiasm for craft beer is exemplified in the slogan of Manuele Colonna's taproom, called Ma Che Siete Venuti A Fà: "When I die I want to be fermented." His taproom opened a door in 2001 for Romans who wanted something other than lager. Roman brewers continue to experiment with styles from around the globe, infusing them with local flavors. Take the popular Queen Makeda Grand Pub. Its namesake Makeda beer is a bitter ale made with orange and bergamot peels from southern Italy, which produce a dry, citrus taste. Breweries such as Birra del Borgo have introduced hoppier beer to ever thirsty Roman beer drinkers. Increasingly, the phrase "Do as the Romans do" means drinking a local craft beer filled with Italian flavors.

meet the brewer
Teo Musso

After making a few trips to Belgium, Teo Musso began constructing a brewery, called Le Baladin, in Piozzo in 1996 using old milk vats in a garage adjacent to his pub. The first beers he brewed, a blonde and an amber, were not immediate hits. But perseverance, clever marketing, and improved beer paid off. Soon he needed more space, so he planned to convert a nearby chicken coop on his parents' farm into a fermentation facility. When he applied for the permit, he found out that the building codes mandated that the fermentation facility be physically connected to the brewery. Undeterred by the setback, Musso installed a 984-foot (300-m) "beer duct" that ran underground, connecting the brewery with the fermentation tanks. Musso has since opened taprooms in Rome, Turin, and 10 other cities, including New York and Essaouira, Morocco.

 on tap with Garrett Oliver

NORTHERN ITALY
Italian Farmhouse Beer

This wine-focused culture is diving headlong into enthusiastic craft brewing. Wild creativity, often based on local food and wine traditions, helps the nation's rich character and *bella figura*—beautiful style—shine through.

ABV 5.5–9% | **IBU** 15–30

Aroma Spicy (it's sometimes actually spiced) and highly aromatic

Appearance Usually golden to amber and often hazy, with copious foam

Flavor Often Belgian-influenced, very dry, with spices and/or edible flowers, and occasional acidity

Mouthfeel Light, dry, and effervescent

Presentation Tulip, white wine, or Teku glass

Food Pairings Charcuterie, cheese, rabbit, pâté

Craft to Try Birrificio del Ducato Nuova Mattina.

ROME
Abbazia Tre Fontane Tripel

The only Trappist abbey in Rome houses Italy's only approved Trappist brewery, Tre Fontane (see page 108). Its beer is based in the Belgian tripel style, but with a local twist: eucalyptus leaves.

ABV 8.5% | **IBU** 25

Aroma Floral, spicy, and clovelike, with a distinctive eucalyptus overlay

Appearance Deep orange and slightly hazy with a well-formed, fluffy foam

Flavor Dry and almost spirituous, with a complex Christmas cake–like flavor showing honey, orange, clove, and eucalyptus oil

Mouthfeel Highly carbonated and warming

Presentation Chalice

Food Pairings Strong cheeses, cured meat, savory biscuits and other nonsugary desserts

Vienna's Old Town, or Innere Stadt, lies at the heart of the city. Its narrow and winding streets are lined with bars and cafés.

AUSTRIA

WHERE TRADITIONS INTERSECT

Once seated at the crossroads of major trade routes, Austria turned into a major world power thanks to its distinct geographic advantage. Historians hypothesize that beer made its way to Austria along these trade routes, traveling from Bavaria and Bohemia around A.D. 1100. The House of Habsburg ruled over most of Europe from its base in the capital city of Vienna, making Austria a thriving hub full of beer from far and wide.

Austria's exposure to other cultures influenced the beer brewed within its boundaries. Breweries existed in Austria prior to the 1300s, though there is no mention of one in official records until 1384. Salzburg's Stiegl Brauwelt, the largest brewery in Austria, opened more than 100 years later. By then lager had taken over the Austrian brewing scene, aided by the cool regional temperatures ideal for producing it.

Under the Influence

When it came to beer, no influence was greater than that of neighboring Germany. Germany's lagering techniques and mechanical refrigeration shaped and defined Austrian beer culture and the styles it would go on to produce. Austrian brewers were never constrained by Germany's purity law (see page 53), though, so they produced a greater variety of styles. In 1841, a year prior to the invention of pilsner, Anton Dreher developed a new style in Vienna that combined the crispness of lager with the amber color of ale. He decided to call it the Vienna lager. Dreher's

AT A GLANCE
Featured Locations

🛢	Brewery
★	Capital
●	City
BAVARIA	German state
BOHEMIA	Historic Czech region
ALPS	Physical feature

Anton Dreher was a Viennese brewer in the mid-1800s. His creation, the Vienna lager, combined the crispness of a lager with the deeper color of an ale.

success allowed him to open breweries in Hungary and Italy. When Carl von Linde's refrigeration technology, the "cold machine," became available in the late 1800s, Dreher was first in line to purchase one. The machine went to his brewery in Italy, not Austria, but Dreher is credited with bringing Austrian brewing into the industrial age.

Those looking to find a fervent passion for Vienna lager will need to travel to Mexico to find it. When Austrians immigrated to Mexico in the late 19th century, they took their knowledge of Vienna lager along with them, and it is the most popular beer style in Mexico today (see page 183).

Meeting Demand

As the popularity of Vienna-style lager waned in Austria, another style took its place: the Austrian märzen. The popularity of this märzen is credited largely to the style's marketing slogan: It was "brewed the Vienna way," as opposed to the Bavarian way. This style is lighter in color and maltiness than its Bavarian cousin and is often compared to helles (see page 57). Much like Bavarian märzen, it is brewed in the late spring and consumed in the fall. Today the Austrian märzen style commands 60 to 70 percent of the country's beer market.

While roughly half of Austria's märzen is produced in breweries owned by foreign companies, such as Heineken International, many Austrian-owned breweries are helping meet the demand for local beer. Globally, the country has Europe's fourth highest consumption rate per capita, at 27.7 gallons (105 L) per year, finishing just behind Germany's 28 gallons (106 L). Of Austria's nearly 200 breweries, around half are considered microbreweries. While märzen and lagers such as pilsner dominate the Austrian beer scene, microbreweries like award-winning Biermanufaktur Loncium are producing non-Austrian beer styles like IPA and stout. New beer is cropping up, but traditional beer continues to be a staple of this country's beerscape.

local flavor
Steinbier: Where There's Flame, There's Beer

Steinbier, an amber to dark ale, was common in southern Austria prior to the early 1900s. Its name means "stone beer" in German and refers more to the process of making it than its taste. Farmers would brew it in wooden vessels, which couldn't be subjected to the fire directly. So to heat the mash and boil the wort, brewers would heat sandstone rocks—of which the area had a plentiful supply—in a fire and place them in the liquid mash or wort.

The hot stones caramelized the wort's sugars and transferred the smokiness of the fire. The process was laborious, made small quantities, and never produced the same taste twice. It was also dangerous, often resulting in burns or a brewery burning down. The last steinbier brewery was closed in 1917, when metal brewing equipment was becoming common, allowing breweries to produce ale and lager in larger quantities.

BEER GUIDE

WHERE BEER LOVERS GO

Austria has many great beers and breweries, but this list of recommendations from Austrian brewers should make it a little easier to choose among them.

1 | Yppenplatz 4

Vienna

In the vibrant district of Yppenplatz, this microbrewery offers some of Vienna's freshest craft beer. Don't expect märzen and Vienna lager; look forward to IPA, porter, Flanders red, and radler instead.

2 | Stiegl Brauwelt

Salzburg

The largest brewery in Austria began with small steps—literally. The original brewery was by a canal, and beer had to be carried down a set of steps to the water for distribution. The new brewery offers tours, a museum, a restaurant, a cinema, and beer tastings.

3 | Starkenberger Brauerei

Tarrenz

This brewery is located in an old castle and has always been run by women. They offer a range of beer, and people come here to drink it and swim in the pool full of heated beer.

4 | Theresienbräu

Innsbruck

This is the brewpub where locals hang out. The

brewery makes only five beer styles, but it makes them well—and fans can only get them here.

5 | Stift Engelszell

Engelhartszell

Founded in 1293, this is the only Trappist monastery (see page 38) producing beer in Austria. It produces two styles: a dark ale made with chocolate and honey and a farmhouse ale with a 7 percent ABV.

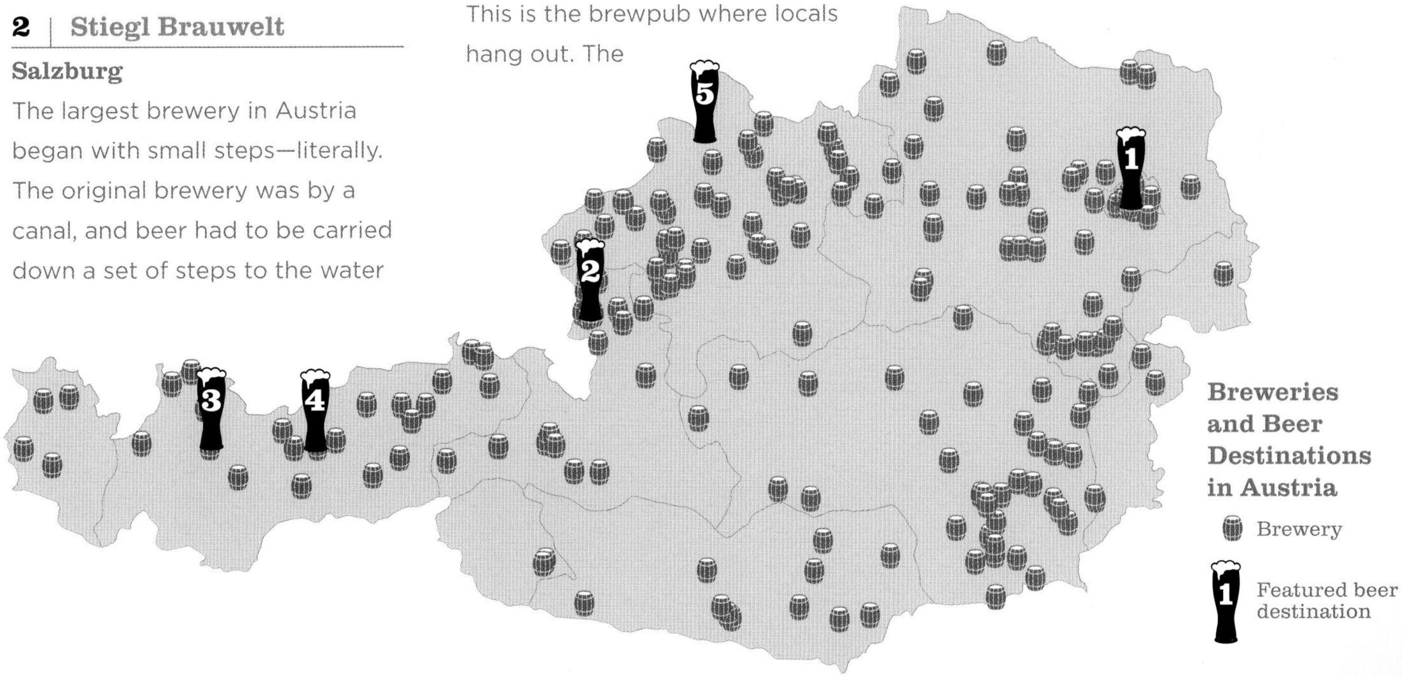

Breweries and Beer Destinations in Austria

🍺 Brewery

🍺 Featured beer destination

Once a busy commercial port, Nyhavn canal in Copenhagen is now home to popular bars and restaurants.

DENMARK

FOR THE LOVE OF PILSNER

L ager rules in this Scandinavian country, which makes it all the more interesting
that Denmark may have given us the English word for ale. Some scholars believe that "ale" comes from the Danish word *øl* (beer) with the
Germanic base *alu* (bitter). Others attribute it to the Vikings who
sailed and conquered far and wide, bringing their word for bitter
"ault" with them. Regardless of which story is true, the history of
beer is most certainly lengthy in Denmark, which has left a stronger impression on the global beer scene than people might think.

As was the case in most of early Europe, women were the ones
who brewed beer, which was considered to be a domestic activity
until religious orders took over the practice in the Middle Ages
(A.D. 500–1500). The end of the Middle Ages saw the rise of the
country's first beer guild, created in 1525 in Copenhagen. Guild
members were responsible for producing beer for the king and
his military, with a daily ration of 2.6 gallons (10 L) per person.
Meanwhile, in the countryside, women resumed their work as
brewers. Low in alcohol, sweet, malty, and dark, *hvidtøl* ("white beer")
was the most common beer brewed in the countryside. Its name comes
from the white malt used to make the beer; the malt is lighter in color because
the barley isn't fully matured before it's malted.

Carl's Lagering Hill

By the mid-1800s clean, crisp lager—the antithesis of hvidtøl—was all the rage in
Denmark, so many of the country's newest breweries focused on producing it. One

AT A GLANCE
Featured Locations

🛢 Brewery

★ Capital

● City

Horses help deliver Tuborg beer to Tivoli Gardens in Copenhagen.

such brewer, Jacob Jacobsen, brought lager yeast back from Bavaria—not an easy feat in a time when refrigeration didn't readily exist to preserve it. He opened a brewery in Valby, just outside Copenhagen, where the water was clean. The area also featured a *bjerg* (hill) that he could dig cellars in to lager his beer. Jacobsen decided to name the brewery after his son, Carl, and the hill that had proved so convenient for his brewing enterprise. That's literally what Carlsberg means: "Carl's hill." Carlsberg Group is now one of the world's largest brewing companies.

A Growing Craft

By the late 1870s, 200 breweries existed in the Danish countryside and 16 in Copenhagen. Tuborg, which opened in 1873, produced Denmark's first pilsner; Carlsberg didn't make pilsner until decades later, in 1904. By the turn of the 20th century Denmark had nearly 400 breweries and pilsner had become—and has stayed—the most popular style in the country.

Macrobrewed lager has long dominated in Denmark, but the craft beer revolution is picking up. In 1990, brewpub Bryggeriet Apollo opened in Copenhagen, reintroducing Danes to ales. Five years later, the first Danish-brewed IPA arrived on the scene, courtesy of Brøckhouse. Ølbutikken ("Beer Shop" in Danish) opened in 2005 and has gone on to become one of the world's most famous bottle shops, acquiring hard-to-get beer such as Three Floyds Brewing Company's Dark Lord from the United States and Cantillon's blueberry lambic from Belgium.

Childhood friends Mikkel Borg Bjergsø and Kristian Klarup Keller are probably Denmark's best-known craft brewers, brewing under the name Mikkeller. They hit international fame in 2006 with their oatmeal stout, Beer Geek Breakfast. Mikkeller has since opened a bar in San Francisco and partnered with Three Floyds in Indiana (see page 154) to open Warpigs Brewpub in Copenhagen. In other words, Danish craft beer is finding its way into the minds and glasses of beer enthusiasts all over the world.

local flavor
Carlsberg Lab and "Good" Beer

While Carlsberg is known for its slogan "Probably the best beer in the world," the world has a lot more to thank the company for than lager: namely its research on beer and yeast. Jacob Jacobsen established Carlsberg Lab in 1875 to further research on beer production. Back then, it was relatively common for brewers to end up with beer that was "off," or "sick," and Jacobsen wanted to figure out why. In 1883, Emil Hansen was examining a batch of sick beer at the lab when he discovered that it contained numerous yeast strains. Hansen was able to isolate these strains and find the one most suitable for brewing good beer, which he named *Saccharomyces* ("sugar fungus"). His work led to a process of propagating yeast strains. Rather than patent the process, Hansen published his work for all to read and emulate, and Carlsberg sent this yeast to breweries around the world. The yeast found in most lagers likely originated from this strain.

BEER GUIDE

WHERE BEER LOVERS GO

For a small country, Denmark produces a significant number of wonderful beers. Try some at these beer spots recommended by Danish brewers.

1 | To Øl

Copenhagen

Tobias Emil Jensen and Tore Gynther have made award-winning beer, pushing the brewing envelope by using raw, unprocessed ingredients. Their bar, Mikkeller & Friends, boasts 40 taps and is ranked among the world's top four bars by RateBeer.

2 | Nørrebro Bryghus

Copenhagen

Founded in 2003 and one of the earliest craft breweries in Denmark, Nørrebro Bryghus is known for brewing foreign-style beer with a Nordic twist. It makes everything from IPA to farmhouse ale to barley-wine, as well as traditional Nordic dishes to pair with its beer.

3 | Rise Bryggeri

Ærøskøbing

Started in 1926, this brewery produces two lines of beer: the classic Ærø series and an organic line. Both are worthy of a visitor's attention.

4 | Skagen Bryghus

Skagen

You can't go much farther north in Denmark than this microbrewery. It is owned by 2,200 shareholders, so visiting is like being invited into a local's home.

5 | Mikkeller Bar

Copenhagen

The outside of Mikkeller's taproom is small and unassuming, but inside the 20 beers on tap are not. Generally, around 10 of the taps pour Mikkeller's creations, while the others pour beer from breweries around the world.

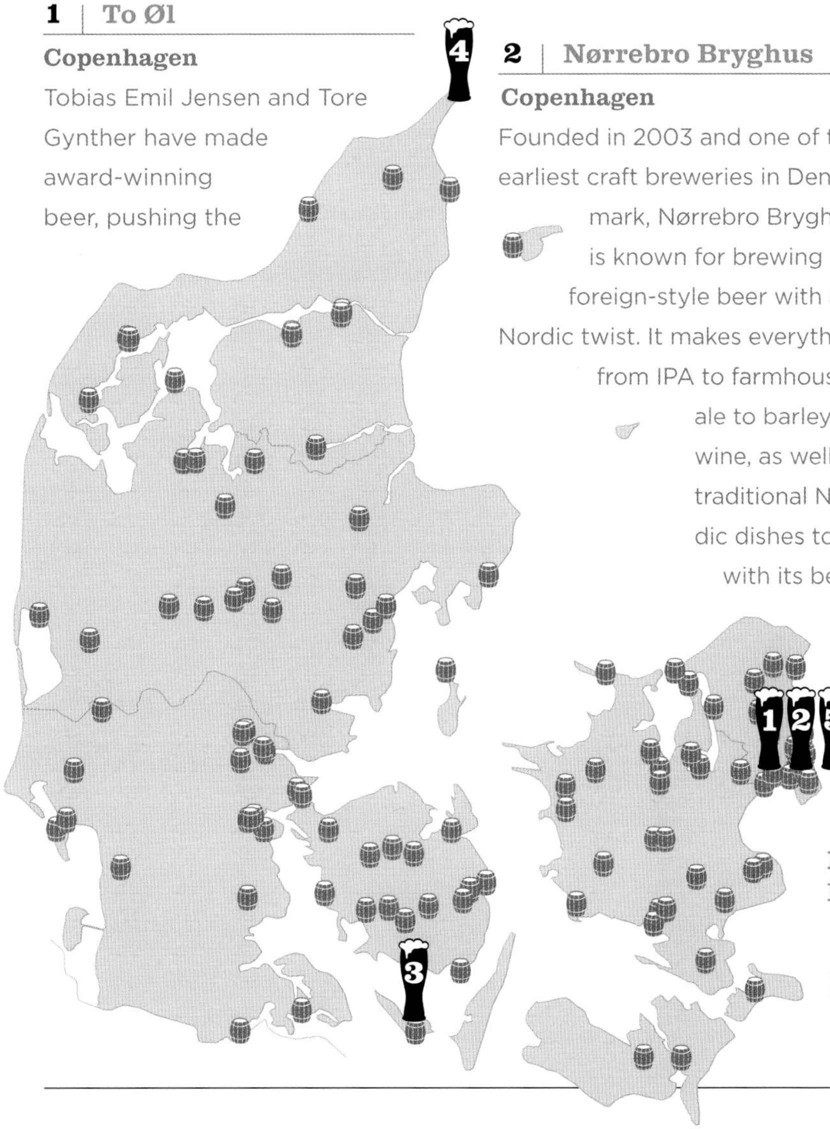

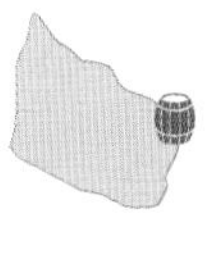

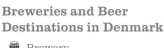

Breweries and Beer Destinations in Denmark

Brewery

Featured beer destination

The windmills of Kinderdijk
are part of a UNESCO world
heritage site.

NETHERLANDS

FLOWING CURRENTS OF BEER

With a quarter of its land at or below sea level, this relatively flat nation has long relied on a vast network of canals to transport goods. Water has shaped its agriculture, its shipping, its economy—even its beer production. So have its fertile lowlands, which proved ideal for growing hops at a time when hopped beer was all the rage in Europe.

Hopped beer was first mass-produced in Germany in the 12th century, then introduced to bordering nations in the 13th century by the Hanseatic League (see page 31). Brewers in Holland (now the Netherlands) had long been using gruit to bitter their beer (see page 72), but they started switching to hops when they flowed through their canals from Germany. By the mid-14th century, Holland was producing its own hops near Gouda, Kampen, and Breda, which did so well that by the end of the century hopped beer had become commonplace. The Dutch provided the English with hopped beer for the next century, until the English started producing hops themselves.

Claims to Fame

Up until the mid-1800s, the only beer style the Netherlands brewed was ale. Then along came a brewer named Gerard Heineken, who bought Amsterdam's Den Hoybergh (Haystack Brewery) in 1864 and decided to brew a *Hollandsch bier*—what we now call a Dutch lager. Five years later, after witnessing its popularity at an international fair in Amsterdam, Heineken decided that Bavarian-style lager was the way to go and constructed a new brewery to make Bavarian pilsner. Heineken beer was exported to other European countries by 1875, followed by South America, Africa, and Asia. The beer finally made an appearance in the United States in 1933. Today, Heineken International is a well-recognized

AT A GLANCE
Featured Locations

- Brewery
- ★ Capital
- City

brand powerhouse and the second largest brewing company in the world.

Another noteworthy piece of Dutch beer history took place in Tilburg, near the Belgian border. In 1891, a Trappist brewery opened in Koningshoeven Abbey and started producing what it called La Trappe ales. In 1969, the abbey licensed Artois Brewery (of Stella Artois fame) to produce its beer. When the agreement ended in 1980, the monks returned to brewing ales, including the only Trappist witbier produced in the Netherlands. Today, La Trappe ales are exported across the globe. But La Trappe isn't the only Trappist brewery in the Netherlands. De Kievet, founded at the Abbey Mary Refuge in 2013, is the world's second newest official Trappist brewery.

Crafting an Identity

Several craft breweries opened from the mid-1980s to the mid-1990s. Looking to their beer-powerhouse neighbor Belgium for inspiration, many produced Belgian-style ale. Enough were successful with this style that the Netherlands' four big macrobreweries—Heineken, Interbrew (now part of AB InBev), Grolsch (now part of Japan's Asahi), and Bavaria—decided to brew ale as well.

The Netherlands now has more than 260 breweries, up from 165 in 2012. While pilsner still accounts for more than 90 percent of the market, the biggest growth has been in the craft beer sector. This formerly ale-only country is producing an increasingly diverse range of styles—everything from IPA to barrel-aged beer.

local flavor
Green Bottle, Red Star

Quick: Name beers that come in a green bottle. The answers may include Grolsch and Carlsberg, and will certainly include Heineken. But Heineken's distinctive green bottle hasn't always looked as it does now. In the 1960s Alfred Heineken, grandson of founder Gerard Heineken, tinkered with making the bottles brick shaped. The bottles, called WOBOs (world bottles), were interlocking and could be used to construct affordable homes. The WOBO project never made it past the prototype stage, though a small WOBO shed was built on Heineken's estate.

Heineken's iconic red star didn't exist when the company first started. The label gained its star in the 1930s—a marketing ploy aimed at catching the consumer's eye. The red star picked up controversial connotations with the spread of communism after World War II, so Heineken changed it to a white star with a red border. It changed back to red again in 1991 with the fall of communism in Europe.

Heineken's beers bear a recognizable red star.

BEER GUIDE

WHERE BEER LOVERS GO

Some things must be done in the Netherlands: Stroll along Amsterdam's canals, amble through tulip fields, and stop by some of these bustling beer hubs recommended by Dutch brewers.

1 | Brouwerij 't IJ

Amsterdam

Located next to the country's largest wooden windmill, this famous microbrewery is hard to miss. Take a tour, then try craft beers like Zatte, a Belgian tripel, and Struis, a barleywine.

2 | The Fiddler

The Hague

One of The Hague's most popular breweries, The Fiddler produces traditional English ales. These outstanding craft beers offer every reason to drink local.

3 | Kaapse Brouwers

Rotterdam

This new arrival in the port city of Rotterdam aims to brew the best beer in the world, many of them old styles made new. It offers five staple beers and a constantly changing experimental beer.

4 | Brouwerij de Prael

Amsterdam

This microbrewery is a few minutes' walk from the central train station, in the red-light district. The beer here is not your typical Dutch variety—it serves milk stout, double IPA, Scotch ale, and barleywine.

5 | Heineken Experience

Amsterdam

It's a museum, brewery, video arcade, movie theater, restaurant, gift shop, and pub all rolled into one. And, yes, it's the perfect place to sample the world-famous Dutch-brewed pilsner. Visitors can even become a certified Heineken beer pourer, replete with a certificate.

Breweries and Beer Destinations in the Netherlands

🛢 Brewery

🍺**1** Featured beer destination

Warsaw's Old Town is
home to many bars
and outdoor cafés.

POLAND

FIGHTING FOR NEW BREWS

Poland's landscape changes from mountain ranges to sandy beaches, and from glacial lakes to some of Europe's last primeval woodlands. But its climate is consistently ideal for growing barley, which is great for producing both vodka and beer.

As was true throughout the rest of Europe, brewing in Poland in the Middle Ages (A.D. 500–1500) was typically a household activity. Unlike elsewhere in Europe, there weren't any monks to take command of the craft. That's because Poles were pagan until 966, when King Mieszko I converted himself (and thus the entire country) to Christianity. The Szczyrzyc Abbey, founded in 1234, included a brewery.

The Beer War of 1380 was perhaps the only war in Poland in which no one was killed. Wrocław's town government fought with the church over its monopoly on the town's beer production and sales. Then the town confiscated some beer from a local monastery—a Christmas gift from the Duke of Legnica—and the church responded by threatening to excommunicate the town's burghers. The dispute was resolved in 1382 when the Polish king and the pope intervened, effectively restoring the beer monopoly the town enjoyed. It would be nearly a century before Poland's first commercial brewery, Warka, was built in 1478.

Porter Goes North

Brewing continued to be a small-scale operation until the 19th century, when Archduke von Habsburg of Austria built his first brewery in Cieszyn. It brewed

AT A GLANCE
Featured Locations

- 🛢 Brewery
- ★ Capital
- ● City

A bartender pours a draft beer in Warsaw's Same Krafty taproom. Poland's craft beer movement has roots in homebrewing.

wheat beer, which was soon replaced by increasingly popular lager. The archduke built a second brewery in Żywiec, replete with the latest brewing technology.

As the archduke was busy constructing breweries, the English began to export porter to Poland, which was vastly different from the local ale and lager. The style that became known as Baltic porter was stronger than English porter. Żywiec Brewery developed its own porter recipe based on the Baltic porters sent over from England, producing a beer that it still brews today.

New Frontiers

After World War II, the Soviets controlled Poland's national government. Industries were nationalized, including the beer industry. Beer production didn't decline, though—quite the opposite. Poland produced about 80 million gallons (3 million hL) of beer in 1950, an amount that steadily rose under communist control. By 1992, three years after communist rule ended, Polish brewers were producing more than 370 million gallons (14 million hL).

The Polish beer industry has experienced tremendous growth in the decades since and now produces more than 1.05 billion gallons (40 million hL) of beer a year. Experts believe the lager market is saturated and that growth will need to come from the craft beer and regional brewery market. Poland currently has 133 breweries, the bulk of them brewing an increasingly diverse range of beer.

local flavor
Resurrecting Poland's Grodziskie

Once on the very brink of extinction, Poland's native beer style is making its way back onto the world's list of styles to try. *Grodziskie* is a low-alcohol wheat-based ale that traditionally has only four ingredients: wheat, water, yeast, and hops (no barley here). Its other distinctive characteristic is its smoky flavor, which comes from wheat malt that has been dried in a smoke kiln. The style is also known by its German name, *grätzer*, and its high effervescence has led some to dub it Polish champagne.

Polish wheat beer was popular as far back as the 14th century, but folklore ties grodziskie's origin story to a 16th-century Benedictine monk. Legend has it that Bernard of Wąbrzeźno arrived in Grodzisk Wielkopolski to find the well had run dry. He offered up prayers, which soon proved fruitful: The water miraculously filled the well again, and brewers could return to their craft. The water was far superior to what had filled the well before, evidenced by the town's higher quality beer. For the next two centuries, this point of pride had the local brewers' guild claiming a monopoly over the town's malt and controlling who could sell its beer. It even regulated the beer's quality: Town elders tested every barrel before it was sold. The drink was popular with locals and tourists alike—a 19th-century travel guide recommended it as a great summer beer to sip while gazing at leafy woodlands.

The style's popularity eventually waned; after World War I, only one brewery still produced it. The last grodziskie brewery closed in 1993, but eight years later Polish homebrewers helped rescue it from the scrap heap of brewing history. The style has seen a revival in the United States, too, where brewers are inserting their own distinctive twists on this Polish original.

BEER GUIDE

WHERE BEER LOVERS GO

From self-guided beer walks to breweries and vibrant taprooms, Poland offers beer enthusiasts a wealth of worthy stop-offs.

1 | Browar Pinta

Żywiec

Located right in Żywiec Brewery's backyard, this craft brewery offers many notable beers: an American IPA called Atak Chmielu (Attack of the Hops), an espresso lager called I'm So Horny!, and an IPA called Ce N'est Pas IPA (This Is Not IPA). They brew only 100 barrels at a time, so the offerings are always fresh.

2 | Ulica Piwna

Gdańsk

Stroll down cobblestone-lined Ulica Piwna, the unofficial "Beer Street" of the Old City in Gdańsk, stopping in to visit Browar Piwna (Brewery Beer), a brewery producing more than two dozen styles.

3 | Same Krafty and Same Krafty vis-à-vis

Warsaw

For those who find themselves in Warsaw's Old Town with limited time to try Polish craft beer, these taprooms are the ones to visit. They are located across the street from each other and offer several Polish craft beers.

4 | Strefa Piwa Pub

Kraków

This serious craft beer lover's taproom offers dozens of local and imported craft beers. The staff is incredibly knowledgeable and willing to share their expert opinions.

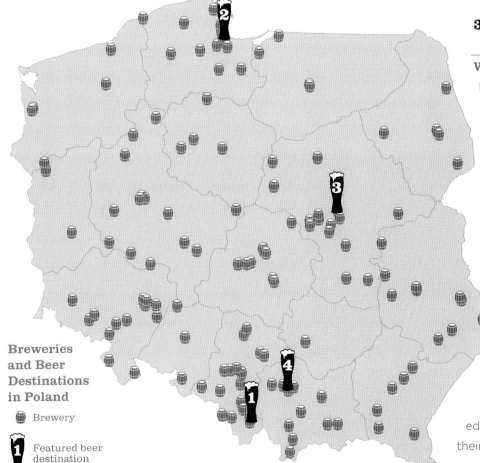

Breweries and Beer Destinations in Poland

🛢 Brewery

1 Featured beer destination

Moscow's Red Square is home to the iconic St. Basil's Cathedral. Recent trends show Russians are drinking less vodka and more beer.

RUSSIA

BEYOND VODKA

While vodka is Russia's most celebrated drink, beer here has a significant past and a bright-looking future. More than two millennia ago, *kvass* (leaven, or fermented drink) was common in Russia. People would put rye bread in a bowl, add water and spices, and leave the mixture exposed to the air. People sometimes added fruit or birch sap to give it extra flavor. A book from the first century A.D. mentions kvass being served at Prince Vladimir's baptism. Kvass can still be purchased in Russia today.

Baltika
Brewery

Kalinkin

● St. Petersburg

Victory Art Brew

Moscow

Ochakovo
Brewery

★

AF Brewery

Salden's

● **Zarechny**

Vladivostok ●

Porter The Great

Russian royalty proved to be influential tastemakers when it came to Russian beer. In 1698, Peter the Great traveled to London and developed a liking for British beer. So when St. Petersburg was built in 1703, the British began exporting it. But Peter wanted stronger beer, so British brewers increased porter's alcohol content, creating a stronger style known today as Russian imperial stout. Nearly a century later, in 1795, German immigrant Abraham Krohn opened a brewery in St. Petersburg to make English ale and porter for Catherine the Great. It merged with a brewery started by Englishman Noah Kazalet, becoming a new enterprise called Kalinkin. In 1822, the government under Tsar Nicholas I imposed tariffs on all goods from England—all, that is, except for porter. Nicholas's tariffs effectively killed the English ale trade, but Russian imperial stout continued to flow.

AT A GLANCE
Featured Locations

🛢 Brewery

★ Capital

● City

A 1909 ad from Bohemia Brewery in Rybinsk features its Canteen Dark, Special Export, English Porter, and March Pilsen beers.

Fast-forward to just after World War I and the Bolshevik Revolution (1917). Prohibition was instituted throughout Russia, though vodka could still be purchased at restaurants. When prohibition ended in 1925, breweries reopened and were mostly nationalized. By and large, vodka, particularly Moskovskaya and Stolichnaya, dominated the alcohol market—beer just didn't pack enough alcohol for Russian tastes. Ochakovo Brewery started operations in Moscow in 1978, expanding into soft drinks, wine, and—more crucially—agricultural businesses that produced barley and malt. It is now the largest Russian-owned brewery. Baltika Brewery started brewing beer in 1990 and was purchased by Carlsberg after the Cold War ended. It is now the largest beer producer in Russia.

Beer Versus Vodka

Vodka is Russia's national drink, but beer is giving it a run for its money. Statistics suggest that beer sales have increased by 40 percent since the turn of the 21st century. While Russians as a whole have a slight preference for vodka, young Russian drinkers (those 18 to 35 years old) prefer beer.

Craft beer is leading the charge in this cultural shift, with the number of craft breweries growing from 13 in 2010 to 98 in 2015. Craft beer experienced a watershed year in 2010, when foreign craft breweries such as BrewDog from Scotland (see page 79) and Mikkeller from Denmark (see page 118) started collaborating with Russian breweries.

On the flip side, the excise tax imposed on beer rose by 200 percent in 2010 and continued to rise in the following years. The Russian economy started to slow in 2013 and has continued to do so, resulting in a steady decline in beer sales. Russian brewers estimate that their craft beer scene is where the U.S. scene was in the early 1990s—still trying to find footing in an evolving market. Craft breweries such as AF Brewery, Salden's, and Victory Art Brew are thriving despite these challenges, crafting beer that not even hard-core vodka fans can resist.

Speakeasy

How to Order Beer in Russia

If you are meeting your friends at the bar, you will need to ask them «где находится паб?» (gde nak-ho-dits-ya pab): "Where is the pub?" Once there, you can tell your bartender «я хотел бы пиво пожалуйста» (YA KHYtel by PI-va pa-ZHAL-sta): "I would like a beer, please."

———

If the bartender offers you a cheap imported lager, you can ask «есть ли у вас какие-либо местное пиво?» (yest' li u vas ka-KI-ye-LI-bo MEST-no-va PI-va): "Do you have any local beer?"

———

Since you appreciate your friends and tour guides, you can say «позвольте мне платить за это» (POZ-vol'te mne PLA-tit' za eto): "Let me pay for this." Don't forget to raise your glass and toast by saying «Ваше здоровье! » (vashe zda-ROV'-ye): "To your health!"

———

Once you're ready for another round, say «Я хотел бы еще пива» (YA KHY-tel by YEESH-che piva): "I would like another beer."

BEER GUIDE

WHERE BEER LOVERS GO

Russia stretches across 11 time zones, so practice strategic beer-cation planning with these brewer-recommended must-sees.

1 | AF Brewery
Moscow

Two of this brewery's founders decided to ditch their jobs at a large macrobrewery and start their own microbrewery—hence the name AF, which stands for "Anti-Factory." These rebels brew much of their beer with what they call a "criminal level of hoppiness." Try their ABV Not IBU: Polaris, a double IPA with 119 IBUs.

2 | Beer Museum
St. Petersburg

Started in 1995 to commemorate the Stepan Razin Brewery (Russia's oldest) on its 200th anniversary, the museum offers visitors a detailed look at Soviet beer history. Heineken closed the brewery in 2009, but the museum is well worth visiting.

3 | Jaws Brewery
Zarechny

This brewery is located in an old Laundromat a few miles from a nuclear power plant—what could possibly go wrong? The brewery produces more than two dozen beers, including an American IPA with the apt name Nuclear Laundry.

4 | Gutov (Russkaya)
Vladivostok

Should you ever find yourself in far-eastern Siberia, stop in at the city's first microbrewery. It makes three kinds of beer—light, red, and dark—and is open to suggestions from patrons when it comes to what type of one-off it might brew next.

Breweries and Beer Destinations in Russia

 Brewery

 Featured beer destination

Old meets new in Girona, a historic city in Spain's Catalonia region that is home to a thriving craft beer scene.

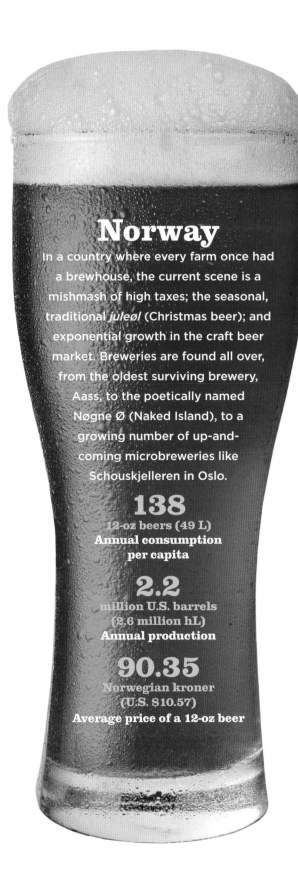

Norway

In a country where every farm once had a brewhouse, the current scene is a mishmash of high taxes; the seasonal, traditional *juleøl* (Christmas beer); and exponential growth in the craft beer market. Breweries are found all over, from the oldest surviving brewery, Aass, to the poetically named Nøgne Ø (Naked Island), to a growing number of up-and-coming microbreweries like Schouskjelleren in Oslo.

138
12-oz beers (49 L)
Annual consumption per capita

2.2
million U.S. barrels
(2.6 million hL)
Annual production

90.35
Norwegian kroner
(U.S. $10.57)
Average price of a 12-oz beer

Sweden

Beer has been in Sweden for millennia, despite the heavy regulations inhibiting it for most of the 20th century. Sweden is home to historic beer styles—the sweet, low-alcohol *svagdricka* and the spicy homebrew favorite *gotlands-dricka*—but American IPA reigns supreme. International collaborations with many of the 150 or so Swedish breweries are all the rage, making Sweden a promising craft beer destination.

149
12-oz beers (53 L)
Annual consumption per capita

4
million U.S. barrels
(4.7 million hL)
Annual production

68.29
Swedish kronor
(U.S. $7.61)
Average price of a 12-oz beer

Numbers were accurate at the time of printing. They are averages, subject to change over time.

Portland, Oregon, is rightfully known as Beervana. More than 80 breweries call the city home, a larger number than in any other U.S. city.

NORTH
AMERICA

Brewery workers prepare beer for delivery in Cleveland, Ohio, after the end of Prohibition in 1933.

BOLD, UNIQUE, AND WILD

North America's contemporary craft beer revolution is rooted in a long history of innovation. Early settlers from Europe mixed Old World techniques with New World ingredients, creating beer that was fundamentally shaped by the landscape itself. As new waves of immigrants arrived, bringing deep brewing knowledge and specific preferences, ale and lager settled firmly into the continent's collective palette. Adjunct lager remains one of North America's most popular styles, but a revived passion for regional ingredients and experimentation ensures that the continent's brewers will continue to innovate.

Beer Pioneers

Though European explorers and pilgrims brought beer to North America's shores, indigenous groups had already been brewing it for centuries. The Native American brewing grain of choice was maize (corn): Apache and Pueblo tribes of the southwestern United States fermented it into weak beer such as *tiswin*, used for healing, bartering, dispute resolution, fiestas, and religious ceremonies. Beer was also brewed in Central America, including a foamy beverage made from fermented maize and cacao that the Maya used to celebrate feasts.

While indigenous groups used beer for ritual and celebration, New World settlers relied on it because, unlike water, it didn't make them sick. Brewers boiled the water during the brewing process, killing waterborne bacteria and other germs (though they didn't know that). Beer was particularly important aboard ships full of settlers because it did not spoil over long months at sea.

Legend has it that beer played a vital part in grounding the *Mayflower* near Cape Cod in 1620. After two months of delays and rough seas, the crew found themselves off course and perilously low on beer. Captain Christopher Jones had a choice: drop his passengers off at Plymouth Rock or risk not having enough beer for the journey home. Pilgrim William Bradford complained that passengers "were hastened ashore and made to drink water, that the seamen might have the more beer."

Though water in the New World was cleaner and likely safer than what settlers were used to, most remained suspicious of it. They favored beer, which meant that building breweries and sourcing supplies was a top priority. Most colonists brought

North America

▨ Country or region in this chapter

The average North American consumes **16 to 20** gallons (61 to 76 L) of beer a year.

brewers with them, and those without a brewer found themselves desperate to acquire one. It's no surprise that the first New World "help wanted" ads, posted in a London newspaper in 1609, were from the Virginia colony of Jamestown seeking brewers. Sourcing ingredients from overseas was expensive, so settlers often experimented with native ingredients like pumpkin and spruce tips.

War and Peace

In 1632, twelve years after the *Mayflower* made its famous voyage, Dutch settlers built one of the New World's first commercial breweries. Its location on the southern tip of New Amsterdam (modern-day Manhattan) was ideal: It had a local water source, access to grains, and available transportation routes via the North River (now the Hudson). Colonial ale wasn't hopped like beer from Europe was, so they soured soon after they were made. Most beer in North America was prepared this way, which meant brewing was a highly localized undertaking.

Everyone drank beer—laboring men, pregnant women, the old and the young. Fashioned after English-style ale, beer was purposefully made weak to be suitable for all-day consumption. Most beer was brewed at home by women or servants or in local taverns. As the colonies grew, taverns became important community-gathering places. Patrons could do many things at these taverns: listen to news and gossip, conduct meetings, hold court, post mail, find entertainment, and take a meal. Visitors could even spend a night. So taverns made ideal breeding grounds for revolutionary ideas about independence from European rule.

celebrations North America's Best Beer Festivals

Mondial de la Bière | MONTREAL | CANADA |
Canada's biggest beer fest provides more than 600 beers, meads, and ciders for some 80,000 attendees. *June*

Portland Craft Beer Festival | OREGON | U.S. |
Only city-made craft beer is allowed at this fest, which is probably a good thing considering the Portland metro area boasts nearly 90 craft breweries. *July*

Great American Beer Festival | DENVER | U.S. |
The GABF is the largest craft beer festival in the United States, with 800-plus breweries pouring more than 3,800 beers for 60,000 attendees (see page 159). It offers visitors a chance to meet brewers from across the country. *September/October*

Guadalajara Beer Festival | GUADALAJARA |
MEXICO | Once an assortment of beer stands in a city square, this festival touts itself as the largest in Latin America, with more than 100 beers and 30,000 festgoers. *October*

Banff Craft Beer Festival | BANFF | CANADA |
Nestled in the Canadian Rockies and held in the Cave and Basin National Historic Site, this fest combines natural beauty with Albertan breweries. *November*

Puebla Beer Fest | PUEBLA | MEXICO | With more than 20,000 attendees, this is one of the largest beer festivals in Mexico and offers local and international beers to sample. *December*

When the Revolutionary War broke out in 1775, beer was an integral part of a soldier's life. George Washington, commander of America's forces, mandated a one-quart (1-L) daily ration of spruce beer or cider per Continental Army soldier.

Locals enjoy craft beer in the Crux Fermentation Project taproom in Bend, Oregon.

The Brewer's Melting Pot

While colonial beer was a local affair, technological advancements in the 17th and 18th centuries meant that beer could be produced and distributed on an ever larger scale. Innovations such as pasteurization and bottling helped brewers make better quality beer that lasted longer. Railways and refrigerated rail cars, which came to the United States and Canada in the mid-1800s and to Mexico in the early 1900s, made it possible to distribute beer on a national scale with less risk of it spoiling.

Another factor that forever shaped the continent's beer culture was the influx of Irish, English, and German immigrants in the 1800s. Their penchant for beer, along with rising wages, helped per capita consumption almost quadruple from 1865 to the end of the 19th century. Germans were particularly influential, using their brewing traditions and a bottom-fermenting yeast to produce a then-novel beer type: lager. Within decades German-style lagers had usurped English ales and local styles as the continent's beer of choice.

A growing market helped big breweries expand, but it also meant that small breweries struggled. By 1915, there were 1,345 breweries producing an average of 44,000 barrels (51,600 hL) a year. Small-time brewing was a relic of the past.

Last Call for Alcohol

In the 19th and early 20th centuries, the beer industry was booming. Multipurpose community taverns were replaced by saloons whose primary purpose was to serve up alcoholic drinks. Saloons became synonymous with gambling, debauchery, and drunkenness, helping spawn the temperance movement. Temperance supporters originally advocated beer as an alternative to spirits, but they eventually pushed for a national ban on the production and sale of all alcohol. The result was Prohibition in the United States (1920–1933) and Canada (time period varied by province), which had a long-standing detrimental effect on the beer industry.

Some big breweries bounced back after Prohibition, but temperance-laced legislation lingered on for decades. While brewing giants such as Anheuser-Busch and Pabst were able to adapt to post-Prohibition commercial changes, smaller breweries struggled. Alcohol manufacturers were barred from owning saloons or bars, which made it impossible for many small breweries to stay commercially viable. Home-brewing anything stronger than 0.5 percent ABV was illegal in the United States until the 1970s, when President Jimmy Carter introduced legislation that ushered in the modern-day craft beer movement. Brewpubs were legalized in Canada's

brewline
Historic Moments in Beer

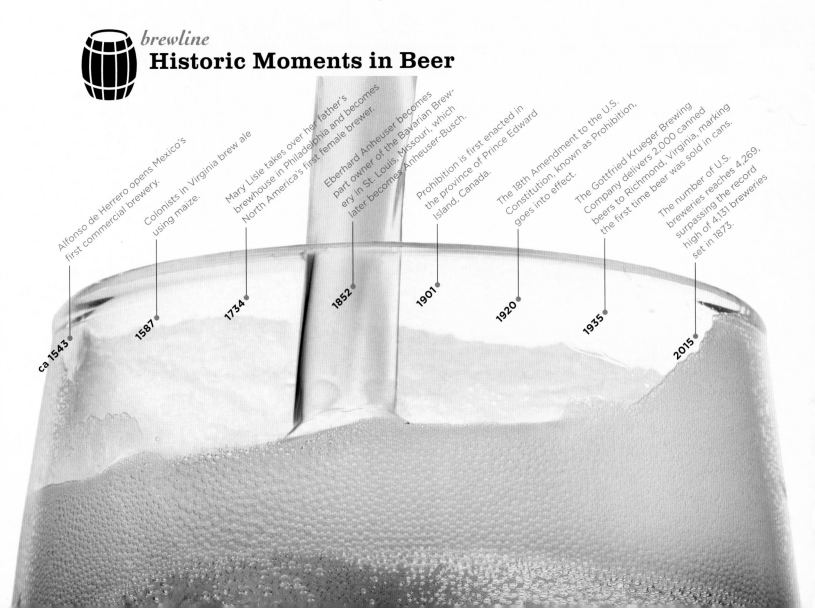

ca 1543
Alfonso de Herrero opens Mexico's first commercial brewery.

1587
Colonists in Virginia brew ale using maize.

1734
Mary Lisle takes over her father's brewhouse in Philadelphia and becomes North America's first female brewer.

1852
Eberhard Anheuser becomes part owner of the Bavarian Brewery in St. Louis, Missouri, which later becomes Anheuser-Busch.

1901
Prohibition is first enacted in the province of Prince Edward Island, Canada.

1920
The 18th Amendment to the U.S. Constitution, known as Prohibition, goes into effect.

1935
The Gottfried Krueger Brewing Company delivers 2,000 canned beers to Richmond, Virginia, marking the first time beer was sold in cans.

2015
The number of U.S. breweries reaches 4,269, surpassing the record high of 4,131 breweries set in 1873.

British Columbia in 1982, eventually expanding to all provinces and territories by 2013. Though Mexico didn't suffer through Prohibition, it has had to deal with cartel-like laws that benefited only certain beer brands.

New York City provides a backdrop for a toast with light lager, North America's most popular beer style.

A Flavorful Revolution

Consolidation has continued on well after Prohibition, with successful small breweries being bought up by ever growing conglomerates. Today, beer brands that were once North American owned are owned by big corporate brewing companies. The U.S.-Brazilian-Belgian firm AB InBev owns Budweiser (U.S.), Labatt (Canada), Modelo (Mexico), and many more. It also owns popular U.S. microbreweries like Goose Island, Elysian, and 10 Barrel—all previously craft breweries that no longer meet the Brewers Association's definition of one. Such acquisitions have led some to question whether these companies' products still count as "craft."

Despite these mergers, the return of independent breweries using local ingredients has sparked a craft beer revolution across the continent. Scores of brewers have fought to make North America's beer scene diverse, and many are using local water, yeast, and cereal grains to infuse their beer with a sense of place. Where beer lovers' choices were once predominately restricted to light beer and lager, they can now find hop-heavy IPA, rich stout, creamy ale, and wild beer with sour, funky flavors. Brewers are creating bold twists on Old World styles, producing some of the world's top-rated beer.

THE CITIZEN

EL HEFE SPEAKS

PENN QUARTER

Belgian Pale Ale 7%

Hefewizen 5.3%

Robust Porter

1 2 3 4

Washington D.C.'s DC Brau Brewing Company only distributes within about 100 miles of the brewery, a practice that harks back to a time when brewing was largely a local affair.

UNITED STATES

ONE NATION, UNDER HOPS

American brewers have a long history of melding Old World styles with New World flavors to create something unique. Shortages of traditional ingredients forced early European settlers to brew with the ingredients at hand, such as spruce tips, potatoes, pumpkin, maize, and birch sap, which lent their beer the flavors of the land in which it was made. When America gained independence in 1776, leaders like James Madison and George Washington chose to eschew imported beer in favor of beer brewed at home. "We have already been too long subject to British prejudices," Washington wrote in 1789. "I use no porter or cheese in my family, but such as is made in America; both these articles may now be purchased of an excellent quality."

In the mid-1800s, immigrants from Germany brought their beer styles and techniques with them, pushing aside the popularity of English-style ale to make way for Bavarian-style lager. As they moved west, adapting their ingredients and techniques to suit the environment, they helped spawn a nationwide love of lager. Brewing became a major industry, with the nation's breweries growing in size and production, though declining in number. By 1915 the United States had more than 1,300 breweries.

This prosperity was destroyed by Prohibition (1920–1933), which wiped out many local styles and most of the nation's breweries. By the 1970s there were only 89 breweries, most of which were large conglomerates flooding the market with light beer and pale lager. That changed in 1978, when President Carter signed H.R. 1337, which legalized homebrewing and kick-started a craft beer revolution. Brewers tinkered with ingredients and techniques in basements and garages, giving rise to microbreweries that brought U.S. beer styles back to life.

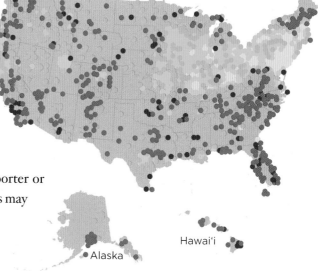

Alaska

Hawai'i

AT A GLANCE
Brewery Locations Over Time

- 1612–1840
- 1841–1865
- 1866–1920
- 1921–1932
- 1933–1985
- 1986–2011

Present-day boundaries are shown on map.

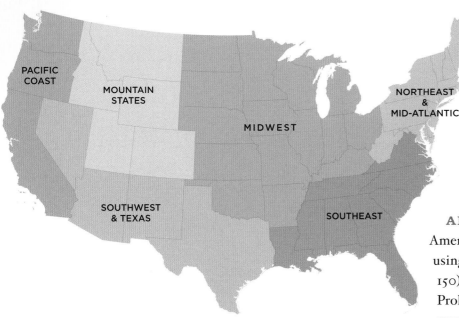

**Beer Style Most
Characteristic of Regions**

- American IPA
- American pale lager
- East Coast IPA
- Session IPA
- West Coast IPA
- Wild ales

MIDWEST Region

Data based on brewer responses.

U.S. Signature Beer Styles

Two characteristics stand out for most U.S. beer styles: hops and experimentation. The following styles aren't the only ones made in the United States, but they showcase the innovative spirit of its brewers and their passion for creating truly regional beers.

AMERICAN HOPPED ALE

American brewers adapted Old World recipes by using local hops—and lots of them (see page 150). While hoppy ale fell out of favor post-Prohibition, the style rose again in California in 1975. Pacific Northwest hops are the backbone of many hop-forward styles like American pale ale and American IPA, which is informally divided into West Coast IPA and East Coast IPA. The former tends to be hoppier, whereas the latter tends to have a more complex malt profile.

AMERICAN ADJUNCT LAGER

This easy-drinking style is the country's most popular and has garnered appreciation worldwide for its low bitterness and light body. Early American brewers modified European lager recipes using native ingredients like six-row barley, adjuncts such as maize, and the once ubiquitous Cluster hops. Light versions originated in New York around 1967 and were popularized by Miller in 1975.

AMERICAN STOUT AND PORTER

American stout and porter take their cues from English and Irish versions, with their dry-roasted finish, but they are often enhanced by smoke, coffee, or chocolate flavors. Bourbon-barrel-aged stout originated in Chicago, where brewer Greg Hall of Goose Island Beer Company first poured stout into Jim Beam oak barrels (see page 157).

AMERICAN STRONG ALE

All varieties of American strong ale have one characteristic in common: an ABV of 7 percent or higher. A notable example is American barleywine, revived in 1975 by Anchor Brewing Company in San Francisco using the traditional parti-gyle brewing technique that draws off the first part of the mash.

AMERICAN WILD ALE

American wild ale uses wild yeast and other microbiota in the air or wooden barrels, or added by design. Its flavor is as unique and variable as the microbiota used in brewing them, with tastes ranging from very ripe fruit to earthen barnyard. Wild ale is a truly avant-garde style with definitively funky tastes.

CREAM ALE AND CALIFORNIA COMMON

Both styles originated in the 1800s, created by brewers looking for ways to meet the demand for lager without having the refrigeration capabilities to brew it. Invented in Pennsylvania's Delaware Valley region, cream ale was made with lager yeast and adjuncts such as rice and maize. Brewers used lager yeast in shallow fermenters, creating a light-bodied ale that could compete with lager. California common, an ale-like lager, was first brewed during the 1800s gold rush. Brewers got around the lack of refrigeration by fermenting lager yeast at ale temperatures, producing a beer with the crispness of a lager and the full body of an ale.

Land of the Free

The U.S. beerscape changed quickly and radically after homebrewing was legalized in 1978. Entrepreneurs and small breweries could once again make regional beers and serve them to the populace. Craft beer pioneers such as Anchor Brewing Company and New Albion Brewery helped brewers find ingredients in small batches, wade through governmental red tape, and learn the ins and outs of small-scale brewing. Craft brewers weren't afraid to create new styles and resurrect forgotten ones. Even so, the craft industry struggled in its early years with regional legal restrictions that made it difficult to get craft beer to the masses. In other places, macrobreweries clamped down on

local flavor
Judging a Style

Debating and categorizing beer styles is a fairly recent phenomenon. Charlie Papazian, founder of the American Homebrewers Association (AHA), enlisted beer aficionado Michael Jackson to help judge home-brewed beers in the 1970s. Jackson obliged by coming up with more than 70 beer styles.

The Beer Judge Certification Program (BJCP), founded in 1985, is another big player in the beer style categorization game. As of 2015, the BJCP recognizes more than 120 different styles, grouped into 34 different categories. Friendly debates over the best beer styles take place in pubs around the globe, but we contend that the best style is whatever one is currently in your glass.

Charlie Papazian in his Boulder, Colorado, office

HOPNATION

AMERICA'S LOVE AFFAIR WITH HOPS

Of the four ingredients needed to make beer, hops is the one that has defined America's beer styles and turned them into objects of cultlike obsession.

While the United States is known for its IPA, the style actually originated in England in the early 1700s (see page 70). British soldiers and expats living in colonial India formed a taste for hoppy beer because it better suited the tropical heat than did the porter that was in vogue in London. It helped that the addition of fresh hops ensured the beer didn't spoil aboard ships sailing from England to India, a journey that could take six months. The popularity of English IPA spread worldwide, but it couldn't stand up to temperance movements, Prohibition, and World Wars I and II. It was rediscovered only during the modern U.S. craft beer movement, evolving to become the full-bodied, hop-bitter, relatively strong beer we know today.

Hoppy U.S. ales have two things in common: a pronounced aroma and a strong bitterness. They get both from the female flowers (cones) of the hop plant, *Humulus lupulus*, a climbing vine closely related to the marijuana plant *Cannabis sativa*. Hop flowers contain essential oils that infuse beer with aromas that can, depending on the hop variety, be citrusy, floral, tropical, fruity, spicy, piney, or earthy. This aroma is complemented by a bold, distinctive bitterness akin to the taste you get when biting into a citrus rind. A beer's bitterness is measured in International Bittering Units (IBUs), and though the IBU scale ranges from zero to infinity, most beers fall somewhere between 5 and 120. IBUs measure actual bitterness, not perceived bitterness, so two beers with the same IBU level may taste different depending on such factors as how much malt was used or their alcohol by volume. Most American pale lagers come in at around 8 to 12 IBUs, whereas most IPAs range from 40 to 70. Flying Monkeys Craft Brewery's Alpha Fornication clocks in at a mouth-numbing 2,500 IBUs, though humans aren't capable of registering any bitterness that's higher than 120 IBUs.

Hops are a major ingredient in beer today, but that wasn't always true. Early brewers preferred gruit, a common mix of fruit and spices such as heather, spruce, ginger, and bog myrtle that helped preserve and flavor beer (see page 72). For centuries, hops defined the difference between "ale" and "beer": ale excluded hops, while beer included them. Then the Bavarian purity law of 1516 (see page 53) declared

Washington State produces much of the U.S. hops crop, harvested in facilities like this one in the Yakima Valley.

hops one of three acceptable brewing ingredients. English law didn't ban non-hop bittering agents until 1710, and hops came to define the bitterness in beer.

The soils and climates of given areas produce hops with differing aromas and bitterness, which means hops have proved instrumental in how the world's beer styles have evolved. Hops from the United States are bold and brash, promoting the hop-forward styles born in California and the Pacific Northwest: American pale ale, American IPA, double (imperial) IPA, triple IPA, and Cascadian dark ale (India black ale).

Hop plants are happiest when grown between 35 and 50 degrees north or south of the Equator, where the soil is rich, the climate is mild, and the rainfall (or irrigation) is abundant. These specifications make the Pacific Northwest the perfect place for cultivating hops. With its dry climate and irrigated flatlands fed by water from the Cascade Range, the Yakima Valley grows around 80 percent of the U.S. hops crop—from the classic "C" hops of Cascade, Centennial, and Columbus to newer, experimental varieties. With so many hops to choose from, the possibilities for brewers creating hoppy beers seem almost endless. ■

The hop plant is a perennial climbing vine that can grow up to 30 feet (9 m). Only the female hop plant produces hop

craft beer distribution. Despite these hardships, craft beer production was growing by 30 to 50 percent a year in the early 1990s, fueled by consumers choosing craft beer over macrobrews. In the mid-1990s, the market experienced growing pains as too many brewers jumped on the craft beer bandwagon, only to fade away because of low-quality products. This thinning had one desirable effect: It separated the chaff from the grain, allowing an industry of quality to reemerge.

The Rise of Craft

In the United States, around 90 percent of the brewing industry remains dominated by macrobrewing giants such as Molson Coors and AB InBev. Even so, craft beer is changing how we define American beer. Beer production in 2015 was down by 0.2 percent from the previous year, but craft beer production grew by 13 percent over the same time period. U.S. craft brewers are arguably producing a wider variety of styles than anywhere else, many using local ingredients and adjuncts. The United States now boasts more than 5,000 breweries and brewpubs, and thousands more homebrewers, crafting styles that challenge our notions of what beer is and can be.

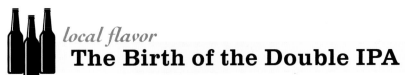

local flavor
The Birth of the Double IPA

It all started in the 1990s when a brewer at the Electric Brewing Company in Phoenix, Arizona, was arrested for marijuana possession. Electric sold its plastic fermenters to a brewpub called Blind Pig Brewing in Temecula, California. That's where brewmaster Vinnie Cilurzo used them to brew Inaugural Ale, the first official double IPA. Concerned the plastic equipment would introduce unwanted flavors, Cilurzo doubled the hops and increased the malt to counteract them. The resulting beer, unveiled on the brewery's first anniversary, was big, intense, and a huge success. Cilurzo experimented further after moving to Russian River Brewing Company, increasing the hops and the ABV. The result was Pliny the Elder, named after the first-century Roman philosopher, one of the first people to write about hops. It is now one of the most sought-after beers in America.

cones, so male plants are culled.

BEER GUIDE

WHERE BEER LOVERS GO

With more than 4,000 breweries and so little time, how do you decide which ones to visit? Start with these recommendations from U.S. brewers and beer business insiders.

1 | Hill Farmstead Brewery

Greensboro, Vermont

Though it's not on any major tourist routes, beer fans drive for hours to get their hands on Hill Farmstead's limited batches of beer for good reason. Grab some of the Biere de Norma, a spectacular barrel-aged bière de Mars. The purchase limit is three bottles, so arrive early.

2 | Three Floyds Brewing Co.

Munster, Indiana

Three Floyds is one of the Midwest's most popular craft breweries, owing in part to its unabashed use of hops: Three Floyds makes five beers with an IBU of 100. Not a hop head? Then come over to the dark side with its Dark Lord, a 15 percent ABV Russian imperial stout. The color of the wax-dipped top will let you know the beer's vintage.

3 | Allagash

Portland, Maine

This brewery makes some of the best Belgian-style beer outside of Belgium. Take the tour to see the coolship, a vessel used in spontaneous fermentation. While you're there, make sure to try the award-winning gueuze (a style of Belgian lambic), Coolship Resurgam. If there's any left, that is.

4 | Russian River Brewing Company

Santa Rosa, California

One word says it all: Pliny. Russian River's Pliny the Elder (see page 153) has been voted the best double IPA in the United States. The beer is hard to find, but the brewery will sell visitors up to 12 bottles. Russian River's triple IPA, Pliny the Younger, is available on draft during the first two weeks of February. Line up early and often.

5 | Crooked Stave Artisan Beer Project

Denver, Colorado

One of Denver's newer brewing projects is making a name for itself in the crowded Denver craft beer market by providing award-winning beer. Try Persica Wild Wild Brett, a barrel-aged American wild ale made with peaches and fermented with *Brettanomyces* yeast.

6 | Jester King Brewery

Austin, Texas

It's outside Austin, in Hill Country, but the wild microbiota on the beautiful property and some of Texas's best beer make it worth the trip. Its Nocturn Chrysalis is a

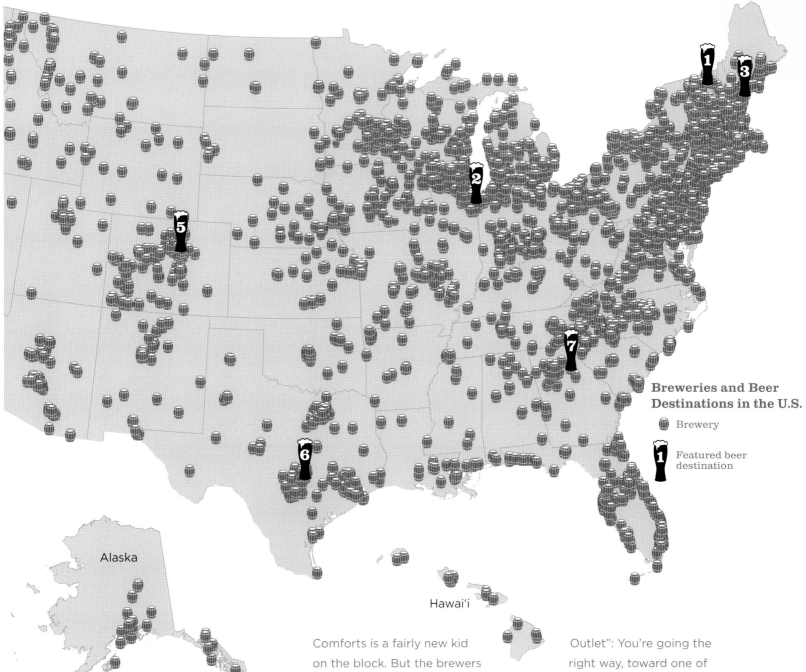

Breweries and Beer Destinations in the U.S.

Brewery

Featured beer destination

Alaska

Hawai'i

sour aged in oak barrels that contain traces of mature sour beer from previous batches, as well as Oregon blackberries.

7 | Creature Comforts Brewing Co.

Athens, Georgia

Located in one of the South's burgeoning beer centers, Creature

Comforts is a fairly new kid on the block. But the brewers have wasted no time in making new friends with their amazing beer. Try their Athena Paradiso, a top-notch Berliner weisse made with guava and passion fruit.

8 | Crux Fermentation Project

Bend, Oregon

Don't be deterred by the signs saying "Private Road" and "No

Outlet": You're going the right way, toward one of Bend's best beer spots. The tasting room at the heart of this brewery is topped only by the quality of its beers. Hook a Chinook is its representative IPA, but there are at least a half dozen other IPAs to try.

Photo

3 *Allagash Sixteen Counties is brewed exclusively with grains grown in Maine.*

LOCAL BREWS
MIDWEST
ON THE RISE AGAIN

The average craft beer uses nearly four times the amount of barley as its macrobrew counterpart.

The Midwest is a vast region, stretching from the Great Lakes of Wisconsin and Michigan to the prairies of the Central Plains and the farmlands of Nebraska and Kansas, but its sometimes-prolific beer production has always been concentrated in its major cities. Milwaukee, Wisconsin, and Chicago, Illinois, were the epicenters of large-scale United States brewing in the late 1800s and early 1900s, run by industry titans who made mass-produced lager a household staple.

The earliest breweries were founded in the 1830s, mainly by the wave of German immigrants who brought a love of lager, German brewing techniques, and European bottom-fermenting yeast with them. Midwestern beer barons like Frederick Pabst, Frederick Miller, and Joseph Schlitz used new technology and business savvy to produce beer in mass quantities and distribute it

widely. By the 1890s, Wisconsin boasted more than 300 breweries producing some two million barrels (2.3 million hL) of beer a year. So much beer was drunk in Milwaukee that men with a pronounced beer belly were said to have a "Milwaukee goiter." Chicago had only around 60 breweries, as many were lost in the Great Chicago Fire of 1871, but they were still producing about three million barrels (3.5 million hL) a year. Breweries became empires that fueled employment and made beer, particularly lager, a pillar of midwestern life.

Prohibition struck the region hard, even though people saw it coming. Groups such as the Wisconsin State Anti-Prohibition Association published pamphlets in the 1880s warning that a prohibition against beer was antibusiness and un-American, but to no avail. Only large breweries that could produce products like "near beer" and malt extract were able to survive. Post-Prohibition, well-known large breweries used their size and competitive advantage to squeeze smaller breweries out of the market. The last brewery in Chicago closed in 1978, leaving the city without one for a decade.

Then, after decades of faltering, midwestern beer rose again in the form of craft breweries. The region's craft beer revolution arguably began with the opening of Chicago's Goose Island Beer Company in 1988, followed by Kansas City's Boulevard Brewing Company in 1989. Today the region boasts more than 1,000 microbreweries. This success has not gone unnoticed by large beer conglomerates and private equity firms; indeed, the large breweries that survived Prohibition have all been acquired. Despite the increasing foreign ownership of many American brands, brewers are staying true to their historical and geographical beer roots. They brew everything from pale ale to stout, but the American adjunct lager remains the region's signature style.

on tap with Garrett Oliver

American Premium Lager

The beer that built the great American breweries of the mid-20th century—and the style that still dominates the country's beer scene today—is a toned-down variant of the German pilsner style, featuring lower hopping than its ancestors.

ABV 4.7–5% | **IBU** 10–15

Aroma Grainy, with light apple and floral notes

Appearance Very pale straw with a frothy white foam

Flavor Light, grainy, cornlike, and slightly sweet, with very restrained bitterness

Mouthfeel Brisk and quenching

Presentation Pint glass or mug

Food Pairings Backyard barbecue

Classic to Try Schlitz Gusto

local flavor
Barrel-Aged Beer

For most of brewing history, brewers relied on wooden barrels to ferment, transport, and serve beer. Though wooden barrels have given way to the metal equipment of today, modern brewers have discovered that aging beer in them—particularly the ones that once carried spirits—can introduce exciting flavors. Credit for creating the first bourbon-barrel-aged beer goes to brewmaster Greg Hall at Chicago's Goose Island Beer Company. In 1992 he got six Jim Beam barrels and aged stout in them, resulting in a beer that inspired excited reviews at the Great American Beer Festival (see page 159). Any beer can be barrel aged, but dark beer is best complemented by the wood's flavors. It takes anywhere from 2 to 12 months for beer to absorb a barrel's flavors, so breweries tend to release them only once a year. People line up for Goose Island's Bourbon County Brand Stout when it hits shelves each year.

Wine and whiskey barrels infuse beer with flavor.

LOCAL BREWS

MOUNTAIN STATES

CRISP, CLEAN TASTE

Pristine peaks and quiet mountain streams are the hallmarks of Colorado, Utah, Montana, and Idaho, but the region's history is anything but tranquil. In the 1850s, Denver, Colorado, was a rugged boomtown thick with pioneers and miners who came to profit from the gold rush and who stayed to enjoy the saloons.

Breweries prospered in the 1880s, as miners proved to be a thirsty lot and beer was seen as a popular alternative to hard liquor. By 1891 Utah's Salt Lake Brewing

on tap with Garrett Oliver

Session IPA

Combining the bitterness and flavor of modern IPA with the lightness and drinkability of "lawnmower beer," session IPA looks to bring the best of both worlds.

ABV 4.5–5.0% | **IBU** 35–45

Aroma Highly aromatic, with citrus, floral, and sometimes garlicky dank notes of American hop varieties

Appearance Pale to deep gold

Flavor Light and flinty, featuring a sharp, well-defined bitterness; good examples avoid acridity

Mouthfeel Light, brisk, and snappy

Presentation Pint glass

Food Pairings Fried foods, tacos, steaks, burgers, oily fish

Craft to Try Oskar Blues Brewery Pinner Throwback IPA

Company was producing 100,000 barrels (117,300 hL) annually, a huge amount for the time. Colorado's first brewery, called the Rocky Mountain Brewery, made beer that prompted the editor of the *Rocky Mountain News* in 1859 to call it "the best we've ever tasted." Fourteen years later, Jacob Schueler and Adolph Coors started a brewery in Golden, Colorado, later named the Coors Brewing Company. Though ownership buyouts by multinational corporations have diluted its regionality, its craggy mountain logo remains.

Breweries faded as mining declined and Prohibition was adopted, particularly in states like Utah. When the Fisher Brewing Company closed in 1967, the state had no more commercial breweries. It took decades for the region's first microbreweries to appear, but they made a big impression. Colorado's employee-owned New Belgium Brewing Company has become the fourth largest craft brewery in the United States, producing 945,000 barrels (1.1 million hL) annually containing everything from hop-heavy IPAs to dark ales and sour beers. Colorado ranks third in the country when it comes to breweries per capita, and it's a key location for the craft beer movement. Utah broke its decades-long brewery drought with Schirf Brewing, now known as Wasatch Brewery, in 1986. The state now has 22 craft breweries.

Brewers here say that the easy drinking session-style IPA is the most characteristic of the region. Session IPA holds on to the taste and aroma of its stronger sibling, but a low ABV makes it easy to drink for hours on end while staring at a snowcapped vista.

Colorado is a linchpin in the craft beer movement, ranking highest in the nation in terms of economic impact.

local flavor
The Great American Beer Festival

Held each September in Denver, Colorado, the Great American Beer Festival (GABF) prides itself on offering the largest number of domestic beers in one place. Charlie Papazian started the festival in 1982 with only 22 breweries in attendance, but it has grown into the country's largest craft beer festival, drawing more than 60,000 attendees each year. With 800 breweries pouring 3,800 different beers, visitors run out of time before they run out of tasting options. The festival also features "meet the brewer" sessions and a beer competition. But be warned: Tickets sell out within hours.

Thousands of beers are on tap at the GABF.

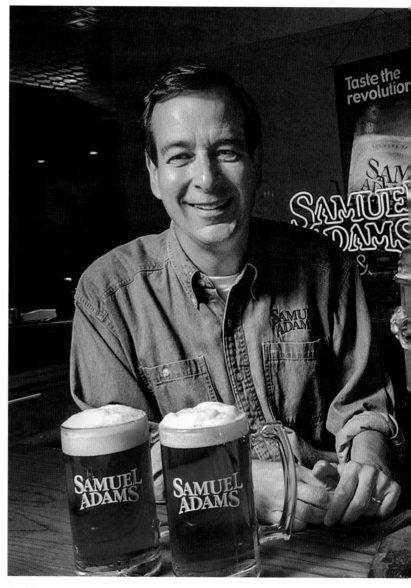

LOCAL BREWS
NORTHEAST & MID-ATLANTIC
HOTBED OF FLAVOR

From New England's rocky coastlines to the stately monuments of Washington, D.C., this center of industry and revolution has long played patron to the beermaking arts. The region saw a lot of national firsts: The Dutch set up the first commercial brewery in New Amsterdam (modern-day Manhattan) in 1632, Samuel Cole opened the first licensed tavern in 1634, and

on tap with Garrett Oliver

American Amber Lager

New York City was the world's third largest German-speaking community in the 1850s, so it's no surprise that Vienna lager gained prominence. As the craft beer movement awakened in the 1980s, American brewers adopted it as a flagship style.

ABV 4.8–5.2% | **IBU** 26–30

Aroma Bready malts and caramel malts, with a floral hop overlay from both kettle hopping and dry hopping

Appearance Bright medium amber with off-white foam

Flavor Snappy bitterness up front, followed by a slightly sweet mid-palate and a hoppy, clean finish

Mouthfeel Medium- to full-bodied, well carbonated, and clean

Presentation Pilsner or Willi Becher glass

Food Pairings Particularly good with ham, steak, pizza, barbecue, and fried food

Craft to Try Brooklyn Brewery Brooklyn Lager

Jim Koch co-founded the Boston Beer Company, which has

local flavor
Ringwood Yeast

Ringwood yeast easily defines New England brewing. It comes from Yorkshire, England, where it was originally used to make English-style ale. Alan Pugsley brought it to Maine in 1992 and put Ringwood at the center of the region's craft beer revolution.

Any yeast will chew through sugars and turn them into alcohol, carbon dioxide, and phenols, but Ringwood does so more aggressively than most. It packs a unique one-two punch since it actually combines two strains of yeast: a fast-attenuating strain that readily converts sugar to alcohol and a fast-flocculating strain that clumps together after fermentation. This powerful combination produces a bright beer with buttery notes and a dry, malty finish.

Massachusetts grew the first commercial hops in 1648. Beer was thought so preferable over hard liquor that in 1815 Thomas Jefferson wrote a letter in favor of making beer the national drink. "I have no doubt," he wrote, "of the desirableness to introduce a taste for malt liquors . . . . It appears to me to need no other encouragement than to increase the number of consumers."

Increase it did. As early as the 1800s, immigrants arriving from Germany and Ireland made the northeast's industrial port cities into brewing hotbeds. Beer money enabled Jacob Ruppert to buy the New York Yankees in 1915, acquire Babe Ruth in 1920, and build Yankee Stadium, which opened in 1923.

These early breweries did well, but one of the most successful arrived much later. The Boston Beer Company opened its doors in 1984 with its flagship beer, Samuel Adams Boston Lager, and is now the second largest craft brewery in the United States. The region's smaller breweries produce fewer barrels, but they keep the region's beerscape interesting. One such brewery is Dogfish Head in Delaware, where owner Sam Calagione worked with a biomolecular archaeologist to analyze beer found in ancient tombs and create his Ancient Ales series.

Despite their success, many of the region's brewers are opting to stay local. Breweries such as Washington, D.C.'s DC Brau aren't distributing any farther than a few states away, while people drive for hours to Vermont's the Alchemist and Hill Farmstead breweries to snap up their limited selections. Beer lovers hoping to sample this region's best offerings may just have to travel to get them.

grown into the country's second largest craft brewery.

LOCAL BREWS
PACIFIC COAST
GREAT AMERICAN BEER RUSH

Seattle, Washington, is one of the craft beer revolution's hot spots and the birthplace of some of its signature styles.

This region's love of beer is no more apparent than in the story of Henry Weinhard and Portland, Oregon's Skidmore Fountain. In 1888, this pioneering brewer was so enthusiastic about his beer that he offered to pump it through the fountain's pipes for its grand unveiling. Such excitement, along with perfect hop-growing conditions, has made Oregon, Washington State, and California the epicenter of the craft beer scene.

It began with the gold rush of the 1840s. Thousands of people came west hoping to strike it rich, bringing a thirst that brewers rushed in to quench. By the 1860s and '70s, settlers such as Weinhard and Gottlieb Brekle were buying up breweries. Brekle turned an old saloon in California into what eventually became Anchor Brewing Company, while Weinhard bought Portland's Liberty

Brewing and became one of Oregon's most influential brewers. Washington State's iconic Rainier beer was first brewed in Seattle back in 1878, 11 years before Washington was declared a state. Long before the craft beer revolution started stirring, this region was developing unique and distinctly American beer.

The proximity to thriving hop farms played a key role in developing the Pacific Coast's distinctive style. The region's clean mountain water, volcanic soil, temperate climate, and frequent rain make it the ideal place to grow hops. Of the 45,000 acres (18,211 ha) of hop farms in the United States, Washington claims 71 percent and Oregon 15 percent. This abundance may have inspired Fritz Maytag—who bought Anchor Brewing in 1965—to combine the English practice of dry-hopping with local hop varieties to produce his Liberty Ale. Sierra Nevada Brewing Company followed suit in 1980, when brewer Ken Grossman created a new style: the intensely hopped American pale ale. But if there is one style this region is famous for, it is the American IPA. Credit goes to Bert Grant of Washington's Yakima Brewing and Malting Company for developing the Northwest's first version of a hoppy IPA. His creation evolved into the unofficial beer style known as West Coast IPA.

This region's brewing culture isn't just enthusiastic—it's prolific. California leads all other states when it comes to the sheer number of craft breweries, with Washington ranked second and Oregon fourth. Portland, Oregon, boasts more than 70 breweries and brewpubs in its metropolitan area—the country's highest number of breweries per capita. Some of the larger craft breweries have been purchased by macrobreweries, but the region's craft brewing renaissance remains undiminished.

on tap with Garrett Oliver

West Coast IPA

Once rejected by both American and European brewers, American hops and their huge, unmistakable aromatics are now the hallmark of modern U.S. craft brewing. The hoppy West Coast IPA is the region's flagship beer style.

ABV 6-7% | **IBU** 55-70

Aroma Highly aromatic, with citrus, floral, and sometimes garlicky dank notes of American hop varieties

Appearance Golden to pale amber

Flavor Very dry, snappy, and bitter, with restrained malt character

Mouthfeel On the lighter side of medium-bodied, with a clean mineral tightness

Presentation Pint glass

Food Pairings Spicy food, aged cheddar, Thai cuisine, fried food

Craft to Try Russian River Brewing Company Blind Pig IPA

meet the brewer
Charles Finkel

Despite his unassuming nature, Charles Finkel looms large in the history of U.S. craft beer. He is considered one of the 12 founders of the modern craft beer revolution, though he started his career in wine. In 1969 he became one of the first people to sell boutique West Coast wines, then went on to pioneer many firsts in the beer industry: He was the first to import Belgian beer, market fruit beer, and revive such styles as oatmeal stout. He and his wife, Rose Ann, own Pike Brewing in Seattle's famous Pike Place Market. This go-to brewpub has a selection of eclectic beers that's eclipsed only by an incredible collection of beer memorabilia; highlights include some of his own beer-label artwork, adorning such brands as Lindemans and Samuel Smith.

Beer memorabilia lines the walls at Pike Brewery Co.

LOCAL BREWS
SOUTHEAST

THE LAST FRONTIER

For all its sense of tradition, the Southeast has been slow to find its way back to brewing. This land of humid swamps, low-slung mountains, and marshlands has such varying laws that while states like North Carolina welcome the craft beer industry, others in the region have been slow to adopt it. Mississippi and Alabama were the last states in the country to legalize homebrewing, which they did in 2013.

It wasn't always so. Virginia's Jamestown Colony brewed some of the continent's first European-style beer in the 1600s. Major William Horton built the first brewery in the Deep South—on Jekyll Island, Georgia, in 1738—and southern statesmen Thomas Jefferson malted grain and brewed with it at his Virginia plantation in the early 1800s. The Civil War (1861–65) destroyed most of the South's handful of breweries, and from the end of the war to the start of Prohibition, only a modest number of breweries opened.

Beer lovers can pedal their way through Asheville, North Carolina's Ale Trail on a "pubcycle."

Some scholars suggest the slow growth may have to do with the region's religious roots; the temperance movement has had a more intense impact on drinking and brewing here than elsewhere. A long-depressed economy and a hot climate didn't exactly help matters. Yet a beer scene has arisen, and it's growing in exciting ways.

In the 1980s and '90s, adventurous new arrivals enlivened the southern brewing landscape. Bavarian transplant Uli Bennewitz missed German lager so much that he helped get brewpubs legalized in North Carolina so he could open his own. An economic boom brought money to the region, and micropubs and breweries emerged where they had never been before.

Some of the Southeast's great brewing successes have been in small towns. Asheville, North Carolina, has become a thriving beer haven, with the second most breweries per capita in the United States. It now boasts 14 breweries, including East Coast outposts from big names in other regions, such as Sierra Nevada and New Belgium. The region may have been slow to blossom, but it is earning a place on the U.S. beer map.

on tap with Garrett Oliver

Florida Weisse

An emerging style based on the German regional sour specialty Berliner weisse, Florida weisse starts with a brisk acidic base and then layers on all manner of citrus and/or tropical fruit flavors.

ABV 3-5% | **IBU** 4-8

Aroma Brightly fruity, often with aromatics of lime zest and other fruits

Appearance Golden to bright pink, orange, or red, depending on the fruits used

Flavor Light, dry, and briskly acidic with notable fruit flavor

Mouthfeel Well carbonated, tart, snappy, and thirst-quenching

Presentation Tulip glass

Food Pairings Goat cheese, panna cotta, shrimp dishes, fish tacos

Craft to Try Coppertail Brewing Company Guava Passion

local flavor
The First Canned Beer

Canned beer is as familiar a sight at U.S. summer gatherings as hamburgers sizzling on the grill and children splashing in the pool, but that wasn't always the case. Canned food was invented in the early 1800s, but canning beer presented challenges that delayed its debut. Early cans weren't strong enough to withstand the internal pressure created by carbonation, and they tended to impart a metallic taste. The world's first canned beer was sold in 1935, and the lucky few who sampled it in Richmond, Virginia, felt that it tasted more like draft beer than bottled beer did. Since then, canned beer has gotten a reputation as being inferior to beer that's been bottled or kegged, but craft brewers are changing that. As more and more quality beer is canned, we are bound to see more variety around the picnic table.

Craft breweries are increasingly turning to canning.

LOCAL BREWS
SOUTHWEST & TEXAS
A BLOOMING THIRST

Skiers enjoying an après-ski beer in the sunshine at the Bavarian Lodge in New Mexico's Taos Ski Valley.

The Southwest's red rock mounds and Texas's dry valleys may not be what springs to mind when dreaming of beer. But the beverage has a long history here, forged by stalwart pioneers in the 1850s despite the challenges of brewing in parched, sunbaked lands. Heat was a major setback, as it tends to spoil beer quickly. Brewing was typically done in winter, when temperatures dipped low enough for beer to both ferment and keep. Though the 1800s brought an influx of German immigrants to the

Southwest, their beloved lager needed consistently cool temperatures to age: a real challenge without refrigeration. It could be produced only in small quantities, but that didn't stop enterprising brewers from trying.

Commercial breweries appeared as early as 1855, when William A. Menger's Western Brewery opened in San Antonio, Texas. Like other breweries at this time, its success was short-lived. Railroads brought beer to the Southwest from other states, which put the squeeze on local breweries. Then came the death knell that was Prohibition. Even Lone Star Brewery, co-founded by Adolphus Busch in 1883 with the latest technology and a very deep coffer, was forced to close for the duration.

Though the number of southwestern breweries did rebound post-Prohibition, they've had to face another threat: consolidation. The venerable Arizona Brewing Company, which survived through many ups and downs post-Prohibition, fell to a final takeover by Canadian Breweries in 1985. Yet there's plenty of hope for the Southwest's breweries. Law changes in Texas, Arizona, and New Mexico have resulted in a tremendous upsurge of microbreweries, some of which are considered the country's most innovative. They specialize in some U.S. signatures: wild (spontaneously fermented) ale and barrel-aged beer. As of 2016, there are 189 such breweries in Texas, 78 in Arizona, and 45 in New Mexico, blooming out of the region's harsh landscape like desert flowers after rain.

on tap with Garrett Oliver

American Wild Ale

These beers are fermented by wild yeast and bacterial strains, giving the best of them great complexity and funkiness.

ABV Varies | **IBU** Varies (but usually relatively low, 5–20)

Aroma Varies, but often a blend of tropical fruitiness and earthy barnyard funk

Appearance Pale to black

Flavor Commonly acidic and with earthy, fruity (though rarely sweet), and somewhat funky flavors

Mouthfeel Runs the gamut of carbonation and palate fullness, but balance, structure, and complexity are prized

Presentation Tulip or stemmed white wine glass

Food Pairings Cheeses and some desserts

Craft to Try Jester King Brewery's Atrial Rubicite

local flavor
Going Wild With Local Ingredients

Of the four ingredients needed to make beer, water is often the only one that's sourced locally. Climate and soil conditions can make it difficult to grow barley and hops, and most of the yeast used in brewing is cultured in laboratories. But in Texas's Hill Country, brewers are doing something rare in the beer world: sourcing all four ingredients from their own backyard. The area's environmental conditions allow barley and hops to grow, and breweries such as Jester King and Live Oak are harvesting local yeasts and microbes from surrounding flora. A process called spontaneous (also known as open or wild) fermentation exposes wort to the air, allowing naturally occurring yeast strains to settle in and work their magic. By blending these natural wild cards with known strains of yeast and bacteria, Hill Country brewers are making funky, flavorful farmhouse ales that truly reflect the pastures and farmsteads of central Texas.

Wildflowers harbor airborne microbes, which help give wild ales their unique flavors.

The Hotel Frontenac is a local landmark in Quebec, a province becoming known for producing outstanding Belgian-style beers.

CANADA

A LAND OF LAGER

Where could a female settler (Marie Rollet), a Jesuit priest (Frère Ambroise), and a militia captain (Louis Prud'homme) be among the first individuals to brew beer for the masses? An early New World settlement in Canada. The country's brewing history dates back to the 1600s, when French settlers brought European beer to New France (now Quebec). Abundant grain supplies and a cool climate aided these early brewers in producing European-style beer.

If statistics are anything to go by, then Canadians love beer. Fifty-seven percent of the nation prefers beer over other forms of alcohol, particularly beer brewed on home soil. Of the 19,350,290 barrels (22,707,133 hL) of beer consumed in Canada in 2015, 84 percent was brewed domestically. Stretching from the rocky shores of Newfoundland to the mountains of British Columbia, Canada offers brewers plenty of space and ingredients to experiment with.

The French brought beer to New France, but it did nothing to improve their relationship with the British colonists and army in Canada. After the French colonists surrendered to the British in 1763 at the end of the Seven Years' War, British rule shaped their brewing practices, bringing about the rise of the commercial brewing industry and the adoption of English brewing techniques. By just prior to World War I, Canada's beer scene had grown to 117 breweries.

Things got complicated when prohibition started taking effect around the turn of the 20th century. Federal laws regulated alcohol production, while various

Yukon (1918-1920)

Northwest Territories (1874-1891)

Labrador (Dependency of Newfoundland)

Newfoundland (United Kingdom) (1917-1924)

British Columbia (1917-1921)

Alberta (1916-1923)

Manitoba (1916-1921)

Quebec (1919)

Nova Scotia (1921-1930)

Saskatchewan (1917-1925)

Ontario (1916-1927)

Prince Edward Island (1901-1948)

New Brunswick (1856, 1917-1927)

AT A GLANCE
History of Prohibition in Provinces and Territories

Extent of Canada in 1927

Alberta Province or territory

(1916-1923) Years of prohibition

1927 Canadian provincial boundaries are shown on map.

Canada-made beer accounts for more than **80%** of the beer Canadians consume each year.

provincial temperance laws regulated its sale and consumption. This difference between federal and provincial law greatly benefited Canadian breweries during U.S. Prohibition, when roughly 80 percent of Canadian-brewed beer was exported legally (though imported illegally) to the United States. By 1931, all but the province of Prince Edward Island had overturned temperance laws in favor of government-controlled systems, many of which are still in place.

The Winds of Change

The decrease in the number of Canadian breweries after World War II was a result of consolidation. By the 1980s only 10 breweries remained, and 3 of them (Labatt, Molson, and Carling O'Keefe) monopolized more than 95 percent of the market. Canada's beer styles dwindled to one: American pale lager. Though lager is still Canadians' preferred beer type, the diversity of available styles has grown.

The 1980s beerscape was certainly homogeneous, but the decade also brought changes that made room for an emerging craft beer scene. Provincial governments faced pressure to grant licenses for microbreweries, while newly formed Canadian organizations promoted a wider variety of beer styles.

The first wave of microbreweries opened in Canada in the 1980s and early '90s, though not all were successful. Those that endured provided the backbone for the craft brewing industry and paved the way for the current craft beer explosion, with hundreds of breweries now operating throughout the country. Most Canadian craft breweries are microbreweries, a trend that harks back to a time when breweries were small and numerous, and styles were full of local flavor.

local flavor
Canadian Ice Beer

What is ice beer, other than a marketing term? At its core is a process called fractional freezing. When beer is taken to subzero temperatures, some of the water within it will freeze while the alcohol remains liquid. Canadian-style ice beer comes from the fractional freezing of American-style pale lager, removing ice crystals, tannins, and bittering particles derived from hops and grain husks, and adding some fresh water back in. The result is a slightly boozier beer with a milder, less bitter taste.

Ice beer was all the rage in Canada in the 1990s. Competitive branding campaigns run by Molson and Labatt catapulted its popularity, and ice beer quickly captured a 10 percent share of the Canadian beer market.

Although ice beer is a distinctly Canadian icon, the process of fractional freezing beer was not invented there. It was developed in Germany in the 1890s—likely by accident. Legend has it that a young brewery employee, tired from a long day at work, left a few kegs of doppelbock outside the Reichelbrau brewyard in Kulmbach, Germany, with plans to cellar them the next day. The casks froze over during the bitterly cold night, leaving them cracked open and the beer an icy mess. The angry brewer forced the young worker to drink his handiwork, which turned out to be an enjoyable punishment. This boozy, sweet beer became the foundation of the *eisbock* style and the predecessor of Canada's ice beer.

With extensive beer lists, taprooms like Craft Beer Market in Vancouver help patrons expand their tastes.

Toasts in Translation

For most of Canada, toasts are fairly simple. In the English-speaking parts of Canada, you raise your glass over the bar or brewery table and just say "Cheers!" In other parts of Canada, make sure you know the local lingo.

————————

In French-speaking Quebec, you raise your glass of **bière** (bee-YAIR) at a **brasserie** (BRA-sir-REE), or pub, or grab one from a **dep** (short for *dépanneur*, a convenience store that sells beer and inexpensive wine), raise it high, and say, **"Santé!"** (soun-TAY).

————————

And then there's the obsolete **"Chimo"** (CHEE-mo). The Anglicized adaptation of an Inuktitut greeting from the Ungava region of northern Quebec, "Chimo" can mean several things: "Hello," "Goodbye," and "Peace be with you." Although politicians officially nationalized the phrase by an act of federal government, the term never quite made it into the Canadian lexicon.

————————

If you happen to meet Her Majesty, Queen of Canada (and of England) or another head of state, it's good to know the **Loyal Toast**. Make sure to stand up if the toastmaster does. Raise your glass—not a bottle, as that would be rude—to eye level. Repeat the words of the host or toastmaster (for example, "The Queen"), and drink some of the glass's contents. **Do not clink glasses.**

BEER GUIDE

WHERE BEER LOVERS GO

Canada is a melting pot of different beer styles and beautiful places to try them. Check out these excellent recommendations from Canadian brewers.

1 | Spinnakers Gastro Brewpub

Victoria, British Columbia

Victoria is a beautiful place to visit innovative breweries that use local and seasonal ingredients. Spinnakers Gastro Brewpub, one of Canada's original brewpubs, pairs small-batch beer with "farm to fork" food, all within a heritage building overlooking Victoria's inner harbor.

2 | Niagara College Teaching Brewery

Niagara-on-the-Lake, Ontario

It may seem strange to have a college listed in a beer guide, but a

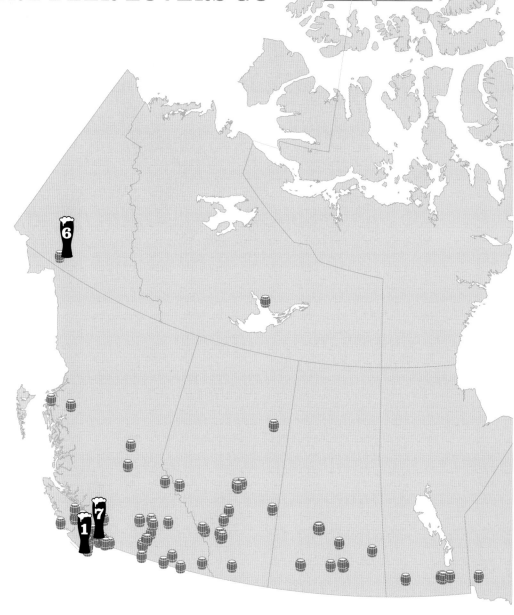

college devoted exclusively to beer is worth noting. Niagara focuses on teaching students how to brew and prepare for careers in brewery operations—and, yes, imbibing class projects is encouraged. Stop in for a student-made lager or ale.

3 | Indie Ale House
Toronto, Ontario

Located in the Junction neighborhood of Toronto, this small brewpub is incredibly prolific. It has four flagship beers and has brewed at least five dozen rare releases, one-offs, and collaboration beers. There's no telling what will be available when you go. Try the Cockpuncher if it's on tap, an imperial IPA with 11 percent ABV and 100 IBUs.

4 | Dieu du Ciel!
Montreal, Quebec

When a brewery's name means "God in Heaven," you know its beer must be good. Dieu du Ciel! makes beer that goes beyond classic styles. If you like hibiscus flowers, Belgian beer, and hefeweizens, then the Rosée d'Hibiscus Belgian hibiscus wheat beer is for you. It's perfect for sipping on the brewpub's terrace on a summer evening

5 | Garrison Brewing Company
Halifax, Nova Scotia

Ancient recipes and forgotten beer styles are revived at Garrison Brewing. The Spruce Beer—a strong ale made with local spruce and fir tips, black molasses, and dates—is an updated yet authentic interpretation of one of North America's oldest beer styles.

6 | Yukon Brewing
Whitehorse, Yukon

Canada's northernmost brewery makes "beer that is worth freezin' for." Take a trip up north to try its award-winning amber ale and unique Up the Creek Birch Sap Ale, created from the sap of 1,500 trees.

7 | Vancouver's Brewing Districts
Vancouver, British Columbia

This coastal city boasts neighborhoods that put breweries on proud display. Check out East Vancouver's dozen breweries or wander through the Brewery Creek district, whose brewing history spans more than 100 years.

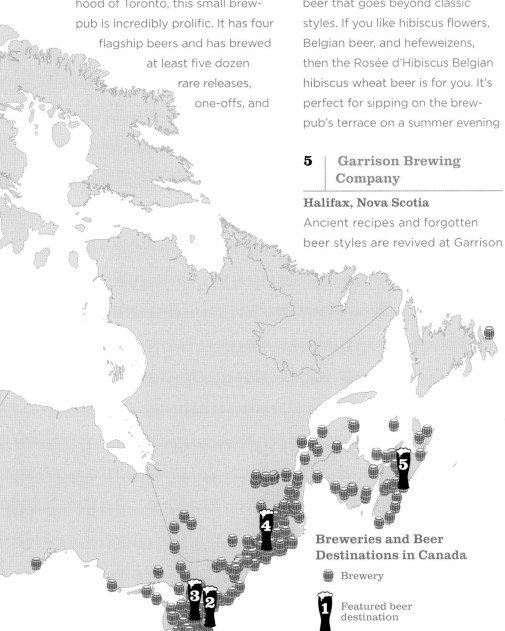

Breweries and Beer Destinations in Canada

🛢 Brewery

🍺 Featured beer destination

Photos

1 *Spinnakers was an early pioneer in the Canadian craft beer scene.* **6** *The downtown area of Whitehorse, Yukon, showcases the city's frontier spirit.*

LOCAL BREWS
WEST COAST & QUEBEC
FRESH HOPS AND OLD WORLD TERROIR

MOUNTAIN MAJESTY   The roots of Canada's craft beer movement run deep in the pine woods and lofty mountains of British Columbia. When the taps ran dry during workers' strikes at Canada's largest breweries in 1979, the government in Canada's westernmost province allowed for a temporary importation of beer from the United States to ease the drought. But it came too late; the people were angry. That anger fueled a swell of policy changes and reform, and soon British Columbia's breweries were producing beer again. One of the craft beer

local flavor
Looser Laws

Beer regulations in French-speaking Quebec echo laws in France more than they resemble laws in the other Canadian provinces. Alongside Alberta and Manitoba, the legal drinking age here is the lowest in Canada: 18 years. Quebec also has the lowest provincial beer taxes, with the average tax on a "2-4"—Canadian jargon for 24 beers—nearly 35 percent lower than in neighboring Ontario. Breweries in Quebec are allowed to sell beer directly to retailers, whereas other provincial governments (save Alberta) control distribution. While many provinces are starting to allow beer to be sold in private stores, beer has been available for years at Quebec's local *dépanneurs* (convenience stores). Those who feel like drinking one beer instead of a 2-4 shouldn't fear: singles can be bought to go. *Santé!*

movement's pioneers was John Mitchell, an Englishman and pub owner who opened Canada's first microbrewery, Horseshoe Bay Brewery, in 1982, and its first brewpub, Spinnakers, in 1984 (see page 172). Fast-forward three decades and there are 100 breweries across British Columbia and dozens of breweries in metro Vancouver, earning the city the title of Canada's Craft Beer Capital.

Beyond brewing, British Columbia has also had a revival in its hop production. Hops were first planted here in 1892, and by the 1940s, the region had become Canada's largest hop-growing region. Industry consolidation and the lower cost of farming elsewhere eventually collapsed British Columbia's hop-farming industry, but a global hop shortage in 2006 started a resurgence of hop farming here. Hop farming has found a new home outside the city of Kamloops, where the climate is most suitable for growing them.

FRENCH FLAIR   The province of Quebec blends classic Canadian wilderness with honored European heritage—it's a place where enjoying good food and drink is the joie de vivre. When many of the first settlers in the eastern province of New France (Quebec) arrived from wine-loving France, they found there were no grapes to be had. Beer became the alcohol of choice by default. Frère LeJeune, the superior of the Jesuit mission in New France, began brewing beer for the mission's consumption in 1647. Four years later Louis Prud'homme received a royal decree to establish the first commercial brewery in what is today Montreal.

British Columbia's Rocky Mountain scenery provides a backdrop for many breweries.

New France's first public administrator, Jean-Baptiste Talon, received permission from Louis XVI to construct a brewery in 1667. The production of wine and spirits increased, and the rise in alcohol abuse became worrisome. In 1762, three years into the British occupation of New France, regulations were imposed on the sale of alcohol to curb its abuse.

In the 1780s, a wave of British loyalists left the newly founded United States and made their way to New France. Eager to tap into this new market, John Molson opened his first brewery in 1786. The 4,000 imperial gallons (4,800 U.S. gallons) he brewed in his first year of operation sold out instantly. Two centuries later, Quebec had six big breweries. But Quebecers have a cultural tendency to go against the grain, including a desire for the unique amid a sea of adjunct lager. It was this desire that helped Unibroue succeed in the 1990s. The brewery produced the first abbey-style beer in North America, introducing consumers to Belgian-style ale. By 2000, Quebec had 90 breweries; by 2015, that number had swelled to 160.

WEST COAST

Fruit Beer

Canada's West Coast brewers have long produced fruit-influenced beers. Not all show notable acidity, but the best find a nice integration between fruit and grain flavors.

ABV Varies, with most 4–7% | **IBU** 5–12

Aroma Fruity and bright, with the variety of the fruit showing through. Wild yeasts are sometimes used to produce earthy, funky aromatics.

Appearance Varies depending on the fruit used

Flavor While many fruit beers were once sweet, they now tend to be drier and more acidic

Mouthfeel Dry, tart, and refreshing

Presentation Tulip or white wine glass, or even a champagne flute

Food Pairings Pork dishes, Caribbean seafood dishes, goat cheese, chocolate desserts

Craft to Try Postmark Brewing Raspberry

QUEBEC

Tripel-Style Golden Ale

Quebec's French heritage has led to an affinity for abbey ale. These beers are prized for their affinity with food—something Quebec approaches with Gallic seriousness.

ABV 9–10% | **IBU** 22–25

Aroma Fruity, spicy, and complex, with clove, orange, and banana notes

Appearance Antique gold, with a dense white persistent foam

Flavor Very dry, showing a false sweetness produced by fruity aromatics combined with alcoholic strength

Mouthfeel Frisky, with champagnelike carbonation that opens into a mousselike texture

Presentation Tulip glass or chalice

Food Pairings Very versatile, from roasted fowl to game meats, pork dishes, grilled vegetables, and cheeses

Classic to Try Unibroue La Fin Du Monde

Mexico City's Palacio de Bellas Artes is the cultural center of the city, home to music, art, and dance.

MEXICO

VIVA LA REVOLUCIÓN

Mexican beer likely conjures thoughts of a pale lager—ideally consumed on an empty beach under a swaying palm tree. But lager wasn't the country's first beer of choice; beer was made here well before the Spanish conquest of the 1500s, with local ingredients like maize and cocoa beans. The Maya and Aztec brewed a low-alcohol beverage called *pulque*, made by fermenting agave sap (called *acuamiel*, or honey water), which was a cure-all for everything from diabetes to sleep disorders. Even so, the Spanish invaders preferred the European beer they brought with them and weren't afraid to try to make their own. Alfonso de Herrero was granted a brewing license from the king of Spain in the 1540s, and though his European-style offerings couldn't keep the business afloat, he earned the distinction of having established what some scholars believe was the first brewery in North America.

It wasn't until the mid-1800s, when Holy Roman Emperor Maximilian I became emperor of Mexico, that the industry truly began to take root. Maximilian preferred dark Vienna-style lager, an influence visible in present-day brands such as Victoria and Negra Modelo. Europeans migrated in droves during his reign, many of them Germans and Austrians who produced the lager style that has remained Mexico's most popular.

From the late 1890s to the 1950s, Mexico's breweries grew in earnest. Reliance on foreign brewers receded as large *cervecerías* (breweries) modernized their equipment and developed technical know-how, largely by creating educational institutes geared toward teaching Mexican students about working in the beer

**AT A GLANCE
Major Brewery Locations
and Opening Year**

- ● FEMSA brewery
- ● Modelo brewery

Orizaba City

(1985) Year opened

Conglomerates FEMSA and Modelo control the majority of the beer market in Mexico.

industry. Yet pulque was still the preferred beverage outside the urban centers, so these breweries embarked on a massive campaign to turn the rural population into beer drinkers. As the local taste for beer grew, Mexico's offerings also started to gain attention well beyond its borders.

Global Recognition

Two key events jump-started the globalization of Mexican beer: the World's Columbian Exposition of 1893 in Chicago and Prohibition in the United States. Cervecería Cuauhtémoc won a prize in the Columbian Exposition's beer competition, proving that Mexican breweries were making great beer. Prohibition (1920–1933) brought Americans rushing across the border in search of Mexico's German-style beer, resulting in brisk local trade and high profits. These in turn attracted foreign companies, which bought their way in and today control 98 percent of the domestic market. In 2011, Mexico became the world's largest exporter of beer, knocking the Netherlands out of the top spot. The United States remains the top export destination.

Battling for Artesanal

With foreign-owned macrobreweries continuing to dominate the domestic beer scene, *artesanal* (craft) beer has yet to catch on with the general public. Similarly, several other beer trends that thrive elsewhere have yet to take hold—beer served on tap, for one. Though craft breweries make up only one percent of the domestic market in terms of total sales (compared with 12 percent in the United States),

local flavor
Michelada: Beer With a Twist

Most cocktail enthusiasts have tried a margarita, but what about a *michelada*? A michelada is a drink made with beer, tomato or Clamato (clam and tomato) juice, lime juice, Worcestershire, teriyaki, or hot sauce, and spices, commonly served chilled in a salt-rimmed glass. The term comes from the Spanish phrase *mi chela helada*, which means "my cold beer." Before making the drink, bartenders often ask patrons what lager they want used. This choice does not alter the final taste, as the sauces, spices, and lime juice pretty much nullify the flavor of the beer. Hoping to capitalize on the beverage's popularity, both the Miller Brewing Company and Anheuser-Busch make their own versions: Miller Chill and Bud Chelada.

Michelada recipes vary widely across Mexico.

the craft industry has grown by 50 percent a year since 2005. The industry's rise goes back to Gustavo González, who started the Cerveza Cosaco microbrewery in 1995 in Mexico City. Since then the number of microbreweries has continued to grow, along with the quality of the beer they produce.

For a number of reasons, the craft beer sector has struggled to gain the same kind of traction as its counterpart in the United States. First, AB InBev and Heineken International exercise tight control over the distribution of beer in the country. One of the largest convenience store chains, a common outlet for selling beer, is owned by a beverage conglomerate called FEMSA, whose beer division is owned by Heineken. Second, the consumer base is small—both in number and as a percentage of the population. Third, potential consumers haven't been educated about craft beer, which is often viewed either as an unknown commodity or a luxury good. In spite of the difficulties microbreweries face, Mexico's craft beer scene is growing more vibrant and diverse. Brewers are making high-quality European lager styles as well as IPA, stout, and porter. They are introducing local flavor to their beer as well, by adding adjuncts such as chocolate and peppers that impart flavors unlike anywhere else.

The booming Mexican craft beer scene attracts both locals and visitors, especially in popular tourist destinations like Costa Careyes in Jalisco.

BEER GUIDE

WHERE BEER LOVERS GO

After years of ubiquitous pale lagers, craft beers are slowly but surely changing Mexico's beer-scape; there's much more than beer in clear glass bottles.

1 | Norte Brewing Company

Tijuana, Baja California

Like a pirate's buried treasure, this brewery is hard to find. But riches await those who venture to the fifth floor of a parking deck in downtown Tijuana! Along with a terrific view of the city, you can enjoy great craft beer such as its Penthouse IPA, which is such a good West Coast IPA you'll swear you are north of the border.

2 | Veracruz Brewing Company

Tejería, Veracruz

The growing Mexican craft beer scene has many wonderful ales for discerning drinkers. This brewery, located in hot, humid Tejería, offers cold, crisp lagers to cool things off. Its lagers include a pilsner and a Vienna lager. The pilsner, called Criolla Pilsen, is one of the best in the country.

3 | Baja Brewing Company

San José del Cabo, Baja California Sur

The southern tip of the Baja California peninsula is hot, windy, and dusty, which means it's the perfect place to enjoy a cold beer. Founded in 2006, Baja Brewing was the region's first craft brewery. Today, it is also the largest. Its beers are popular with locals and tourists alike. Try the flagship Cabotella, a blonde ale, which the brewers have dubbed a "Mexican ale," or the hoppy Mexican IPA. Take a trip to the rooftop cantina at Cabo Villas Beach Resort for good brew with a view. *Salud!*

4 | Cervecería Calavera

Tlalnepantla, Mexico City

Located just west of the city, this craft brewery is like most in Mexico in that it produces the requisite pale ale and stout. But unlike at most craft

breweries in Mexico, the founder and brewer hails from Denmark, and he makes a Belgian dubbel and tripel. Try their standout Maquahuitl, a black IPA made with coffee and dried chilies.

5 | Cervecería Teufel

Oaxaca, Oaxaca

An increasingly popular question in the craft beer scene is "What beer do I pair with that food?" At Teufel the pairing is done with mescal, a distilled liquor made from an agave plant. Not keen on

mixing alcohols? Try Teufel's 77 Agave Honey Ale, a hoppy, copper-colored ale made with agave syrup.

6 | Cervecería Minerva

Guadalajara, Jalisco

If you're going to Guadalajara, a trip to Minerva is a must. It's taking on the two big beer conglomerates in Mexico (and winning), but it still has the gumption to take risks, like making ale aged in old tequila barrels. The Imperial Tequila Ale is about as unique a beer as you will find in Mexico. It's actually quite smooth, with hints of oak and malts. No salt or lime required.

Photos

1 *Dia de los Muertos celebrations honor the dead, often with gifts of alcohol.* **4** *Sidewalk cafés are popular places for enjoying a cold beer.* **5** *Music is an important part of the culture in Oaxaca.* **6** *Traditional dance is a fixture in Guadalajara.*

Breweries and Beer Destinations in Mexico

🛢 Brewery

🍺 Featured beer destination

LOCAL BREWS
BAJA & GUADALAJARA
A GROWING THIRST

BEER ON THE BEACH　Separated from the rest of Mexico by the Sea of Cortez, Baja California is a 760-mile (1,200-km) stretch of lonely deserts, ocean views, and inviting beaches perfect for enjoying a swim and a beer. The peninsula's geography has much to do with why Baja California is one of Mexico's craft beer hot spots. Its proximity to San Diego, California—a beer haven—gives Baja California access to the area's brewing knowledge and makes collaboration possible. This accessibility has also made the region a popular destination for U.S. tourists, who bring a thirst for craft libations. Whether they're ordering a beachside beer in Cabo or signing up for a brewery tour in Mexicali, these tourists are eager to enjoy what Mexico has to offer.

Brewers in Baja California tend to fall into one of two categories: Expats who come for the laid-back lifestyle and decide to start a brewery, and Mexican nationals who go to the United States to learn the brewery business and then return home to start their own. The result of this cross-border mingling is beer offerings that go well beyond lager: black IPA, smoked saison, English-style ale, and more. No matter which part of the peninsula visitors venture to, Baja California will open their minds about the depth and variety of Mexico's beer.

Patrons enjoy a beer at sunset at the Baja Brewing Company bar in San José del Cabo.

RAISING THE BAR With more than four million inhabitants, Guadalajara is Mexico's second largest city—a buzzing cultural hub full of vibrant restaurants, busy galleries, and an emerging middle class that make it a prime place for a growing craft beer scene. The Federal Competition Commission's recent ruling limiting macrobreweries' exclusivity deals with stores, restaurants, and bars is great news for Guadalajara's small breweries, as it gives them a fighting chance to get their beer into the public's hands. Cervecería Minerva, a brewery based in Guadalajara, teamed up with beer giant SABMiller to contest exclusivity deals. Grupo Modelo, one of the defendants in the lawsuit, is owed by AB InBev, which now happens to own SABMiller as well. Cervecería Minerva is perhaps the best known craft brewery in Guadalajara, if not in all of Mexico. It brought home a gold medal from the 2010 World Beer Cup for its pale ale, proving that Mexican brewers could compete with those in the rest of the world. Minerva co-founded the Guadalajara Beer Festival, which is a great place to sample the country's beer delights.

meet the brewer
The López Sisters

Ximena and Karla López, two sisters who started Azteca Craft Brewing in Tijuana with their father, Joel, don't subscribe to the belief that the key to business success is a store's visibility. This difficult-to-find brewery is located in the basement of an outdoor mall, with no signs to alert customers to its presence. The sisters found a better form of advertising than a couple of billboards: They imported the latest brewing equipment from neighboring San Diego, California, and let the scents of the brewing process lure in customers. The first time the sisters added hops to their wort, the smell filled the mall and drifted outside. Hundreds of people descended, intrigued by the wonderful smell emanating from somewhere below them. Word spread, and now the brewery has a steady stream of beer-loving patrons.

on tap with Garrett Oliver

GUADALAJARA
Vienna Lager

Mexico spent three years as part of the Austro-Hungarian Empire and emerged with Vienna lager firmly entrenched in its brewing heritage. Mexican versions are not as richly flavored as the original, but many are credible and great with food.

ABV 4.8-5.5% | **IBU** 12-18

Aroma Caramel, burnt sugar, bread, and apples

Appearance Full amber

Flavor Lightly caramelized and slightly sweet, with burnt sugar notes reminiscent of Cracker Jack candied popcorn or the surface of a crème brûlée

Mouthfeel Round and soft, with a clean finish

Presentation Tumbler

Food Pairings Mole dishes, bean dishes, roasted meat

Craft to Try Cervecería Minerva Viena

BAJA CALIFORNIA
Cucapá Chupacabras Pale Ale

Founded in Mexicali in 2002, Cucapá is one of the leading breweries of Mexico's nascent craft beer revolution. It looks to the north and to Europe for inspiration while bringing its own sense of balance.

ABV 5.8% | **IBU** 45

Aroma Piney and slightly dank, with strong orangey notes

Appearance Full amber with reddish highlights

Flavor Bread, caramel, fruit, and hops, with a richly malted center

Mouthfeel Relatively full-bodied and creamy compared with its American counterparts

Presentation Willi Becher glass

Food Pairings Hard cow's milk cheeses, carnitas, tacos, pizza, spicy Thai cuisine

WHAT'S BREWING

in

NORTH AMERICA

Belize

With the Caribbean Sea to the east and dense jungle dotted with Maya ruins to the west, beer is popular in Belize. This tropical country heralds the highest consumption per capita in all the Americas and boasts the oldest brand, Belikin, touted as the "beer of Belize."

263
12-oz beers (93.3 L)
Annual consumption per capita

255,700
U.S. barrels (300,000 hL)
Annual production

3.50
Belizean dollars (U.S. $1.74)
Average price of a 12-oz bottle

Caribbean

While the region has well-known brands such as Red Stripe (Jamaica) and Carib (Trinidad), craft beer is becoming more popular. The region's geography makes transporting craft beer from one island to another cost-prohibitive, so the craft beer market is highly localized: If visitors want a local island beer, they have to travel there to try it.

8 to 175
12-oz beers (3–62 L)
Annual consumption per capita

2
million U.S. barrels (2.4 million hL)
Annual production

5.42
euros (U.S. $5.75) or
68.02 Haitian gourdes (U.S. $1.02)
Average price of a 12-oz bottle

Costa Rica

While the first brewery in Costa Rica opened in 1908, it wasn't until nearly a century later that craft beer entered the scene with a dozen or so craft brewery start-ups. While several beer styles are available, the country remains dominated by lager. Each March, the Festival Cerveza Artesanal showcases craft beer.

15
12-oz beers (5.4 L)
Annual consumption per capita

1.4
million U.S. barrels (1.7 million hL)
Annual production

775.54
Costa Rican colónes (U.S. $1.39)
Average price of a 12-oz bottle

Panama

As in other Central American countries, Panama's beer scene is populated by a few widely available lagers. Craft beer is just starting to arrive here. Three craft breweries, producing mostly ales, offer beer drinkers a little something different.

216
12-oz beers (76.6 L)
Annual consumption per capita

1.9
million U.S. barrels (2.2 million hL)
Annual production

0.67
Panamanian balboa (U.S. $0.67)
Average price of a 12-oz bottle

Numbers were accurate at the time of printing. They are averages, subject to change over time.

CHAPTER
3

SOUTH AMERICA

Before they had delivery trucks, breweries in Valparaiso, Chile, distributed beer via horses, as this man is seen doing in 1922.

REINVENTING TRADITION

All it takes to make beer is a little spit. At least that is true of an indigenous South American beer style called *chicha,* which predates the arrival of Europeans. The Inca used to chew starches such as yucca and maize, then spit them out and let them ferment into a beverage consumed at feasts and given as an offering to the gods. People in Chile were making potato chicha as early as 13,000 B.C. The Mapuche still make a version of it today—a testament to how indigenous beer styles continue to reflect South America's diverse landscapes and culture.

Great Migrations

Beer made from grains like barley and wheat arrived with European explorers in the late 15th century. Portugal claimed the east and Spain the west, in accordance with the Treaty of Tordesillas (1494), but the English and the Germans had the biggest impact on the continent's beer.

While the English did not colonize lands in South America, aside from Guyana (formerly known as British Guiana), they still managed to spread their culture and their love of English-style beer across the land. Britons established breweries throughout the colonial period (roughly 1500–1800) in what became Chile, Argentina, and Brazil, introducing locals to porter and ale while supplying British expats with a taste of home. The German diaspora, or Deutschstämmige, started in the late 1800s. Germans brought lager with them, preferring to brew it in the cold climate of southern Patagonia, where a large percentage of the present population claims German ancestry. Little did they know that a South American ingredient was most likely responsible for the lagers they so dearly loved back home.

Epic Journeys

Long before the Germans brought lager to South America, this southern continent gave Europe an unexpected gift. In the 1500s, Argentine yeast from Patagonia found its way aboard ships bound for Europe—probably attached to wooden barrels. These accidental stowaways might seem innocuous, but they hybridized with a European yeast strain to create something new—a yeast that fermented

South America

▮ Country in this chapter

beer at cooler temperatures. This new yeast ultimately led to the invention of lager—a beer type that accounts for more than 90 percent of the world's beer market. You could say the German diaspora to South America in the 1800s was a homecoming for this hardy, game-changing yeast, rather than an introduction.

Go Global, Drink Local

Global beer conglomerates such as AB InBev and Heineken International, and their pale lagers, dominate today's South American beer scene. Imported craft beer is becoming more common, but high taxes make them less appealing than their domestic counterparts. That said, the domestic craft beer scene in South America is growing. Breweries are cropping up in surprising places, from the world's southernmost brewery in Ushuaia, Argentina, to what is arguably the world's most isolated brewery on windswept Rapa Nui (Easter Island) some 2,300 miles (3,700 km) off Chile's coast. Many are producing world-class beer.

South American brewers take advantage of many fruits, grains, bacteria, and yeast strains endemic to the continent to put a novel twist on European and U.S. beer styles. In Chile, Cervecería Cruzana brews beer with quinoa (technically a

The South American craft beer market has grown by **25%** a year since 2010.

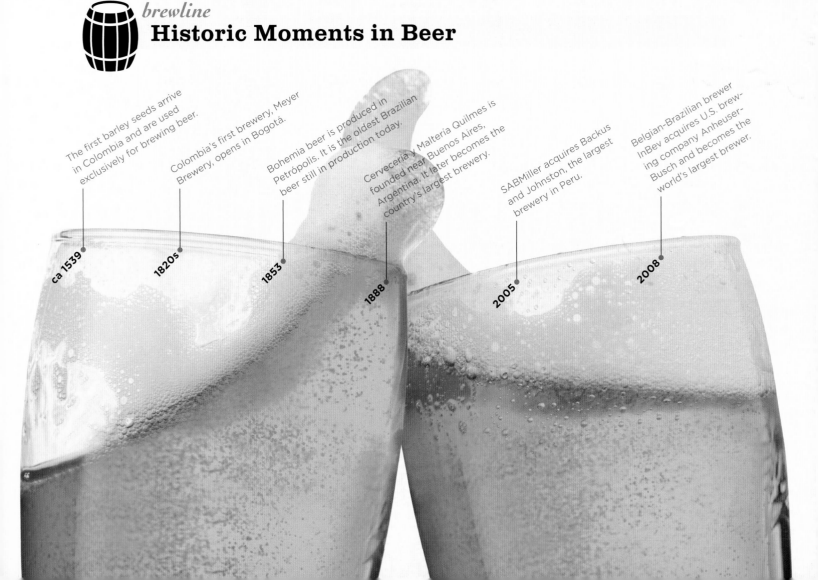

brewline
Historic Moments in Beer

The first barley seeds arrive in Colombia and are used exclusively for brewing beer.
ca 1539

Colombia's first brewery, Meyer Brewery, opens in Bogotá.
1820s

Bohemia beer is produced in Petrópolis. It is the oldest Brazilian beer still in production today.
1853

Cervecería y Maltería Quilmes is founded near Buenos Aires, Argentina. It later becomes the country's largest brewery.
1888

SABMiller acquires Backus and Johnston, the largest brewery in Peru.
2005

Belgian-Brazilian brewer InBev acquires U.S. brewing company Anheuser-Busch and becomes the world's largest brewer.
2008

celebrations South America's Best Beer Festivals

Beer Week | PAYSANDU | URUGUAY | Celebrated by locals and tourists for more than 50 years, Semana de la Cerveza (Beer Week), held on Easter week, includes beer tents, music, food, and both local and imported styles to try. The town's population nearly doubles during this holiday week. *March/April*

Beer Day Festival | BUENOS AIRES | ARGENTINA | This festival has become so popular with the *porteños* (locals) that it now spans two days. More than 25 of the country's breweries are represented, pouring more than 80 beers. *May*

Festival Internacional de la Cerveza Cusqueña | CUSCO | PERU | Sponsored by local brewery Cusqueña, this festival immerses visitors in the culture of what was once the Inca capital. Try some *chicha* (see page 199), and enjoy the festival's Latin music stars. *May/June*

Oktoberfest | SANTA CRUZ DO SUL | BRAZIL | What started as a tobacco festival in the fall turned into an Oktoberfest celebration (see page 54), thanks in part to the city's large German population. It's now one of the largest Oktoberfests in the world. *October*

A ceremonial keg tapping at Oktoberfest in Argentina

---

seed, not a grain) from the Andes. Szot, a microbrewery near Santiago, can thank a nearby rose garden for its Wild Lager, created when wild bacteria from the roses infected a batch of steam beer. Kross Brewery honors the country's booming wine industry by making its grand cru with local wine yeast.

In Argentina, innovative Juguetes Perdidos Cerveza Artesanal (Lost Toys Craft Beer) ages its beer in wine and whiskey barrels and never produces the same beer twice. The country's brewing innovations have resulted in new beer styles such as the IPA Argenta, made exclusively from Argentine ingredients (see page 194). In Brazil, Cervejaria Caçadorense brews Xingu, a black beer made from maize and cassava that has won two gold medals from the prestigious Beverage Testing Institute of Chicago. Opa Bier makes a German-style weissbier with a kick—the addition of guarana, a fruit from Brazil's Amazon region with seeds that contain twice as much caffeine as coffee beans.

The list could go on, but the point is this: South American brewers have begun to master and contribute to the evolution of European and U.S. beer styles. Lager remains popular, but an increasing number of South American beers once again reflect the land and offer flavors found nowhere else.

Tango dancers often perform on the streets in the La Boca neighborhood of Buenos Aires.

ARGENTINA

AN EXPANDING REPERTOIRE

Argentina's landscape is magnificently varied, from the agriculturally productive pampas at its heart to the towering mountains and glaciers at its southern edges. This diversity is reflected in its beer, some of which nicely captures Argentina's history and geography. The land is good to the beer industry: The local farms of El Bolsón in Patagonia produce nearly three-quarters of the country's hops.

The first commercial brewery in Argentina was Compañía Cervecería Bieckert, founded in Buenos Aires in 1860. Emil Bieckert, a German baron, immigrant, and entrepreneur, opened the brewery and brought the first ice factory to Argentina. Bieckert's German-style lagers were enough of a hit with the local population that other companies took notice. When an English company offered Bieckert one million pounds for his brewery in 1889, he quickly accepted. German-born businessman Otto Bemberg, who made his living importing textiles and exporting Argentina's cereal grains to Europe, saw an opportunity in the growing demand for beer. The Bemberg family started Quilmes in 1890 just outside Buenos Aires. Import duties imposed on foreign beer (35 Argentine cents per liter for kegged beer and 25 cents per bottle) favored local products, creating a protected environment in which breweries like Quilmes, known for its dark beer, could grow. And grow they did: By the turn of the 20th century, Quilmes had become a titan, producing four million gallons (15.1 million L) of beer annually and controlling roughly two-thirds of the Argentine beer market. In 1920, the company entered the malt business and was soon providing malted barley to nearly every brewery in the country. By 1984, Quilmes needed capital to expand its operations, so it sold 15 percent of

AT A GLANCE
Featured Locations

🛢	Brewery
★	Capital
●	City
Pampas	Physical feature

the company to Heineken International. Today, AB InBev has a 91 percent stake in this storied brewery, which is still the country's largest.

Going Big

While Quilmes is the best known beer brand in Argentina, other large breweries have a presence, and one thing these breweries have in common is their German origin. German immigrant Otto Schneider arrived in Argentina in 1906 and went to work at Compañía Cervecería Bieckert as an assistant brewer. His stay at Bieckert's brewery was short, as other breweries wanted him as their head brewer. After 25 years as head brewer at Cervecería San Carlos and Cervecería Sante Fe, Schneider opened his own brewery, Cervecería Schneider, in 1932. It was the most technologically advanced brewery in the country at the time. Two of his beers became wildly popular: Schneider, a Bavarian pilsner, and Munich, a Munich dunkel.

By the turn of the millennium, Chilean beer giant Compañía Cervecerías Unidas S.A. (CCU) had bought out Cervecería Schneider, and within a decade two foreign-owned brewing conglomerates, AB InBev and CCU, collectively controlled more than 90 percent of the Argentine beer market. Hence lager dominated the country, leaving drinkers little in the way of choice. The scene was set for the rise of a diverse craft beer culture, one that would produce new styles and push local expectations about what an Argentine beer can be.

local flavor
The Birth of IPA Argenta

In 2015 the Argentine Homebrewers Association submitted two new beer styles to the Beer Judge Certification Program for consideration. One was the Pampas golden ale, a blonde ale that only uses pils malt, which remains relatively uncommon. The other, the IPA Argenta, is making beer lovers sit up and take notice. An interpretation of an English IPA with hoppy and bitter notes, this Argentine original is unique in its ingredients, combining wheat and up to three varieties of Patagonian hops: Cascade, Mapuche, and Nugget. Argentine Cascade hops are quite different from their loud American counterpart as they are low in alpha acids (just 3.2 percent) and mellow in character. The resulting beer has relatively little bitterness with a hop-rich aroma and notes of pepper, spice, and lemongrass.

The IPA Argenta has a characteristic amber color.

Changing Taps

The contemporary craft beer revolution in Argentina began in 1998 in the coastal town of Mar del Plata, 260 miles (420 km) south of Buenos Aires. That's where Leo Ferrari and his wife, Mariana, learned to make beer in his mother's kitchen. After suffering from setbacks such as bad yeast and scorched malt, they finally produced a beer worthy of selling. Their brewery, Antares, was the first craft brewery in Argentina. Leo Ferrari grew quite successful, winning several international awards and becoming a certified beer judge. Today, Antares has more than 20 pub franchises across Argentina selling locally produced Antares beer.

Buenos Aires's first brewpub, Buller Brewing Company, opened in 1999. It catered to locals as well as tourists who came to see Recoleta Cemetery's famous permanent residents (including former first lady Eva Perón and Carlos Saavedra Lamas) and had a thirst for something different from mass-produced lager. Buller's success helped pave the way for other craft breweries in Buenos Aires by highlighting a growing market for craft beer.

Not far from Recoleta, in the colorful neighborhoods of tango-parlor-filled San Telmo and wealthy, park-dotted Palermo, breweries and brewpubs now serve some truly great Argentine craft beer. With brewers aging beer in wine and whiskey barrels and creating entirely new styles, there is more variety here than ever.

Taprooms such as On Tap in Palermo Viejo, Buenos Aires, play a vital role in increasing breweries' exposure to new patrons.

BEER GUIDE

WHERE BEER LOVERS GO

The craft beer scene is booming in Argentina, making it difficult to decide what beer hubs to visit. These suggestions from local brewers will ensure beer lovers have a great beercation.

1 | Cerveza Berlina

San Carlos de Bariloche

With its glacial lakes and towering nearby mountains, Bariloche is one of the most beautiful cities in Argentina. Family-owned and -operated Cerveza Berlina is a craft beer jewel. It's the largest craft brewery in Patagonia, but the Ferrari brothers (no relation to Leo Ferrari at Antares) still oversee the production of their award-winning beer, including their famous Patagonia IPA.

2 | Cervecería El Bolsón

El Bolsón

Argentina's first hop plantations were established in El Bolsón, located 75 miles (122 km) south of Bariloche and home to a brewery that bears its name. In addition to offering the usual beer-style suspects, Cervecería El Bolsón produces a chili pepper beer (order a chaser to go with it), a smoky winter triple bock, and fruit beer made with local produce, including raspberries and cherries. This brewery also distinguishes itself with its well-known selection of gluten-free beer.

3 | Buller Brewing Company

Buenos Aires

In the heart of the Recoleta neighborhood, this was the first brewpub in Buenos Aires. Fermentation tanks greet those who enter the bar, where you can see the brewers at work. A dimly lit seating area, designed for intimate conversations, is a great perch from which to enjoy one or more of the six beers on tap.

Outside, a small patio is ideal for people-watching. Try the Rubia Invitada, a refreshing blonde ale.

4 | Buenos Aires Craft Beer Walk

Buenos Aires

This city isn't called the Paris of the South for nothing—it is filled with buildings, cuisine, and culture that fuse European design and Latin sensibilities. What better way to explore the historic neighborhoods of Palermo and San Telmo than by taking a leisurely stroll? The Craft Beer Walk passes four craft breweries, where you can stop in to sample locally made beer and some traditional Argentine snacks.

godfather of Argentine beer, Leo Ferrari, in the 1990s. The brewery has a Bar Factory, where you can sample the wide range of styles made in its many Argentine brew-pubs and breweries.

6 | Tierra del Fuego's Breweries

Ushuaia

Go to Tierra del Fuego (Land of Fire), where the Andes meet icy waters, and discover the world's southernmost breweries. Beagle, Cape Horn, and Hain breweries name their beer after the local geography and history. There's Beagle's Fuegian Ale; Cape Horn Stout; and Hain's Kulán Cocoa Ale, named after the nomadic Selk'nam culture's male initiation ceremony, called Hain, and the Kulán (female spirit) who tries to thwart the males' initiation.

Breweries and Beer Destinations in Argentina

🛢 Brewery

1 Featured beer destination

5 | Antares

Mar del Plata

This coastal province is where Argentina's craft beer revolution got started, so it's not surprising that its nickname is the Happy City. Antares is still ground zero for the city's beer scene, started by the head brewer and the

Photos

1 *The cathedral of San Carlos de Bariloche is one of the city's iconic sights.* **3** *Buller Brewing Company's range of tasty beers comes in flights for easy sampling.*
5 *Antares is a leader in Argentina's craft beer movement.* **6** *Former general store Ramos Generales in Ushuaia is a great place to try the area's beers.*

LOCAL BREWS
BUENOS AIRES & PATAGONIA
CITY BREWS AND COOL CLIMES

A VIBRANT SCENE Buenos Aires's sleek metropolitan charm provided the perfect backdrop for the country's first brewery and, now, for its craft beer revolution. Organizations such as Somos Cerveceros, which provides assistance to the homebrewing community, and individuals such as Martín Boán, a beer consultant and the owner of Bierlife, have been instrumental in fostering and developing the craft beer industry with everything from brewing classes and brewery design to helping the national government develop craft-beer-friendly policies. It's no wonder there are so many breweries scattered about Buenos Aires producing world-class beer. Taprooms are also springing up around the city, with more than a dozen opening between 2014 and 2016. These places fill a vital role in the distribution of beer, providing consumers with a hub where they can try beer from many different breweries. Make sure to hop into one of the city's many *parrillas* (steak houses) and grab a local pint.

The award-winning Australis microbrewery was the first Patagonian brewery invited to the World Beer Cup.

HIGH-ALTITUDE BEER You will be hard-pressed to find a more beautiful setting in which to drink beer than Patagonia, which is also one of South America's best places to brew it. The many German immigrants who arrived in the late 1800s had no artificial refrigeration, but Patagonia's cool climate proved ideal for brewing German lager. It was also particularly well suited to growing barley and hops.

Beer production in Patagonia has increased every year since 1997, with no apparent end in sight. Towns such as San Carlos de Bariloche and El Bolsón are home to many craft breweries, several of which produce German-style beer. Breweries such as Cervecería Blest (Argentina's first brewpub), Cerveza Berlina, and La Cruz are reporting a continued increase in production and sales.

Despite the growing popularity of local beer, only a handful of breweries are exporting what they produce. Until more start sending beer abroad, beer lovers will have to book a vacation to southern Argentina to try some.

local flavor
Making Chicha

Chicha can be found all over South America, and its brewing process is fairly simple: chew, spit, ferment. Early South American brewers discovered that natural ptyalin enzymes in saliva break down plant starch into sugar, which can then be fermented to become beer. Chicha has always been made from various chewed plants, such as the potatoes grown around Lake Titicaca, a large, deep lake nestled high in the Andes. Most modern-day chicha uses maize, especially *choclo*, the Peruvian giant maize. Amazonian *masato*, made from chewed and boiled yucca, is traditionally used as a source of food (think liquid porridge). Spit drinks also made for good bonding time among brewers, as they are exceptionally time-consuming to make. Those feeling adventurous enough to try some need only to visit the continent and look out for a red flag, signifying that chicha is for sale.

BUENOS AIRES
IPA Argenta

An emerging style based on the American IPA, this style uses a significant portion of wheat in the mash and emphasizes Argentine-grown hops, which show strong citrus notes.

ABV 4.8–6.0% | **IBU** 40–60

Aroma Big grapefruit and tangerine aromatics from Argentine hops

Appearance Honey-colored, with sturdy white foam

Flavor Brisk, dry, and firmly hoppy, with gentle fruit through the center

Mouthfeel Sharp and frisky, with a mineral tang

Presentation Willi Becher glass

Food Pairings Choripán (chorizo sandwich), empanadas, grilled meats with chimichurri, ceviche

Craft to Try Antares IPA Argenta

PATAGONIA
Cerveza Berlina Patagonia Golden Ale

The American-inflected golden-ale style is widely brewed and often features citrusy Argentine hops. When it comes to Patagonia's golden ale, San Carlos de Bariloche–based Cerveza Berlina has led the charge.

ABV 4.5% | **IBU** 23

Aroma Gently malty with top notes of orangey hops

Appearance Bright, full gold with a rocky white foam

Flavor Dry, bright, refreshing, slightly fruity, and bready through the center

Mouthfeel Brisk and soft

Presentation Pint glass

Food Pairings Very versatile, pairing well with fried food, empanadas, and seafood

The Arco do Teles archway opens on the historic Travessa do Comércio in Rio de Janeiro.

BRAZIL

SUN-DRENCHED DRINKING

With its dense rain forests, sunny beaches, and energetic cities, Brazil is full of balmy places to enjoy a cold local beer. Long celebrated for its samba dancing and Carnival festival, Brazil took center stage for the 2014 World Cup and the 2016 Summer Olympics. But its place in the beer world has always been clear: It produced AmBev, which merged with InterBrew and Anheuser-Busch to form AB InBev, the world's largest brewing company.

Beer is everywhere in Brazil, and has been since the beginning of its beer history. It's a pity that the Portuguese, who colonized Brazil in the early 1500s, didn't bring any with them. As it was, beer was introduced in 1634, compliments of the Dutch, who were seeking to establish trade with Portugal's largest colony. This arrangement was short-lived: The Dutch withdrew 20 years later, leaving Brazil without a European beer source for around 150 years. It took Napoleon Bonaparte and the Peninsular War in Europe to reintroduce one.

Mere days before the French Empire invaded the capital city of Lisbon in 1808, the royal court of Portugal escaped to Brazil. The English later backed Portuguese and Spanish forces for control of the Iberian Peninsula. The amicable relationship between England and Portugal led to a beer revival in Brazil's major cities, sparked by the wares of English merchants. English-style ales were the drink of choice until the German diaspora of the 1800s brought German-style lager. Bohemia brewery started making the country's first beer in 1853, and it is still produced today. Though the warm climate encouraged beer appreciation, the lack of refrigeration made brewing it difficult at best.

AT A GLANCE
Featured Locations

🛢 Brewery
★ Capital
● City

Partygoers at Rio's Carnival can use **empty beer cans** to pay for rides on public transportation.

The tropical climate didn't cause trouble just for the production and storage of lager; it also made it impossible to grow barley and hops. Importation became a necessity, which made brewing an expensive prospect. Heat, light, and age—the three destroyers of beer—hurt quality and sales, as did the Brazilian upper classes' penchant for imported wines and the lower classes' preference for *cachaça*, a liquor derived from sugarcane.

By the late 1880s, improved quality (thanks in part to the invention of the ice-cooling machine), decreased prices, and the steep importation duties limiting foreign beer spurred a rash of local breweries to create a lager beer market. The two largest breweries in Brazil—Cervejaria Brahma in Rio de Janeiro and Companhia Antarctica in São Paulo—formed during this decade, and reigned supreme as two of the country's most popular brands for more than 100 years.

Native Twists

Craft breweries started to pop up in the 1990s, with brewers favoring German styles—reflecting the legacy of the early German immigrants—but it was hard to compete against the macrobrewed lagers. Pioneering breweries like Baden Baden in São Paulo and DaDo in Porto Alegre focused on ale to pave the way for a craft beer scene.

More than 300 breweries can be found in Brazil today, though pricey start-up costs are making "gypsy brewing"—the practice of using an established brewery's space and equipment so brewers don't have to buy their own—increasingly popular. Brewers have created a vibrant scene and have a penchant for creating wild and wacky beer with distinctly Brazilian underpinnings. The high price of hops in Brazil has played a role in encouraging brewers to seek out other options. The country is rich in native ingredients that make for interesting adjuncts—Brazilian coffee,

Speakeasy

Brazilian for Beer

Brazil's Portuguese is not the same as Portugal's Portuguese, but you can get by just fine if you master some of these choice phrases.

———

If craft beer is what you are seeking, you will want to go to a microcervejaria (ME-crow ser-VEH-ja-ree-AH), which means "microbrewery," and ask for **uma cerveja, por favor** (OO-mah ser-VEH-ja, pohr faw-VOHR): "One beer, please."

———

Given the unrelenting Brazilian heat, a useful and common phrase to know is **uma cerveja estúpidamente gelada, por favor** (OO-mah ser-VEH-ja e-STU-pid-a-ment-e he-LA-da, pohr faw-VOHR): "One stupidly cold beer, please."

———

If you want a particular type of beer, you'll have to know how to ask for it. If you want a draft beer, ask for **chope** (SHOW-pea), which can be found at one of the country's many **chopperias** (SHOW-pear-ee-ahs), or draft beer bars.

———

No matter where you choose to drink, don't forget to toast by saying **sáude** (SOW-udge): "Cheers!"

Brazil nuts, cassava, guava, tapereba (akin to passion fruit), açai, and tropical woods such as amburana used for barrel aging—and radical beers are becoming more commonplace. Some brewers have gone so far as to experiment with wild yeast strains, creating beers that are reminiscent of styles such as saison and wild ale.

Despite the small but increasingly noticeable craft scene, big beer brands still dominate in Brazil. AB InBev brands include Brahma, Antarctica, Bohemia, and Skol, all of which have a big presence in Brazil. Regardless of who makes it and how it is made, beer is an integral part of any Brazilian gathering.

Rio de Janeiro's Santa Teresa neighborhood is full of bohemian cafés and bars, many of which are hubs of activity during Carnival.

Party Cold

Beer is the country's most popular alcoholic beverage, especially pale lagers served ridiculously cold. The mass-produced lager's dominance is most apparent during Carnival, the religious-turned-secularized celebration prior to the Christian fasting season of Lent. Outside of the six-day celebration, beer is common thanks to relaxed regulations and a relatively low national drinking age of 18 years. Whether drinking a glass at the local *chopperia* (draft beer bar) or a bottle from the nearby supermarket or bakery, Brazil offers beer drinkers a land of beer plenty.

BEER GUIDE

WHERE BEER LOVERS GO

Beer is threaded through Brazilian culture, but not all of Brazil's drinking establishments are created equal. That's why these recommendations from local brewers come in handy.

1 | CiBrew
Recife

This relatively new craft brewery is producing some outstanding beer, but what really makes CiBrew stand out are its Growler Days. Fill up a growler with one of the brewery's rare beers to take home and enjoy at your leisure. Many beers sell out fast, so arrive early to avoid disappointment.

2 | Cervejaria Nacional
São Paulo

The distance between tank and tap here is the shortest in Brazil, they say, thus making its beer the freshest around. São Paulo's big-city diversity is reflected in Cervejaria Nacional's English-style porter, American IPA, and German weissbier. Its beers are named after Brazilian legends, including a stout named after the one-legged, pipe-smoking prankster Saci, whose antics are superseded only by his ability to grant wishes to anyone who steals his magical red cap.

3 | Cervejaria Wäls
Belo Horizonte

Surrounded by mountains—hence the town's name, which means "beautiful horizon"—is Wäls, regularly named Brazil's best craft brewery. Wäls made only pilsners for its first eight years in operation, but it really took off after the owners decided to branch out and brew styles such as its award-winning dubbel. Wäls now offers some of the best Belgian beer made outside Belgium. Like many well-established craft breweries in Brazil, Wäls is now owned by giant beer conglomerate AB InBev.

4 | Bruxa Cerveja Artesanal
Florianópolis

Located in Santa Catarina state's capital city, Bruxa (Portuguese for "witch") brews many different styles. Try the Bierland Bruxa Blond Ale, named in honor of noted scholar Franklin Joaquim Cascaes's work on the island's witch folklore.

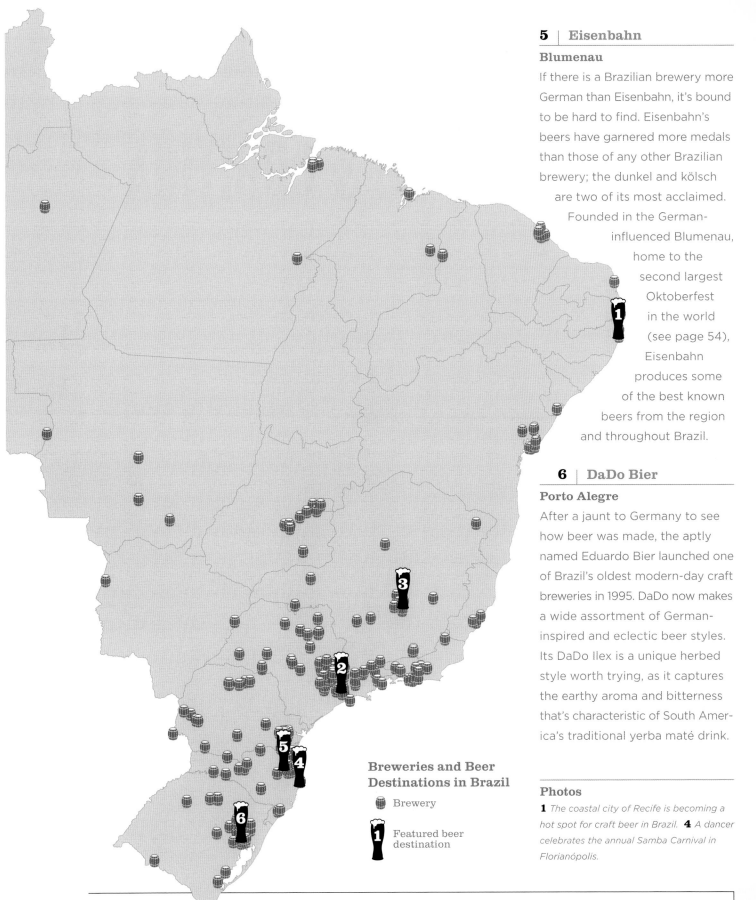

5 | Eisenbahn
Blumenau

If there is a Brazilian brewery more German than Eisenbahn, it's bound to be hard to find. Eisenbahn's beers have garnered more medals than those of any other Brazilian brewery; the dunkel and kölsch are two of its most acclaimed. Founded in the German-influenced Blumenau, home to the second largest Oktoberfest in the world (see page 54), Eisenbahn produces some of the best known beers from the region and throughout Brazil.

6 | DaDo Bier
Porto Alegre

After a jaunt to Germany to see how beer was made, the aptly named Eduardo Bier launched one of Brazil's oldest modern-day craft breweries in 1995. DaDo now makes a wide assortment of German-inspired and eclectic beer styles. Its DaDo Ilex is a unique herbed style worth trying, as it captures the earthy aroma and bitterness that's characteristic of South America's traditional yerba maté drink.

Breweries and Beer Destinations in Brazil

🛢 Brewery

1 Featured beer destination

Photos

1 *The coastal city of Recife is becoming a hot spot for craft beer in Brazil.* **4** *A dancer celebrates the annual Samba Carnival in Florianópolis.*

LOCAL BREWS
RIO DE JANEIRO & CURITIBA

BEER BY THE BEACH

BRIGHT BREWING   In Rio de Janeiro, with its bright beaches spread out under the watchful eyes of the Christ the Redeemer statue, an exciting beer scene awaits beyond the ubiquitous lager shops. Neighborhoods such as Botafogo, with its sweeping bayside vistas, and Catete, once the headquarters of colonial Brazil, have their own amazing taprooms. Birreria Escondido, in Botafogo, was named after the California city where Stone Brewing is headquartered—an homage to a craft beer brand that the owner loves. In addition to selling craft beer, he also carries the occasional homebrew on tap.

Despite the rise of craft beer here, macrobreweries continue to rule; expect to see Antarctica, Brahma, and Skol pilsners on the beach, alongside the region's growing number of craft creations. In the shadow of the macrobreweries is Rio's growing homebrewers' association. Amateur brewers share information, recipes, and ingredients; hold competitions; and host bottle exchanges. Most of its members hold down regular jobs and brew for fun on the side. For most, opening their own brewery is just a pipe dream—it's well known that the craft beer industry here is a wealthy person's game. Nevertheless, homebrewers from Rio have fared well in national homebrewing competitions and continue to show promise when it comes to introducing new styles and flavors.

HOMEGROWN   Brazil's eighth largest city, Curitiba is located in the southern state of Paraná and is home to breweries that include Cervejaria Way, Micro Cervejaria Bier Hoff, and DUM Cervejaria. The city boasts a strong homebrewing scene: DUM Cervejaria was founded by three friends who started out

local flavor
Carnival Warm-up

Pre-Carnival parties in Rio are often sponsored by big beer companies.

homebrewing in their backyard. From these humble roots, Curitiba's craft beer scene has grown to become internationally recognized. Curitiba's WikiBier Festival, held each November, is one of the few beer festivals that actually includes a competition category for home-brewers. In 2016, the city hosted the South Beer Cup VI competition, the largest and most important craft beer competition in South America.

Even craft breweries from the United States have viewed Curitiba as a potential gateway into Brazil's craft beer market. Brooklyn Brewery's lager, for example, is one of the region's best-selling beers, thanks to its reasonable price and high quality. A growing local passion for craft offerings is an enticing prospect for breweries from other countries. Before long, there will likely be many more imports vying for drinkers' attention.

Rio de Janeiro is famous for its Carnival, the six-day celebration leading up to the beginning of Lent. At Carnival, beer drinking is serious business: 4 percent of Brazil's annual beer consumption happens during the celebration. Brazilians start the festivities weeks in advance, hosting *bloco* (neighborhood) parties that often have dress-up themes. Macro-breweries sponsor these parties, paying the city to be the official beer vendor. AB InBev brand Antarctica has served as a sponsor for the past few years, filling the parties with vendors wearing bright blue hats to match Antarctica's beer cans. This sea of blue makes it easy to spot any alternatively colored contraband.

on tap with Garrett Oliver

RIO DE JANEIRO
Tropical Fruit Beer

Brazilian markets are full of tropical fruits, some familiar and many not. Brazilian brewers use this bounty in new and delicious beer styles, many of them based on American wheat beer.

ABV 4.5–5.5% | **IBU** 16–24

Aroma Bright tropical-fruit character, often featuring the native mango

Appearance Golden to honey orange

Flavor Fruity, off-dry, and mildly tangy, with hops in a supporting position

Mouthfeel Light and refreshing

Presentation Tulip glass

Food Pairings Feijoada (meat and bean stew), acarajé (bean fritters), fish tacos, goat cheeses

Craft to Try Nóbrega Brewing Company Vais de Manga?

CURITIBA
Bodebrown Wee Heavy

It's a long way from Curitiba to Scotland, but Brazilian brewers are just as engaged by international styles as brewers anywhere. Cervejaria Bodebrown has made a name for itself as one of Latin America's best breweries, moving easily among the brewing traditions of Germany, the U.K., and Belgium with offerings like this Scottish strong ale.

ABV 8% | **IBU** 20

Aroma Caramel, baking dark bread, molasses, roasted malts, prunes

Appearance Deep russet brown with a rocky tan head

Flavor Sweet, rich, gently balanced, with notes of caramel, chocolate, dark fruit, and wood

Mouthfeel Round, soft, and silky

Presentation British half-pint glass

Food Pairings Feijoada, aged Gouda and Gruyère cheeses

The trendy Barrio Bellavista neighborhood in Santiago is home to many bars and taprooms.

CHILE

FOG AND HONEY

The most famous part of Chile's beverage story may be the introduction of grapes and the wine industry that resulted. Even so, beer has always been important in this long, narrow country. When European ships bearing Spanish conquistadores and explorers (and later missionaries and settlers) arrived on Chile's shores, they were likely surprised by the beer they found there: weak, fermented drinks made from masticated cereal grains. The Mapuche women of south-central Chile chewed up grains to make *muday*, a cloudy beer important at social gatherings, ceremonies, and even burials. Europeans preferred to imbibe their own imported beer styles.

While originally the English and their porter dominated, an influx of German immigrants in the mid-1850s established Bavarian-style breweries throughout the southern part of the country. German beer styles quickly achieved mass appeal, and by the turn of the 20th century, lagers dominated as far north as the port city of Coquimbo and as far south as Punta Arenas.

The industry by this time had been spread quite thin and consolidation began to take hold. Two breweries, Anwandter and Compañía Cervecerías Unidas S.A., became the country's largest by purchasing their competitors. But even Anwandter could not survive the Valdivia earthquake of 1960, which registered at a magnitude of 9.5—one of the most powerful earthquakes ever recorded. The brewery closed as the factory lay in ruins. However, that is not where the Chilean beer story ends. A contemporary craft beer scene has emerged over the past few years, showcasing innovative styles, such as beer tinged with honey, and techniques that capture distinctly Chilean flavors that are slowly turning this wine-drinking nation into a land of beer drinkers, too.

Map labels:

Atacama Desert

PACIFIC OCEAN

Cervecería Atrapaniebla
Coquimbo
Compañía Cervecerías Unidas S.A.
Kross
Valparaíso
Szot ★ Santiago
← Rapa Nui (Easter Island)
Talagante
Cervecería Cruzana

Anwandter
Valdivia
Puerto Montt

Patagonia

Punta Arenas
Austral
Strait of Magellan

AT A GLANCE
Featured Locations

🛢 Brewery
★ Capital
● City
Patagonia Physical feature
Strait of Magellan Water feature

Going Local

Chile's artisanal beer scene is relatively small, overshadowed by the prolific wine industry and lager-dominated macrobreweries. But an increasing number of microbreweries are producing high-quality craft beer with innovative techniques and processes, especially where and when water is scarce. Water-starved Chilean breweries have been known to brew beer from rainwater, including the *cervecería* on the island of Rapa Nui (Easter Island) located some 2,300 miles (3,700 km) from the mainland.

While nearly all beer styles are made in Chile, extremely hoppy beer is the exception rather than the rule. Chileans are more apt to drink lager and sweet-tasting beer, with honey beer a favorite among the craft beer scene. Most beer-making ingredients here are still imported, but breweries are beginning to use local ingredients to give Chilean beer a sense of terroir. Chile's oldest and southernmost brewery, Austral, makes good on the idea of capturing local flavors by brewing an ale using calafate, a Patagonian berry with a potent mythology that suggests all who taste it will become entranced by the region.

A brewer at Cervecería HBH in Santiago cleans out spent grains, which are given to a local farm to feed livestock.

Festive Spirit

Beer festivals are the place to go for local beer. Many small breweries do not sell to the public, and they use these festivals as a chance to solicit discerning beer drinkers' opinions on what they're brewing. Armed with social media, interesting stories, and unique ingredients, many of these breweries serve up their own takes on traditional beer styles, including marijuana beers, sweet honey ales, and malt-driven IPAs. The most established breweries, apart from the country's mass-market brews, are those located within southern Chile's beer scene, where the German brewing legacy still holds strong.

local flavor
Making Fog Beer

Southern Patagonia—a name that some historians argue means "Land of the Bigfeet," so called because of the native giants Ferdinand Magellan found there—encompasses high mountains, deep fjords, and serene lakes. Its northern reaches hold the Atacama Desert, some portions of which haven't seen rain for hundreds of years. Desert plants must pull their moisture from the fog that rolls in on early mornings when Pacific Ocean winds find their way to land. This fog, known locally as *camanchaca*, contains misty drops of water so small (0.0001–0.004 inches,

or 3–102 micrometers) that they might never be able to turn into rain.

Enter Cervecería Atrapaniebla ("catch fog brewery"), whose nets condense the camanchaca into water that is used to make beer. Though the brewers aren't the first to use camanchaca—many villages in the area rely on these nets for their precious daily water supply—they are the first to brew with it. They make about 200 U.S. barrels (240 hL) of ale each year, which they describe as a "heavenly brew." Considering its water comes from a cloud, this description seems apt.

BEER GUIDE

WHERE BEER LOVERS GO

In a land known for wine, Chilean brewers recommend visiting these beer hot spots to sample the best of what's brewing.

1 | Cervecería Hernando de Magallanes

Punta Arenas

Located 100 miles (160 km) from the Strait of Magellan, this brewery is one of the latest additions to the capital of Chile's southernmost region. This modern-looking brewery offers craft beer with character and distinctive labels that give homage to the days of European exploration. Production is small, but the tastes are big, with a focus on intensive, hop-forward styles.

2 | Szot

Talagante

Located on the outskirts of Chile's capital city, Szot is a Belgian-built brewery outfitted with secondhand equipment that produces some of the country's best craft beer. A visit to the brewery offers access to everything from stout and barleywine to pilsner and wild ale.

3 | Casa Cervecera Altamira

Valparaíso

The beautiful coastal town of Valparaíso, just a 90-minute drive from Santiago, is home to Casa Cervecera Altamira—a little gem of a place that brews outstanding beer. Located at the foot of the Queen Victoria Funicular that climbs up to the neighborhood of Cerro Concepción, Altamira's museum documenting the early days of Chilean brewing gives beer-history buffs ample excuse to make the trek.

4 | Cervecería HBH

Santiago

Nondescript from the outside, and located just off Plaza Ñuñoa, this brewery is worth a stop because it's one of the first microbreweries in Santiago. The brewery's name pays tribute to the German *hofbrauhaus* (court brewery). Its beer styles offer a nod to those found in Bavaria and include a blonde pilsner, an amber märzen, and a dark-colored bock.

Breweries and Beer Destinations in Chile

🛢 Brewery

🍺1 Featured beer destination

WHAT'S BREWING

in

SOUTH AMERICA

Colombia

In 1910, Colombia's *chicherias* (*chicha* bars) produced 9,250 gallons (35,000 L) of chicha a day. So how did macrobrewers get people to swap out this indigenous style for European beer? Hygiene. They made labels promoting the purity of beer, and the market followed. AB InBev dominates the market today, but several award-winning microbreweries have sprung up around Bogotá.

116
12-oz beers (41 L)
Annual consumption per capita

767,000
U.S. barrels (900,000 hL)
Annual production

2668.57
Colombian pesos (U.S. $0.93)
Average price of a 12-oz bottle

Ecuador

Pilsners reign supreme in Ecuador, especially those brewed by AB InBev–owned macrobrewery Cervecería Nacional Ecuador. Ecuadorians' beer choices are growing with an increasing number of craft breweries, found mainly in Quito and Guayaquil. Twenty new microbreweries opened in Quito from 2015 to 2016, promising locals a more colorful palette of beers from which to choose.

56
12-oz beers (20 L)
Annual consumption per capita

4.9
million U.S. barrels (5.8 million hL)
Annual production

$0.93
U.S. dollar
Average price of a 12-oz bottle

Peru

Peruvian brewing dates back to A.D. 600, when the Wari (a Peruvian tribe that predates the Inca) made *chicha* from purple maize and pepper berry. AB InBev controls much of Peru's modern beer market. Local craft breweries such as Cherusker Cervecería Alemana and Roche's Brewing Company have been cropping up in the more populous areas of Lima and Cusco.

79
12-oz beers (28 L)
Annual consumption per capita

11.2
million U.S. barrels (13.1 million hL)
Annual production

4.45
Peruvian nuevos soles (U.S. $1.37)
Average price of a 12-oz bottle

Venezuela

A prolonged economic crisis in Venezuela may limit the availability of beer throughout the country, which boasts the continent's highest consumption rate per capita. Cervecería Polar, which rules the market with its pilsner beer, leaned on international investors for loans in 2016 to enable it to buy barley, hops, and cans.

248
12-oz beers (88 L)
Annual consumption per capita

15.5
million U.S. barrels (18.2 million hL)
Annual production

8.68
Venezuelan bolivars (U.S. $0.86)
Average price of a 12-oz bottle

Numbers were accurate at the time of printing. They are averages, subject to change over time.

The rapeseed fields in Luoping, Yunnan Province, China, surround the region's mountains.

CHAPTER
4

ASIA

Geishas, icons of Japanese culture, pose in the mountainous city of Nikko for a Kirin beer advertisement in the 1920s.

A FERTILE LAND FOR BEER

This massive continent covers 9 percent of Earth's surface and accounts for around 60 percent of its population. It holds what seems like every type of environment: the bone-chilling, subarctic lands of Siberia; the steamy tropical forests of Indonesia; the extreme heat of the Gobi in northern China and southern Mongolia; the snowcapped peaks of the Himalaya, and more. Only about 20 percent of these lands are considered arable, and much of what is grown here are cereal grains. Many of beer's ingredients are of Asian origin, making it an important continent when it comes to beer's history.

Place of Origin

Imagine a beer made with barley, broomcorn millet, a grain called Job's tears, snakegourd root, lily, and yam. If this seems like an unusual ingredients list, that's because it's from 5,000 years ago. Researchers found traces of this beverage near the Chan River in Shaanxi Province, China, where evidence suggests that the people who lived there had a complex understanding of how to brew beer. But Asia's archaeological evidence of brewing goes back even further than that. Bits of pottery discovered in northern China's ancient settlement of Jiahu revealed that the world's oldest known fermented beverage—a Neolithic grog containing wild grapes, hawthorn, rice, and a honey known as *kui*—was brewed in Asia as far back as 9,000 years ago. At the same time, barley and wheat were being cultivated in the fertile lands of Mesopotamia, situated between the Tigris and Euphrates Rivers around what is now Iraq. Beer shows up in Mesopotamia's archaeological record around 5,000 B.C., and it's turned up in a variety of forms: traces of sediment in a wide-mouthed jug from Iran's Zagros Mountains; the ancient "Hymn to Ninkasi" beer poem etched on clay tablets in Sumer (now southern Iraq); and an assortment of ancient vessels used to malt, mash, and ferment grains. Such evidence suggests that Asia is where beer was born, then shaped by its wildly varied landscapes and ingredients.

Beer's major grain, barley, is believed to have originated around 8000 B.C. in western Asia, near present-day Israel and Jordan. Some historians think that

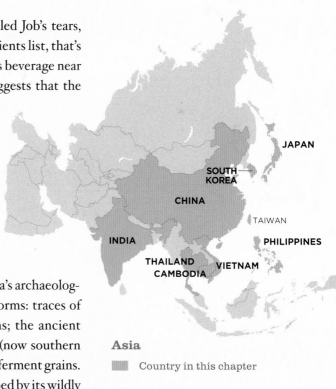

Asia

▨ Country in this chapter

Mijiaya, China, is home to the world's **oldest** known brewery, which operated between 3400 and 2900 B.C.

barley proliferated so extensively because people took it with them as they migrated, specifically so that they could brew beer. Rice originated in Asia as well and was used to make beer in China and Japan. It is still a common adjunct, often included in popular lagers because it imparts little flavor. Popular beer-centric crops such as sorghum and millet also grow well here. Some scholars now think hops may have originated in Asia. China is the only country in which all three species of hops are found—including *Humulus lupulus*, the species used in beer—making it the place from which hops likely sprang. Hops from China and Japan together account for around 7 percent of the world's hop acreage.

Asia's terroir and cultural tastes often show up in its beer by way of indigenous spices such as ginger, lemongrass, peppercorns, nutmeg, and cinnamon. It isn't wholly uncommon to find beer with tea in it, too. Brewing beer with tea probably started in Japan but has since spread throughout Asia and beyond. Ale, particularly the hoppy styles, is most commonly brewed with tea, which adds subtle astringent notes that contrast the hops' bitterness.

An Uncapped Market

Today's Asian beerscape is full of the pale, European-style lager originally introduced and popularized by colonial powers. The English brought ales such as porter to India and Malaysia; the Dutch brought beer to Indonesia; the French introduced beer to Laos, Cambodia, and Vietnam; and the Spanish brought it with them to the Philippines. These colonial introductions led to the creation of local breweries like Dyer Breweries in India, which opened in 1830 and was Asia's first commercial brewery. They also led to a beer market that continues to be dominated by adjunct lagers such as Snow Beer in China, Kirin in Japan,

local flavor
Did Lager Yeast Come From Asia?

A group of Chinese scientists have spotted something interesting about lager's history—something too small for the naked eye to see. Lager yeast, or *Saccharomyces pastorianus,* is widely known to be a hybrid of *Saccharomyces cerevisiae* (ale yeast) and *Saccharomyces eubayanus* (a yeast that is, among other things, resistant to cold). The prevailing school of thought in the microbiology world is that the latter originated in Patagonia, where some experts think it was inadvertently transported to Europe on cargo ships in the late 1400s or early 1500s and started the lager revolution in continental Europe.

But in analyzing the genes of *S. eubayanus,* Chinese scientists found that they contain three distinct genomic lineages: Tibetan, West China, and Sichuan strains. They believe the Patagonian strain that made such an impression on Europe was actually part of the Tibetan lineage, whose DNA shows a very close match to lager yeast. China is the only place in the world where all three of the *Saccharomyces* species are found, which suggests it may in fact be a Chinese native. So while South America may have given the world European lager, it may be China we have to thank for it.

San Miguel in the Philippines, Singha in Thailand, and Tiger Beer in Vietnam. These lagers are the nearly ubiquitous products of multinational brewing conglomerates headquartered in Europe or Japan. Seventeen of the world's 40 largest breweries are headquartered in Asia, and macrobreweries control more than 90 percent of the market in many Asian countries.

Given its massive population, it's no surprise that Asia produces a huge amount of beer. Asia produced more than 603 million U.S. barrels (708 million hL) in 2014; for comparison, Europe produced 474 million U.S. barrels (556 million hL), while North America produced 270 million U.S. barrels (317 million hL). Asia's numbers are impressive, but they also mark a 2.3 percent decrease over the previous year.

While Asia's overall beer production is decreasing, craft beer production is experiencing a steady rise. Though governments in several Asian countries have instituted policies aimed at curbing alcohol consumption, beer sales continue to grow. Take Vietnam, for example, where craft beer sales are climbing at double the pace of the country's gross domestic product. Even so, run a finger down a global list of beer consumed per capita and Asia won't appear until the 45th line down: South Korea at 12 gallons (46 L). Asia's overall beer consumption rate— 8 gallons per capita (29 L)—seems scant when compared with Europe's 16 gallons (59 L). Such numbers indicate there is room to grow for both large brewing conglomerates and small craft breweries.

Young professionals enjoy a celebratory toast at Jing-A Brewing Company's taphouse in Beijing.

Large breweries are expanding into Vietnam and Myanmar, while AB InBev has started buying up breweries and taprooms in Hong Kong. For microbreweries, the growing Asian population represents an expanding market. The beer industry predicts that 70 percent of the global beer market's growth will occur in Asia, with the Asian beer market reaching a value of more than $220 billion by 2020.

The lure of Asia's burgeoning beer market has attracted the attention of breweries on other continents, too. The Brewers Association reports that U.S. craft beer exports to Asia have increased by nearly 40 percent since 2013. The market is certainly receptive to craft offerings, but Asia's craft breweries haven't had an easy time finding a place in the local market.

Jumping Policy Hurdles

Craft beer's progress in Asia has hit some speed bumps. Its growth has been tempered by several major factors, the biggest of which is government policy. In countries with a more liberal approach to beverage taxation such as the Philippines, the craft beer scene is thriving; in countries with tougher regulations, high taxation and a requirement for breweries to produce a minimum volume annually have made craft brewing a difficult business. South Korea's government lifted its minimum

brewline
Historic Moments in Beer

The oldest known evidence of fermented beverages is linked to this date, in the settlement of Jiahu, China.
7000 B.C.

The Sumerians brew beer, evidenced by a recipe in a Sumerian poem.
5000–4000 B.C.

Colonial India receives first shipments of beer from England.
A.D. 1711

Edward Dyer opens Asia's first commercial brewery in the Himalaya.
1830

Norwegian-American William Copeland founds Japan's Spring Valley Brewery, later renamed Kirin.
1869

Southeast Asia's first brewery opens in the Philippines.
1890

Malayan Breweries becomes the first commercial brewery in Singapore.
1931

The Chinese government bans the use of formaldehyde, once used in 95 percent of China's beer.
2001

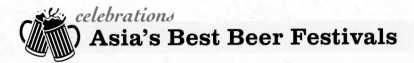

celebrations
Asia's Best Beer Festivals

Beerfest Asia | SINGAPORE | Asia's largest beer festival offers more than 500 beers, 100 of which are brewed specifically for the event. More than 20 countries are represented here. *June*

Outcast Craft Beer Festival | HO CHI MINH CITY | VIETNAM | Though relatively small, this festival is pretty impressive, considering that craft beer was almost nonexistent in Vietnam a few years ago. Six local craft brewers offer visitors convincing evidence that craft beer is happening and here to stay. *August*

Qingdao Beer Festival | QINGDAO | CHINA | The "Asian Oktoberfest" is one of the larger beer festivals on the continent. It's a three-week festival, replete with opening and closing ceremonies, that attracts brewers from around the world. *August*

Oktoberfest of the North | PYONGYANG | NORTH KOREA | Visitors need special permission to attend this government-sponsored festival, which promotes North Korea's Taedonggang Beer Factory. After its first year, in 2016, local media reported that all 100 tourists "enjoyed it greatly." *August*

Beijing Autumn Craft Beer Festival | BEIJING | CHINA | This festival offers visitors a taste of the country's best craft breweries. Stars such as Boxing Cat and Great Leap Brewing will be here to pour you a locally made beer. *September*

Great Japan Beer Festival | YOKOHAMA | JAPAN | It's the largest of five Great Japan Beer Festivals (collectively known as Beerfes), with almost 9,000 people and more than 70 breweries attending, including several from the United States and Europe. *September*

Beertopia | HONG KONG | CHINA | This is a beer/foodie/electronic dance music lover's dream. It's also Hong Kong's largest beer festival, with 119 breweries serving up more than 500 different beers, 65 of which are brewed in the city. *November*

---

volume requirement in 2014. Since then, craft breweries have had more freedom to grow and introduce South Koreans to beverages other than the wildly popular rice liquor *soju.*

Another critical factor holding craft beer back is price. With most countries in Asia still developing and incomes relatively low, craft beer is a luxury good that most can't afford. In Vietnam, a glass of indigenous *bia hoi* lager retails for under the equivalent of 50 U.S. cents, while a bottle of craft beer comes in around the equivalent of four dollars. Cost is becoming less prohibitive in China, where a swelling middle class now has some 300 million people.

Despite these hurdles, local craft beer enthusiasts will find something to try in every Asian country. Even North Korea has a craft brewery—the government purchased it from the U.K., shipped the building home, and had it reassembled for their brewing pleasure. Asia's craft beer scene will continue to grow for the foreseeable future. Breweries and brewpubs alike are catering to a more discerning drinker who appreciates beer that reflects the eclectic cultures and local ingredients that define the continent.

The palatial Forbidden City lies at the center of Beijing, a metropolis quickly becoming a craft brewing hot spot.

CHINA

DYNASTIES AND DRINK

Roughly the size of the United States and with four times its population, China is the world's most populous country. It also has a brewing tradition that stretches back 9,000 years to when the Neolithic Yangshao people used remarkably advanced technology to create some of the world's oldest known beerlike drinks.

Chinese beer has a history of being fortifying, sacred, and a source of debauchery. The Xia dynasty's tyrannical King Jie (1728–1675 B.C.) created a lake of Chinese alcohol to please a concubine. During the Shang dynasty (1600–1046 B.C.), oracle inscriptions—primitive Chinese characters carved on animal bones or tortoise shells and used in divination by fire—were adorned with fermented beverages like the sweet, low-alcohol rice or millet beer called *li* or *lao li*. The Shang dynasty also saw the rise of *qu*, a fermentation starter made from partially cooked wheat or millet and inundated with mold, yeast, and bacteria. Fermenting qu produced *chiu*, the strong beer that became the prevailing Chinese style. Chiu remained culturally embedded in Chinese society—gastronomically, religiously, and artistically—as a source of inspiration for generations of writers, poets, and artists.

New styles and methods of producing beer and beerlike alcohols continued to emerge as the centuries passed. Fermented winelike beers, such as *huangjiu,* and *baijiu,* an intoxicating beverage made from millet or sorghum, were used in rituals,

AT A GLANCE
Featured Locations

- 🛢 Brewery
- ★ Capital
- ● City

Harbin Brewery

Beijing Yangjing Brewery

Great Leap Brewing

★ Beijing

CR Snow

Tsingtao Brewery

● Qingdao

Shanghai ●

TAIWAN

● Hong Kong

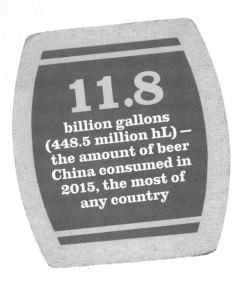

11.8 billion gallons (448.5 million hL) — the amount of beer China consumed in 2015, the most of any country

A worker oversees the production line at Beijing Yanjing Brewery, which brews the city's most popular beer and is one of China's largest beer producers.

ceremonies, and celebrations and as a conduit to the spirit world. The masses drank a millet beer called *shu* during the Han dynasty's golden age (200 B.C.–A.D. 200), while the Tang dynasty (618–907) saw the introduction of a rice beer called *sang-lo* from China's southern region and an unfiltered beer called *pei,* nicknamed "floating ants" because of the grains that floated within it. A sorghum beer called *kaoliang* was brewed during the Sung dynasty (960–1279). Indigenous beer was gradually replaced altogether by rice wine and rice liquor. Recipes for rice beer stopped being handed down from generation to generation and by the end of China's last imperial dynasty in 1912, indigenous beer was all but lost.

Making a Comeback

Contemporary brewing started with the introduction of Western beer styles in the early 1900s by way of the Europeans who leased enclaves in Chinese port cities. Or, in Hong Kong's case, it arrived when the country became a British colony after the First Opium War (1839–1842). Western-style commercial breweries began to pop up all over China. One of the first commercial breweries was Harbin Brewery in Manchuria (now Northwest China), established in 1900 by a German looking to supply beer to the Russians working on the Trans-Manchurian Railway. But earlier breweries did exist, as noted in an 1869 account in the *London*

and China Telegraph of an English-style beer "of excellent quality" brewed in Shanghai by Messrs Evans and Company.

In 1958 Zhu Mei, the minister of light industry, penned a pamphlet introducing beer and brewing to the masses and calling for the construction of hundreds of small-scale breweries. There was a tragic irony in the pamphlet's timing: It was the first year of the Great Chinese Famine, which killed up to 45 million people. Even so, people were interested in starting breweries. But until economic reform hit the Middle Kingdom in 1978, China had only 90 of them, and beer remained a luxury. Decades later, China has more than 900 breweries and beer has worked its way back into China's drinking lexicon.

One of today's best known beer exporters, Tsingtao Brewery, was founded in 1903 by English and German investors from Hong Kong who set up a Reinheitsgebot-style brewery (see page 53) in the trading post of Tsingtao (also spelled Qingdao). It was taken over by the Japanese in World War I, owned briefly by the Tsui family, nationalized after World War II, and then privatized in the 1990s. After surviving more than a century of turmoil, Tsingtao is now China's second largest beer brand. The largest is behemoth CR Snow, whose namesake beer, Snow, is now the world's best-selling beer.

An International Influence

China produced 12.4 billion gallons (471.5 million hL) of beer in 2015—more than anywhere else in the world. Large breweries like Beijing Yanjing Brewery pump out more than a billion gallons (37 million hL) of beer a year; China makes more than three times the amount of beer brewed in the United States and nearly five times the amount brewed in Germany. The Chinese also drink the most overall (though not the most per capita), consuming almost a quarter of the world's commercial beer.

China's most popular beer style is a pale lager that is commonly low in alcohol, light in taste, and made with the addition of rice. This trend toward the bland isn't surprising, given the country's drinking customs. Drinking small quantities—repeatedly and for prolonged periods—is both a social norm and a cultural expectation, especially during Chinese business banquets.

Despite all this drinking, craft breweries are rare in China. That's due in part to laws that regulate beer bottling to those that can bottle 12,000 beers an hour, as well as health and safety laws that prohibit off-site bottling. More often than not, craft breweries like the popular Great Leap Brewing exist in the form of brewpub restaurants that can take advantage of the ability to serve beer on-site, bypass excise taxes, and produce beer in the gray areas where laws do not yet exist.

The majority of China's craft beer is imported or foreign owned. This expat influence shows up in the form of German-style beer halls serving up traditional lager and wheat beer; in the popularity of Belgian-style beer; and in a U.S.-style willingness to use unorthodox ingredients and redevelop indigenous styles.

(see page 53)

Chinese Banquet Etiquette

Drinking in China commences when the host or highest ranking person at the table makes a toast. These toasts, which continue throughout various courses, are called **gānbēi** (gahn-bey), which means "dry the cup" or "empty the glass." The bigger the group, the greater the number of toasts there will be.

___

While drinking heavily exhibits **jiudan** (geo-dan), or "drink courage," drinking in excess is frowned upon. Fortunately, toasts of **"Suiyi"** (soy-yee), or "As you wish," allow diners to take a sip rather than down a glass. You should always raise your glass during a toast, but respect is imperative. Keeping your glass lower than other people's is one way to show it. This practice can get interesting, as everyone's glasses continue to lower until they touch the table. On the off chance you get thirsty, don't drink between toasts; it's considered greedy.

BEER GUIDE

WHERE BEER LOVERS GO

While China is Asia's most populous country, its breweries and brewpubs are relatively sparse. These recommendations from brewers in China represent the country's highlights.

1 | Black Kite Brewery

Hong Kong

The Gallie brothers have one high-flying goal: to make unique and exciting beer with ingredients from all over the world. What better way to do that than create a smoked rauchbier that tastes like bacon? Drop by their brewery on the south side of Hong Kong Island and sample their takes on classic styles such as hefeweizen, pale ale, porter, and IPA, plus whatever seasonal beer they have on hand.

2 | Great Leap Brewing

Beijing

Opened in 2010, China's first microbrewery has a name that encapsulates brewer Carl Setzer's massive contribution to China's fledgling craft beer industry. Beers such as Honey Ma Gold, an ale brewed with honey collected from near the Great Wall and Szechuan peppercorns, are infused with local ingredients that reflect the flavors of the Middle Kingdom. Visit their modern brewery and restaurant, or go on a hunt for the original brewpub. It's nestled in a small, nicely converted outdoor courtyard in a maze of narrow alleys that hark back to the 13th and 14th centuries.

3 | Liquid Laundry

Shanghai

A spin-off of Boxing Cat Brewery and touted as Shanghai's first gastropub, this posh lounge with a distinctive pub feel is worth the elevator ride it takes to get there. Sit near the floor-to-ceiling windows and watch tai chi or Chinese square dancing performers in the park across the street. Enjoy the beer brewed on-site, original Boxing Cat beer, or a rotating assortment of sought-after imports.

4 | Moonzen Brewery
Hong Kong

This brewery's husband-and-wife team chose the name Moonzen (Chinese door gods) for the same reason they name their beer after other Chinese gods—because they believe that every story has a beer and that the best beer is local and pure. Their beers are all brewed with Chinese ingredients. Visit their tasting room and try the Jade Emperor IPA, Moon Goddess chocolate stout, or Kitchen God honey porter.

5 | NBeer Pub
Beijing

What appears to be a run-of-the-mill office building on the outside is a hidden gem with an in-house brewery, more than three dozen taps offering a medley of Chinese craft beer, and a wall-to-wall refrigerator containing some 900 beers from around the world. This brewpub's vast selection is thanks to its well-connected owner, who is co-founder of the Beijing Homebrewing Society.

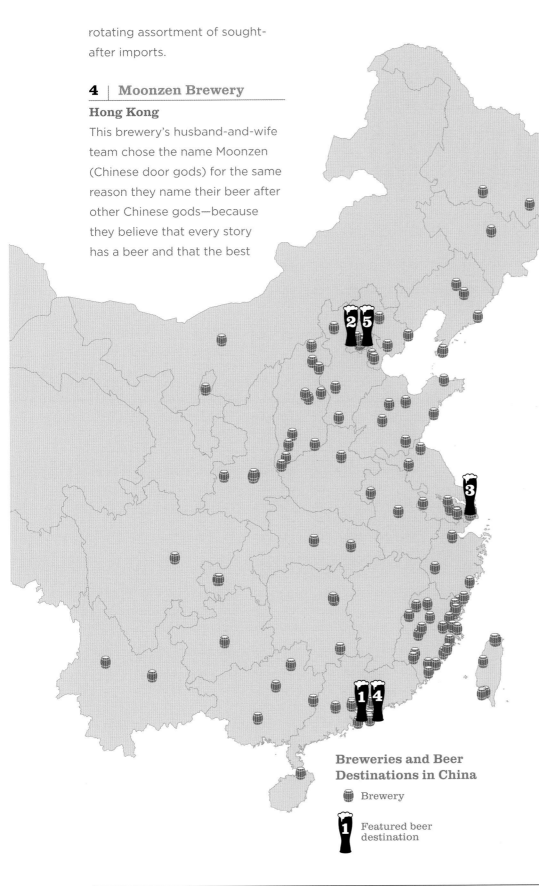

Breweries and Beer Destinations in China

🛢 Brewery

🍺 1 Featured beer destination

Photos

1 *Black Kite Brewery produces an assortment of unique beers.* **2** *Great Leap Brewing is Beijing's first craft brewpub.* **5** *Dozens of local craft beers are on tap at NBeer Pub.*

BEIJING, SHANGHAI & HONG KONG

EAST MEETS WEST

DOWN NARROW ALLEYS Wandering down Beijing's and Shanghai's narrow *hutongs* (alleys) and passing by the elaborate red doors of traditional *siheyuan* (courtyard residences) feels like stepping into a distant past. But many of these cities' industries, including craft beer, are barreling forward into the future. Signs of China's burgeoning craft beer revolution are everywhere. One of those signs is the growing visibility of brewing gems like Great Leap Brewing. Great Leap is known for using locally sourced ingredients such as a berry from the Chinese prickly ash that creates a spicy buzz on the tongue. Other craft breweries here have experimented with endemic ingredients such as Tibetan barley, purple rice, coffee beans from the southwestern Yunnan Province, jasmine tea, rose petals, and the blossoms of the sweet osmanthus bush.

The beer scenes in Beijing and Shanghai also embrace flavors from farther afield. Alongside the noodle shops of Beijing's Huguosi Snack Street, a beer oasis called

A Chinese ship—called a junk—tours around Hong Kong, where the beer scene is gaining in popularity.

NBeer Pub serves hundreds of foreign beers in addition to its local offerings. This love of foreign flavors is even more pronounced in Shanghai, where brewpubs and bottle shops (most owned or run by expats) sell European- and American-style beer in quirky neighborhoods and high-end hotels located far from downtown. Most Chinese still do their drinking at dinner, but the Western pub tradition is gaining ground. These cities hold a growing number of bottle shops, beer bars, taprooms, and clubs, all offering an increasingly diverse range of choices.

BREW FUSION Hong Kong is a place where ancient mountains frame futuristic-looking skyscrapers, and where Eastern tradition fuses with Western ideas. Some of this fusion can be traced to the First Opium War (1839–1842), which brought English ships carrying bread, pigs, poultry, and, of course, English beer. But it was a local rice liquor called *sam shu* that British soldiers ended up drinking too much of while on the mainland, resulting in fights with locals that deepened hostilities. The sudden jump in the city's beer-loving population saw the number of beer barrels imported soar from around 1,000 in 1851 to almost 10,000 in 1866. This swelling tide brought English-style porter, ale, and eventually lager to Hong Kong's shores.

Though lager has long dominated Hong Kong's beer scene, an explosion of craft breweries, brewpubs, and taprooms are introducing the city to a variety of tastes. Brothers Daniel and David Gallie named their Black Kite Brewery after a distinctly local feature—the fork-tailed bird of prey that can often be seen gliding over their city's high rises—but they serve up English-style IPA, porter, and ale. Black Kite illustrates how cultural fusion can create a winning recipe.

meet the brewers
The Raphaels

Can beer be fierce? It is at Moonzen Brewery, where it's named after the gods. Michele and Laszlo Raphael, the wife-and-husband team behind this brewery located in one of Hong Kong's former industrial hubs, look to

Chinese folklore to name their beer. Their IPA is named after the Jade Emperor, ruler of heaven. The honey porter is named after the Kitchen God, who is customarily given honey before he reports to the Jade Emperor in order to sweeten his words (or seal his lips). The amber ale, with hints of peach, is named after the Monkey King, who once stole the Peaches of Immortality from the Heavenly Queen Mother of the West. The brewery's name comes from the Cantonese word *mun san* (door gods), whose images are meant to ward off evil spirits. Michele hints at what makes Moonzen unique: "The saying goes that every beer has a story. We think that every story has a beer."

BEIJING & SHANGHAI
Jing-A Full Moon Farmhouse Ale

Jing-A Brewing Company brews not only Western styles but also a range of beer based on Chinese ingredients and food traditions. Jing-A Full Moon Farmhouse Ale starts with a Belgian base and then adds peppercorns and herbs used in Chinese moon cakes.

ABV 6.2% | **IBU** 20

Aroma Oranges, ginger, *hui hua* (sweet osmanthus flower), peppers

Appearance Deep hazy gold with a fluffy white head

Flavor Dry, light, and orangey, with a zing of ginger and Szechuan peppercorn

Mouthfeel Light-bodied and well carbonated

Presentation Pint or Willi Becher glass

Food Pairings Robust fish dishes, chicken dishes, and pork dishes

HONG KONG
Tea IPA

Hong Kong, long a bustling crossroads of commerce and culture, now has a modern brewing scene that crackles with energy. Many brewers look to integrate Chinese ingredients into existing styles, creating completely original aromatic profiles.

ABV 4.5–6.5% | **IBU** 35–55

Aroma Tropical fruit, hops, and distinctive notes of grass and tea

Flavor Light-bodied, often with firm bittering and fruity tea notes through the center

Mouthfeel Dry and sharp, with moderate carbonation

Presentation Tulip or Willi Becher glass

Food pairings Spicy food, pork dumplings in hot oil, tacos, Thai cuisine

Craft to Try Moonzen Rose Oolong Session IPA

Mount Fuji is a sacred mountain and an active volcano. The surrounding land is home to deep springs filled with soft water, used in brewing traditional sake and lager.

JAPAN

THE DRINK OF CHOICE

The Japanese call their country *Nippon* (source of the sun), a place where each new day brings renewal and reinvention, and one that is—quite literally—always moving. Many of Japan's almost 7,000 islands are made from the tops of volcanic mountains jutting up from the ocean's depths, each sitting on or near the edge of four tectonic plates. These plates constantly creep, lock up, and lurch, causing around 1,500 earthquakes annually.

Its capital city of Tokyo is the largest in the world, as deeply rooted in ancient tradition as in the latest fashion trends and forward-thinking technological gadgets. Japan is well known for its sake made from rice, mold, yeast, and water, but beer is actually the popular drink of choice. In fact, Japan's population drinks around three times as much beer as it does sake. Beer is a cultural fixture, even recognized as the go-to drink in popular manga and anime.

The Rise of Beer

The Dutch introduced beer to Japan in the 1600s, but trade restrictions eventually cut off the Dutch supply. Things changed when the United States went on a mission to open Japan to trade, resulting in the 1854 Treaty of Kanagawa that brought tourism, trade, and beer back to the islands. Japan's first brewery, Spring Valley Brewery, was established in 1870 near a spring in the fishing village of Yokohama. The brewer, Norwegian-American William Copeland, was quick to adopt new techniques such as pasteurization. He also dug a cave into the side of a nearby hill so as to properly lager his German-style beer. Some say he wasn't as good a manager as he was a brewer, and he ended up selling the company to the Japanese. Renamed Kirin, the oldest brewery in Japan is now

AT A GLANCE
Featured Locations

🛢 Brewery
★ Capital
● City
Hokkaido Physical feature

4

The number of Japanese beer companies that put braille on their beer cans

one of its four major breweries, a list that includes Asahi, Suntory, and Sapporo, Japan's oldest beer brand.

In 1901, a beer tax nearly wiped out Japan's 70 breweries. Politicians saw the alcohol tax as an easy source of revenue, but it struck the beer industry a mighty blow. Gone was Japan's German-style beer made with high-quality ingredients and high production standards. Lighter, cheaper beer—mass-produced with less taste, color, and bitterness—flooded in to take its place.

Most of the beer consumed in Japan is still mass-produced lager or a low-malt beer called *happoshu*. Recent attrition in the sales of these beers has coincided with increased interest in *ji-biru* (craft beer), especially with major breweries picking up stakes in U.S. beer companies.

The craft beer scene is small but growing. The industry started to take off after the 1994 deregulation of brewery licenses, which relaxed tax laws linked to production limits, making it easier for smaller breweries to open. Many breweries emerged only to fail, thanks to poor management and even poorer beer quality. Homebrewing beer with more than one percent alcohol by volume is illegal in Japan, so homebrewing wasn't around to support and bolster the craft beer scene in its early days. Craft beer is currently on its second upswing now that

 local flavor
Judging a Beer by Its Barley

"Is this really a beer?" That's a perfectly valid question in Japan, where a beverage is defined as a "beer" depending on how much malted barley it contains. If it has more than 67 percent, it's a beer. Less, and it's a

Breweries like Sapporo make a range of beers, from premium malt beers to cheaper, lower-malt *happoshu*.

popular low-malt beverage called *happoshu* (bubbling spirits). Rice, maize, *kaoliang* (sorghum wine), potato, starch, or sugar are the usual stand-ins for barley malt. Imported Belgian beer and North American craft beer are often designated as happoshu, despite having more than 67 percent malted grains.

Most Japanese happoshu is made with 25 percent malt—far less than the 67 percent threshold. That's because the amount of malt in a beverage determines how big a tax is added to its retail price. Low-malt happoshu is popular because, well, it's cheap.

There is a third beer type, called *daisan* (third) beer, that has no malted barley. Daisan is made from soy or pea protein and tastes like beer, but with a metallic finish. This beer category has the lowest taxation rate, so a can of daisan is usually half the price of a can of Japanese lager. Look for the word *mugi* (barley) in a beer's list of ingredients. If mugi is missing, it's a daisan beer.

Beer lovers revel in the craft beers at the annual Great Japan Beer Festival.

the first wave of poor-quality producers is gone. Many breweries and brewpubs are using local ingredients to create Japanese interpretations of European- and American-style beer. Japanese beer drinkers are noticing, and they are starting to weave craft beer into the fabric of their drinking culture.

Raise a Glass

In Japan, drinking is both a social and traditional activity. It's common to mix business dinners with drinking. Proper etiquette requires diners to fill everyone's glass except their own. Drinking includes a pecking order, with juniors filling their seniors' glasses and women filling men's glasses. These sessions commonly end with a full glass, as an empty glass will never stay so for long.

Drinking etiquette becomes more relaxed after dinner. Diners usually move to more casual locations such as dance clubs, karaoke bars, or casual gastropubs called *izakayas*. Most of these establishments are conveniently clustered around train and subway stations and stay open until the morning, when trains resume their migrations around the metropolis. Beer is also sold at convenience stores and from vending machines. Revelers often stay out into the morning hours sampling Japan's beer delights—long enough to raise a toast to the sun and experience firsthand the source of Japan's nickname.

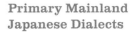

Speakeasy

How to Order Beer in Japan

Primary Mainland Japanese Dialects

■ East
■ Kyushu
■ Mix of East and West
■ West

In Japan, drinking usually begins over dinner, with cheers of **"Kampai"** (KAM-pie-e), meaning "Bottoms up," made over the first round of **biru** (BEE-ru), or beer, and **sake** (sah-KEH), a traditional fermented rice drink.

Politeness is ingrained in the language, so learning how to say "Please" will go a long way. **"Onegaishi-masu"** (one-GY-she-mas) is the formal way of saying it, while **"Kudasai"** (ku-DA-sigh) is less formal.

Considering that drinks might be served into the wee hours of morning, make sure to ask when last call is: **"Lasto orda wa nanji desu ka?"** (lasuto ooda wa NAN-gee des ka).

BEER GUIDE

WHERE BEER LOVERS GO

Though small in size, Japan's craft beer movement is taking big strides when it comes to experimentation. Experience its growing list of offerings at these Japanese brewer–recommended hot spots.

1 | Popeye
Tokyo

Started as a Western-style *izakaya*, Popeye is now one of the "it" places to go if you want to investigate Japan's microbrews. Try one of the 70 varieties of craft beer on tap. Those unsure of what to drink can order a flight (10 beer samples), which also includes a side dish.

2 | Atsugi Beer Brewery
Atsugi

This brewery is nestled at the base of the Tanzawa Mountains and is home to a one-man brewing show. Hideki Mochizuki does it all, from creating recipes to serving his beer. While he is particularly fond of German styles, he also makes an award-winning framboise lambic, as well as an American double IPA called Hopslave. Be sure to try the Shiso, an ale made with Japanese basil.

3 | Abashiri Beer Brewery
Abashiri

What do you get when you brew beer using melted icebergs from the frigid Sea of Okhotsk, blue seaweed, natural gardenia flower pigment, and Chinese

yam? A blue beer that tastes like a pale lager. Love it or hate it, it's uniquely Japanese. So, too, are the brewery's origins, stemming from a Tokyo University of Agriculture research project that aimed to produce wheat beer.

4 | Minoh Beer Brewery
Osaka

This brewery was a gift from a father to his two daughters, who now produce award-winning beer, including a double IPA and a Minoh Cabernet (part beer, part wine). Those who want to visit their on-premises bar should be prepared to wait, as it has only three seats.

5 | Hitachino Brewing Lab

Tokyo

Though the Kiuchi Brewery is well known for producing outstanding beer such as its Saison du Japon and Nipponia, a Belgian golden ale, it also has a brewing lab. It's tucked away in the brick and mortar of Tokyo's old Manseibashi railway station. Visitors can indulge in some Kiuchi specialty and seasonal batches, or they can brew their own beer under a brewer's guidance.

6 | Rokko Beer Garden

Kobe

While Kobe is known for its beef, its craft beer is starting to make a name for itself. The actual brewery is located in the foothills of Mount Rokko, but Rokko Beer Garden is more conveniently located in downtown Kobe. Tucked in the basement of an office building, it's decorated to make visitors feel like they are

in a Japanese garden. The Rokko Porter, a London-style porter with a 5 percent ABV, is the antithesis of Japan's mass-produced lager.

7 | Baird Brewery Gardens Shuzenji

Izu

Baird was the smallest brewery in Japan to obtain a license when it opened in 2001. Its success has led to several expansions, including the most recent one, the brewery gardens: The brewery is now replete with an orchard (for fruit adjuncts) and a hops yard. Be sure to try the Suruga Bay Imperial IPA and Shuzenji Heritage Helles while sitting in the tasting room of this craft beer paradise.

Breweries and Beer Destinations in Japan

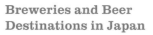

Brewery

Featured beer destination

Photos

1 *Popeye is the quintessential destination for beer enthusiasts in Tokyo.* **3** *Abashiri is home to a brewery of the same name, as well as an annual drift-ice festival.* **4** *The picturesque Minoh Falls are located outside Osaka, Japan.* **5** *You can learn about the brewing process over a pint at Hitachino Brewing Lab.*

LOCAL BREWS
TOKYO & OSAKA
BEER TO DINE FOR

MIXING OLD AND NEW In Tokyo, the juxtaposition of the old and new is present in its temples and high-rises, emblematic of Japan's dichotomous culture. For decades, Japanese beer could be summarized by the German-inspired lagers produced by the country's four main breweries: Asahi, Kirin, Sapporo, and Suntory. These four beer giants are headquartered in this manic capital city, and all vie to be the country's top brewery. Their mass-produced lagers take on the role of the "everyday beer" in a city where space is limited but the nightlife isn't. But Tokyo is becoming a haven for craft

local flavor
Rice Lager

When Japan became a global powerhouse in the 1980s, its young generation of drinkers started seeking a drink to complement their diet, which shifted from plant-based to one higher in both calories and meat. In response to plummeting sales, beer giant Asahi surveyed 5,000 Japanese on what they wanted to drink: The consensus was beer that was rich and sharp. The company used a new, highly attenuated yeast and a longer fermentation time to create a lighter, drier, crisper-tasting beer. Japanese rice lager was such a hit when it came out that grocery stores often sold out of it. It didn't hurt that "dryness" (crispness) has a cultural implication as something individualistic, which may be the best way to describe this style.

beer drinkers, especially after the relaxation of laws in the 1990s that kick-started an influx of smaller breweries and the birth of Japan's *ji-biru* (craft beer). New breweries, brewpubs, and taprooms are springing up in Tokyo neighborhoods, many tucked in the quiet back alleys and away from the glitzy technicolor mazes of the densely populated urban centers. And while Tokyo is known for being expensive—premium pricing, added taxes, and table charges are common when dining out—a growing number of patrons are splurging on Japanese microbrews instead of mass-produced Japanese lagers.

A BEER FOR ALL DISHES Osaka is the "nation's kitchen," so called because of its historic position as a trade city next to Kyoto, Japan's former capital. While the city has a long culinary history, the lack of an indigenous beer culture—and thereby a lack of social and historical construct about what constitutes a beer—has given rise to a wide variety of styles in Osaka (and the rest of Japan, for that matter), and done so almost to a fault. Some of its beer represents the world's recognized styles to perfection. Others are an oddity of color, ingredients, and presentation that defy any beer-style categorization. Despite Japan's motley range of offerings, one thing is for certain: Its beer goes well with food. Foodies in Osaka love pairing beer with local dishes. What beer pairs well with soy? Flanders red. How about a salty-broth ramen? Perhaps a pale ale. Miso soup? Try a fruity, peppery Trappist tripel. So ingrained is the art and importance of beer pairing that beer giant Asahi, which originated in Osaka and still brews there (as well as in Tokyo), has designed beers to be paired with specific foods of the region.

Unlike in the United States, where the craft beer culture was honed by homebrewers, Japanese craft beer culture has been driven by sake brewers and their knowledge of fermentation. In most of Japan, sake was once the favored alcoholic drink—but no longer, and certainly not in Osaka. The region's focus on breweries, brewpubs, taprooms, and bars is helping shape the art of making beer styles that fit in nicely with the innovative and indulgent culinary nature of Japan's "kitchen city."

Eccentric and colorful bars are typical in Osaka's vibrant Dotonbori entertainment district.

on tap with Garrett Oliver

TOKYO
Asahi Kuronama

A version of pilsner dominates in Japan, but there is also a particular affinity for the relatively obscure German *schwarzbier (kuronama)* style of black lager. Asahi has been brewing its kuronama black beer for at least 20 years, and rival Sapporo released its own version, Sapporo Premium Black, in 2016.

ABV 5% | **IBU** 20

Aroma Caramel, with light coffee and dark chocolate notes and a floral hop overlay

Appearance Deep brown to black

Flavor Relatively dry with deceptively light roast and caramel notes, despite the dark color

Mouthfeel Soft, smooth, and round; very drinkable

Presentation Pilsner or Willi Becher glass

Food Pairings Steak, burger, roasted meat, grilled vegetables, freshwater eel, *tonkotsu* (pork cutlet) ramen—versatile

OSAKA
Yuzu Ale

While the beers of Japan tend to have a German influence, craft brewers are starting to reach for Japanese culinary elements. Principle among these regional ingredients is the yuzu, a small citrus fruit with a distinct lime-like aroma and electric acidity. Refreshingly, some yuzu ales are wheat-based.

ABV 4.5–8.0% | **IBU** 12–18

Aroma Yuzu zest aroma; lime-like and bright, with notes of other citrus

Appearance Pale gold, often with some haze

Flavor Light-bodied, low in bitterness, and very dry and fruity, with a slight tanginess

Mouthfeel Light-bodied, bright, and effervescent

Presentation Tulip glass

Food Pairings Salad, seafood dishes, Thai cuisine, sushi and sashimi

Craft to Try Minoh Yuzu White

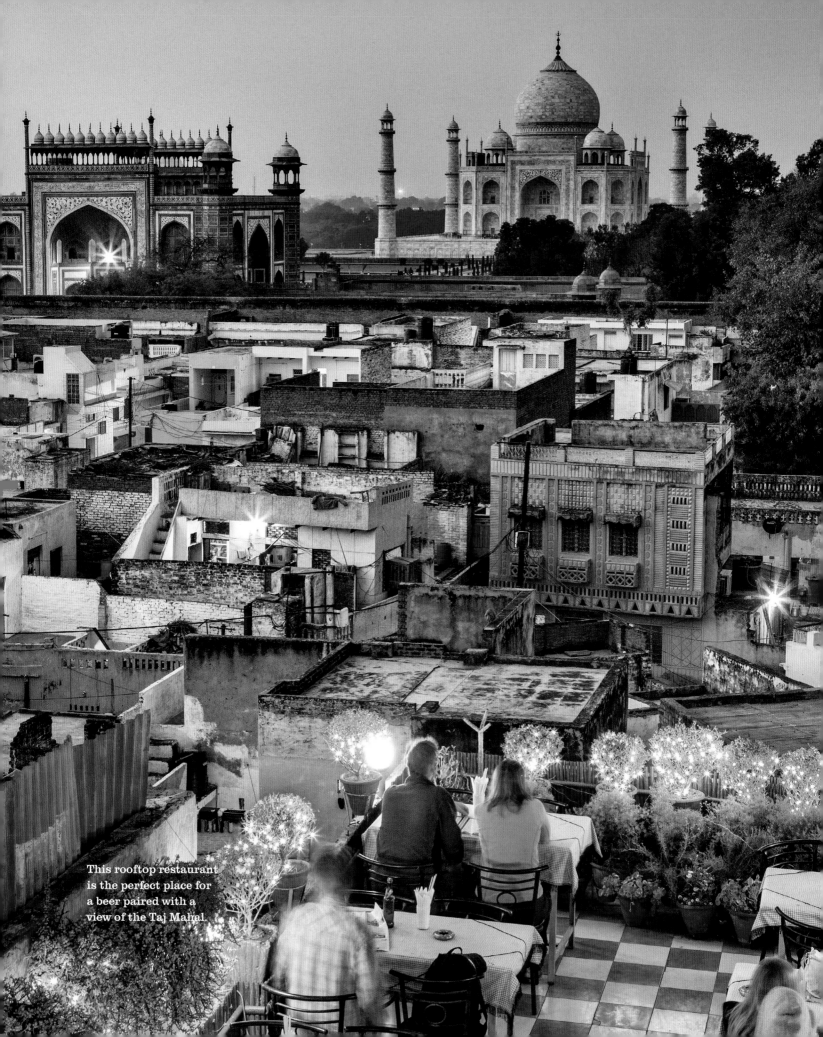

This rooftop restaurant is the perfect place for a beer paired with a view of the Taj Mahal.

INDIA

REDEFINING FLAVOR

India is a nation rich in geographic and ethnic diversity. This subcontinent includes the Himalaya, the Indian Ocean, and the fertile deltas and plateaus that lie in between. It is home to hundreds of distinct cultural groups, each with its own language and faith. But there is a unifying sentiment here regarding the historic presence of the British, expressed in phrases that go something like this: "They were only good for tea, trains, and the education system they left behind." But the British also introduced whiskey to this Southwest Asian country, a drink that remains very popular. India is the world's top consumer of whiskey. Indians consume about 396 million gallons (1.5 billion L) of it each year. Beer isn't as popular, but it is gaining headway with consumers.

Before the British arrived, Indians brewed indigenous beer with rice and millet. *Handia* is an indigenous rice beer predominantly produced in eastern India. The drink is traditionally made by women, who mill the rice and boil it down to a paste. Once it dries, it is mixed with *ranu,* an herbal root, and then left to ferment. Though handia is served during festivals, a number of bars sell it too.

Expat Imports

British colonialists did not care for handia, choosing instead to import beer from home. English porter and pale ale were two of the more dominant beer styles, first imported as early as 1711 (see page 70). It took more than a century for the first commercial brewery to open its doors here, though. In 1830, Edward Dyer founded a brewery in the small British outpost of Kasauli, in the foothills of the

AT A GLANCE
Featured Locations

🛢 Brewery
★ Capital
● City
SRI LANKA Non-subject country

Bengaluru is famous for nightlife, including places such as Le Rock Pub Cafe.

Himalaya. Lucky for Dyer, its elevation of 6,300 feet (1,920 m) meant the climate was good for fermenting beer. Dyer started by brewing a pale ale he called Lion. By 1882, some 50 years after Dyer opened his brewery, the number of breweries in India had reached a dozen.

In 1915 five small breweries in southern India merged to become the United Breweries (UB) Group, which thrived by providing the thirsty British Army with a constant stream of cheap beer. The UB Group grew by acquiring rival breweries in the 1950s and 1960s, but it wasn't until 1978 that it created the brand, Kingfisher, that would go on to dominate India's beer scene. Kingfisher Strong, a 7.1 percent ABV lager, launched in 1999, is the best-selling beer in India and part of what earned the UB Group a 51 percent share in the Indian beer market. Strong beer is popular in India—over 80 percent of all beer sales—with high ABVs that range upward of 8 percent. But its overall sales can't compete with local whiskeys and other spirits.

Finding an Audience

Prohibition is still in effect in some states, such as Mahatma Gandhi's home state of Gujarat. In others there is a minimum production threshold that's nearly impossible for microbreweries to meet. The drinking age varies from 18 to 25, and taxes on beer range from 50 to 85 percent per bottle. But inventive Indian brewers are finding creative ways around these laws. Dissatisfied with existing brewing facilities in India, Bira 91's owners rented a brewery in Belgium, where they combine grains from Belgium and France with hops from the Himalaya. Despite the distance and the heavy import duty, the beer has a strong customer base in India.

India's craft beer revolution started in 2009 with the Doolally Taproom near Pune. The country now has roughly 60 microbreweries and brewpubs, with Bengaluru (Bangalore) and Mumbai-Pune as its craft beer hubs. India's craft beer scene increased by 1,000 percent from 2009 to 2015, but there is still room in this $3 billion beer market for craft beer to make its mark.

Speakeasy

How to Order Beer in India

It's easy enough to order a beer in English while in India, as the language is commonly spoken, but knowing a few beer-related Hindi phrases will certainly serve you well.

If hopping into an auto rickshaw or taxi without a particular beer destination in mind, you may want to ask, **"Jahaan pab hai?"** (ja-HA-an pab hi), or "Where is the pub?"

Once you're there, request a menu from your server or bartender: **"Main biyar menoo dekh sakate hain?"** (min BIbi-yar me-NOO dek se-KA-ka-te hin), or "Can I see the beer menu?"

If whatever is on tap will do, just ask for **"krpaya ek biyar dee-jie"** (ker-PA-ya ek BI-yar dee-GEE-eh): "one beer, please."

You may not want your time at the pub to end, but eventually you'll have to pay up. Ask for the check by saying **"Kya main chek kar sakata hoon?"** (kya min chek ka se-KA-ta oun): "Can I have the check?"

BEER GUIDE

WHERE BEER LOVERS GO

India's craft beer scene is small, but there are several wonderful beer spots to visit. Here are the places that many Indian brewers recommend.

1 | Arbor Brewing Company

Bengaluru

Wait—isn't there an Arbor Brewing Company in the United States? Indeed there is, and this brewery is a collaboration between that iconic Michigan brewery and an Indian partner. With seven staple beers, monthly seasonals, and 10 rotating beers, this is the brewery with the most styles in India. Its hefeweizen, Bangalore Bliss, goes down easy on a hot summer day.

2 | Doolally Taproom

Mumbai

Nondescript wooden furniture and industrial lights don't tamp down the excitement of the crowds at this popular spot. Patrons gather around board games, drinking fresh beer shipped in from nearby Pune.

3 | 7 Degrees Brauhaus

Gurgaon

The brewery's name comes from the temperature at which it serves its German-style beer. Its most popular feature is a Bavarian beer garden replete with chestnut trees.

4 | The Biere Club

Bengaluru

The first craft brewery in Bengaluru serves up traditional craft beer styles such as ale, lager, and stout, as well as experimental brews. If you are lucky and your timing is right, you may be able to try a seasonal style, like mango beer. The beer styles are rotated often, so make several trips if you want to try them all.

Breweries and Beer Destinations in India

🛢 Brewery

🍺 Featured beer destination

Fishermen harvest clams
during the early morning
hours at Tan Thanh Beach.

VIETNAM

FINDING BREWING AND INDEPENDENCE

This Southeast Asian country bordering the eastern edge of the Indochina Peninsula is one of Asia's largest consumers of beer. And though it's long been dominated by macrobrews and *bia hơi* (gas beer), it's full of increasingly pleasant brewing surprises. Microbreweries like Pasteur Street Brewing Company are making European-style beer with hints of Vietnamese flavors; it won the 2016 World Beer Cup gold medal for its chocolate stout brewed with local chocolate.

Beer came to Vietnam in the mid-19th century, when it became a French colony. Before that, a rice liquor known as *rượu đế* (grass liquor) was the common alcoholic drink. That changed when the French imposed a high tax on rượu đế while keeping the prices low on imported French beer. The country's first brewery, Hommel, was founded in Hanoi in the 1890s. It produced only 40 gallons (150 L) a day, but the beer was fresh.

North and South

When the French left Vietnam in 1954 and the country split into the communist North and the free South, Hommel fell into disrepair. Brewers from fellow communist country Czechoslovakia helped the North Vietnamese government restore Hommel, and by 1958 the renamed Hanoi Brewery was producing a lager called Trúc Bach, named after one of the many lakes in Hanoi. In South Vietnam in the 1930s, Brasseries et Glacières de l'Indochine opened a brewery that produced 33 Beer, named after the 33-centiliter (11.2-oz) bottles it came in. The French were the ones who had originally brought 33 Beer to Vietnam, and it was brewed using French and German ingredients.

In the years following the Vietnam War (1955–1975) and the reunification of

AT A GLANCE
Featured Locations

🛢 Brewery
★ Capital
● City
Indochina Peninsula Physical feature

Crates of beer are delivered to the central market in Hội An. This bustling shopping area is on the banks of the Thu Bồn River.

the North and South, North Vietnam continued to enjoy good relations with fellow communist countries Czechoslovakia and East Germany, and many Vietnamese brewers spent time in both countries. Thus Czech and German beer styles are common in Vietnam, especially in and around Hanoi, where 50 breweries produce these styles.

An Expanding Market

Vietnam's population has embraced beer, which makes up 98 percent of the alcohol consumed. From 2005 to 2015, per capita beer consumption rose from 5 gallons (19 L) to 10 gallons (38 L), partly thanks to an exploding economy. But between the macrobrews that constitute 99 percent of the market and the healthy number of bia hơi brewers, beer lovers didn't have much choice. Things changed in 2014 when Louisiane Brewhouse opened its doors in the coastal city of Nha Trang. That opening led to a string of others in various locations, including Pasteur Street, Fuzzy Logic, Platinum, Phat Rooster, Tê Tê, and Gauden. Many of these breweries are run by American expats who see the potential in the emerging Vietnamese craft beer movement and tend to take their cues from the U.S. scene by producing hoppy IPAs. But these brewers don't just want to bring U.S. beer to Vietnam; they want to infuse it with local Vietnamese ingredients.

Craft brewers are not yet able to compete with macrobreweries and bia hơi stands when it comes to price, so they have turned their attention to education. They believe that the more knowledgeable beer drinkers are about craft beer, the more likely they are to invest their money in this growing industry. And though the craft beer scene is still in its infancy, the rise of modern beer gardens, trendy beer bars, and beer clubs is influencing what people are drinking, and how.

local flavor
The People's Beer

Bia hơi (gas beer) is a great example of how necessity is the mother of invention. Vietnam's most popular alcoholic drink prior to the 1960s was a low-alcohol wine made from rice, but then the government banned it during the Vietnam War to ensure there was enough rice for people to eat. Brewers adapted to wartime rations by inventing bia hơi, a low-ABV beer made with equal parts barley and rice. There is no denying this fizzy beer is fresh, with bia hơi made in the morning and consumed that same day.

Since its inception, bia hơi has provided people with affordable beer, but now it seems as if everyone drinks it. It is usually delivered by motorcycle, strapped to the back in drums that range from 2 to 100 liters (0.5–26 gallons). Throughout the day and into the night, crowds of locals and tourists gather on plastic stools at bia hơi shops and makeshift bars in Hanoi's Old Quarter. These improvised watering holes provide places where people can congregate to discuss everything from politics to fashion. Bia hơi is well established, and cheap at only 30 U.S. cents per glass. Its low price point makes it a budget-friendly alternative to the more expensive macrobrewed beers, craft beers, and even bottled water.

BEER GUIDE

WHERE BEER LOVERS GO

Fancy something other than cold lager? You're in luck: The craft beer market is growing in Vietnam. Try out these beer hubs, all recommended by local brewers.

1 | BiaCraft

Ho Chi Minh City

This craft beer bar has partnered with a number of independent local brewers to produce some truly winning brews. Its recent collaboration with Pasteur Street resulted in a beer called What the Heo?, a breakfast stout made with bacon.

2 | Hoa Vien Brauhaus

Hanoi

One of Hanoi's oldest breweries, this is a favorite hangout for expats who want to get away from the crowded bia hơi stands. While you can try the brewery's own craft beer, its claim to fame is that it's the only place in Vietnam to get Pilsner Urquell (see page 84) on draft.

3 | Louisiane Brewhouse

Nha Trang

Louisiane Brewhouse eschews the city's hustle and bustle in favor of a beachside locale. Its four regular beers are made to be paired with food from its kitchen. Try the seasonal Passion Beer, a unique Vietnamese take on the radler.

4 | Pasteur Street Brewing Company

Ho Chi Minh City

The trio of American expats who started Pasteur Street in 2011 have brewed 70-plus styles, all featuring flavors from their country of origin. Try the Spice Island Saison, made with local lemongrass, ginger, and pepper, or the award-winning imperial chocolate stout.

5 | Platinum

Ho Chi Minh City

Platinum's head brewer has worked in 12 countries and created famous brews like James Squire's Golden Ale from Australia. Many consider his pale ale, with its distinctive hop flavors, the best in the city.

Breweries and Beer Destinations in Vietnam

🛢 Brewery

🍺 Featured beer destination

WHAT'S BREWING

in
ASIA

Cambodia

Asia's eighth largest beer-producing country is part of the Asian craft beer revolution, with breweries, taprooms, and beer gardens springing up. Craft beer production is still limited, as brewers focus on quality and sustainability, but breweries such as Cerevisia Craft Brewhouse, Botanico, Himawari, and Tawandang German Brewery are leading the way.

6
12-oz beers (2 L)
Annual consumption per capita

5.1
million U.S. barrels (6 million hL)
Annual production

3,647.64
Cambodian riels (U.S. $0.92)
Average price of a 12-oz bottle

Philippines

Don't be fooled by the dominance of San Miguel in Asia's seventh largest beer-producing country. The craft beer scene here is alive and kicking, and craft beer production is on the rise. Most of the country's craft breweries are based in Manila, but signs of a thriving beer culture are cropping up in Baguio City, Cebu, and Palawan.

56
12-oz beers (20 L)
Annual consumption per capita

11.9
million U.S. barrels (14 million hL)
Annual production

37.34
Philippine pesos (U.S. $0.75)
Average price of a 12-oz bottle

South Korea

Asia's fifth largest beer producer is
awash in pale lager. But when an
article published in the *Economist* in
2012 claimed that North Korea's beer
was better, it sparked a craft beer
movement in the South. A flowering of
expat- and Korean-owned craft breweries suggests that the beer scene
here is growing in leaps and bounds.

138
12-oz beers (49 L)
Annual consumption per capita

18.2
million U.S. barrels (21.3 million hL)
Annual production

2,609.94
South Korean won (U.S. $2.30)
Average price of a 12-oz bottle

Thailand

This tourist destination ranks fourth
in Asia's list of top beer producers.
Almost all beer brewed here is lager
brewed by one of five breweries.
Yet there are a handful of craft breweries producing American-style ales.
Hops are being grown in Thailand,
which has generated domestic and
international attention.

56
12-oz beers (20 L)
Annual consumption per capita

20.1
million U.S. barrels (23.6 million hL)
Annual production

74.35
Thai baht (U.S. $2.16)
Average price of a 12-oz bottle

The harbor in Sydney, Australia, was home to both the country's first British colony and its first privately owned commercial brewery in the late 18th century.

CHAPTER 5

AUSTRALIA & OCEANIA

BULIMBA
GOLD TOP
LIGHT BITTER
PALE ALE
SPECIALLY SUITABLE FOR
TROPICAL CLIMATES
BOTTLED BY
Queensland Brewery Ltd

Queensland Brewery, founded in 1888, produced two popular beers: Bulimba Gold Top and Silver Top.

UP AND BREWING

Oceania, which consists of Australia, New Zealand, and several island nations and territories in Melanesia, Micronesia, and Polynesia, has about 40 million inhabitants—roughly the same population as the much smaller Poland. But small numbers don't matter when it comes to the quality of a region's beer. Oceania produces some of the world's most sought-after beer, despite the formidable challenges posed by Australia's searing deserts, New Zealand's craggy shores, and the South Pacific's thick humidity. Oceania's brewers are putting these island countries on the beer map.

Times of Trial

European explorers commonly carried beer onboard their ships because it was a safe and healthy alternative to water. Captain James Cook, the first European to make landfall in eastern Australia, in 1770, was reported to have left England on his initial voyage to the Pacific with some four tons of beer. In doing so he brought alcohol to Oceania.

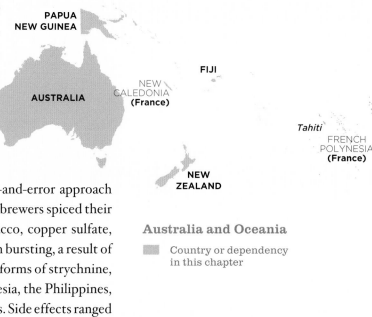

Australia and Oceania

▓▓▓ Country or dependency in this chapter

Colonial brewing was encouraged from the start, as it helped build up agriculture and create employment. A hot climate ill-suited for brewing, and compounded by a limited supply of traditional ingredients, promoted a trial-and-error approach that was experimental at best and dangerous at worst. Some brewers spiced their beer with substances aimed to increase intoxication: tobacco, copper sulfate, opium, and *Cocculus indicus* (which also prevents bottles from bursting, a result of secondary fermentation in warm climates). Some even used forms of strychnine, a poison from the seeds of a deciduous tree native to Indonesia, the Philippines, and China, to water down pale ale during financial downturns. Side effects ranged from hallucinations to aggressive behavior, but the most common was a severe case of diarrhea. It wasn't until the 1880s that most adulterated beer was eradicated, though beer poisoning still took place from time to time.

Breweries started popping up in the late 1790s in Australia, the mid-1830s in New Zealand, and the mid-1910s in island nations such as Tahiti. Australia and New Zealand enjoyed a distinct geographical edge over the rest of Oceania,

in that they could grow hops and barley. The rest of Oceania was too warm to produce these critical beer ingredients, so they needed to be imported.

Beer's popularity grew, despite the difficulties in making it, and today it is Oceania's most popular alcoholic drink. Though a few historic interpretations of the region's native styles have survived, the prevalence of Australia's sparkling ale and New Zealand's draught is much smaller than that of pale ale and IPA.

Australia and New Zealand continue to dominate Oceania's beerscape. Australia has more than 300 breweries, while New Zealand has more than 100. Foreign-owned macrobreweries Kirin Company and Heineken International, and their ubiquitous lagers, are king on most of Oceania's islands, especially where the weather is warm. When asked which country has the better beer scene, Aussie and Kiwi brewers tend to agree: Australia has better local ingredients, but New Zealand produces better craft beer. Australia grows slightly more hops than New Zealand and far more malted two-row barley, though only around 20 percent of Australia's malted barley is consumed domestically. Globally, Australia's crops make up 30 percent of the world's malted barley trade.

Hop Haven

Hop production is relatively new in Australia and New Zealand, but these countries have some of the best known hop regions outside Washington State's Yakima

brewline
Historic Moments in Beer

James Cook brews the first beer in New Zealand. — **1773**

James Squire grows the first hops in Australia. — **1804**

The first commercial brewery opens in New Zealand. — **1835**

Polynesia's first commercial brewery opens in Tahiti. — **1914**

A four-month beer boycott in Greymouth, New Zealand, starts over outrage at a rise in beer prices. — **1947**

New Zealand's Morton Coutts invents the continuous fermentation process. — **1953**

What many consider Australia's first successful craft brewery, the Sail and Anchor Pub, opens in Fremantle, Western Australia. — **1984**

A hailstorm in Australia reduces the country's total hop yield by nearly 30 percent. — **2015**

The Great Kiwi Beer Festival | CHRISTCHURCH | NEW ZEALAND | Is there anything better than strolling through a park on a summer's day and drinking craft beer? With more than 200 craft beers to choose from, the South Island's largest beer festival leaves visitors spoiled for choice. *January*

MarchFest | NELSON | NEW ZEALAND | This outdoor festival features live music and kid-friendly events. All the beers on offer make their world debut here, commissioned for this one-day event. *March*

Great Australasian Beer SpecTAPular (GABS) | MELBOURNE AND SYDNEY (AUSTRALIA) | AUCKLAND (NEW ZEALAND) | This beer fest is so large it has to be held in three cities over three weekends. More than 150 breweries attend, pouring hundreds of beers—120 of which are exclusive to GABS. *May–June*

Beervana | WELLINGTON | NEW ZEALAND | Beervana is Wellington's chief craft beer festival, featuring 60 Kiwi breweries serving more than 300 beers. Wellington's sister city of Portland, Oregon, is honored through taps serving its American IPA, wild beer, and sour beer. *August*

Hundreds of beers are featured at the GABS.

Western Australia Beer and Beef Festival | PERTH | AUSTRALIA | What could possibly be bad about combining beer and beef? This festival offers more than 75 craft beers to sample while dining on various cuts of beef. *September*

Sydney Craft Beer Week | SYDNEY | AUSTRALIA | With more than 100 events in 75 different venues, Beer Week organizers have thought of everything. A highlight is the *Crafty Pint* magazine's Pint of Origin, which brings beer from smaller Australian breweries to pubs throughout the city. *October*

Valley and Bavaria's Hallertau. New Zealand's Nelson Sauvin hop is in high demand by many Northern Hemisphere brewers, while Australia's most popular hop is Galaxy. But Australia's weather is not always kind to hop farmers, and hailstorms can destroy a large percentage of the crop. A storm in December 2015, for instance, destroyed 40 to 50 percent of the Galaxy crop and reduced the yields of hop varieties like Enigma and Topaz.

Luckily, brewers in Oceania have always been a resourceful bunch. They have taken lower local hop yields as an opportunity to experiment with different hop varieties, setting themselves up to brew Oceania's next great beer. Judging by the number of European and American brewers lining up to collaborate with their Aussie and Kiwi counterparts, Oceania is emerging as the world's foremost up-and-coming craft beer region.

The Twelve Apostles are wonders of geology located off the Great Ocean Road in Victoria.

AUSTRALIA

A SPOT AT THE BAR

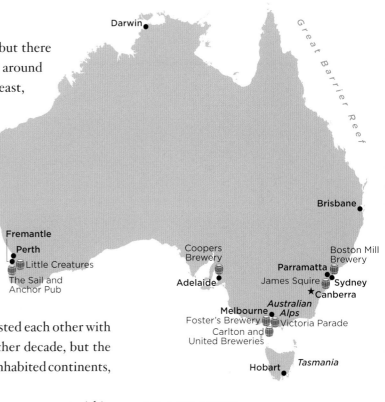

Darwin

Great Barrier Reef

Brisbane

Fremantle
Perth
Little Creatures
The Sail and
Anchor Pub

Coopers
Brewery

Adelaide

Boston Mill
Brewery
Parramatta
James Squire
Sydney
★ Canberra
Australian
Melbourne Alps
Foster's Brewery Victoria Parade
Carlton and
United Breweries

Hobart Tasmania

Australia's midsection has a lot of sun-scorched desert, but there is far more here than the hot and dry. Diversity prevails around its edges: the snowcapped Australian Alps to the southeast, the massive Great Barrier Reef to the northeast, and the temperate rain forests of Tasmania to the south. Most of Australia's 23 million people live within 31 miles (50 km) of the coast, which is where most of the country's brewing happens. The world's smallest continent is enthusiastic about beer and is producing an impressive array of it.

In 1788, 18 years after the British explorer James Cook reached the eastern shores of Australia, Captain Arthur Phillip—along with 751 convicts and their children, plus 252 marines and their families—founded the penal colony of Sydney. To celebrate its founding, Phillip and his officers toasted each other with glasses of English porter. It wouldn't be made here for another decade, but the toast solidified that beer had finally made it to all the world's inhabited continents, and it wouldn't be leaving anytime soon.

The darker side of this achievement was that alcohol abuse was rampant within the colony, particularly when it came to imported rum. The colonial government hoped that cheap beer would mitigate the problem, or at least provide a healthier alternative to hard liquor. In 1804, Australia's first and last government-run brewery was built in Parramatta, New South Wales, in the same general locale as Australia's first pub, opened a few years prior by former convict James Larra. From the outset,

AT A GLANCE
Featured Locations

- Brewery
- ★ Capital
- • City
- *Tasmania* Physical feature

the brewery was plagued with technical issues and a lack of ingredients. Only two years later, the government sold it to its resident brewer, Thomas Rushdon.

Avant-Garde Brewers

When the government failed in its attempt to provide local beer to the colonists, enterprising immigrants took up the charge. As in the other burgeoning beer scenes of the 1900s, the lack of refrigeration and transportation meant that brewing was a local affair. John Boston, an English surgeon and apothecary, didn't have access to local hops, so, guided by an encyclopedia, he brewed using malted maize and apple stalks. He founded the Boston Mill Brewery in 1796 on Bennelong Point, near the site where the Sydney Opera House now stands. It is widely considered Australia's first privately owned commercial brewery, but Boston's beer wasn't very good. He met an untimely end when, in 1804, he sailed on a ship to Tonga, where the locals—or so the legend goes—invited him to a dinner at which he ended up being the meal.

James Squire, a convict sent to Australia for stealing five hens and four cocks from a neighbor's yard, gifted the colony with its first hops. Squire started brewing soon after his arrival, receiving lashings for stealing horehound—an herb with bittering qualities used as a substitute for hops. Upon his emancipation, Squire was granted 30 acres (12 ha) of land in 1795 on the Parramatta River, where he established a brewery, tavern, and eventually a hop plantation. His cultivation of Australia's first

---

Speakeasy

A Beer by Any Other Name

With the exception of South Australia, a pint of beer is the same size as an English pint: 20 imperial fluid ounces (1.2 U.S. pints). South Australia's pints are 15 imperial fluid ounces (just under 1 U.S. pint).

———

If you're looking for a more diminutive serving, you can ask for a **seven** in New South Wales, Northern Queensland, and the Northern Territory. That will get you seven U.S. ounces (200 mL) of beer.

———

Not sure what beer to try? Ask for a **paddle**. It's called a flight in the United States, but Australians call it a paddle because of the common shape of the vessel that holds the glasses.

———

Can't make it to the pub? You can always stop by the **bottle-o** (drive-through beer store) and pick up some **tinnies** (cans).

———

Draft beer generally comes in two sizes— small and large—but the names used for each vary depending on what state you're in.

Beer Serving Sizes

VICTORIA   State

Term for a large beer

Term for a small beer

---

hops was so important that he was awarded a cow from the governor's herd. Squire's pioneering efforts live on today through his eponymous James Squire beer.

A Thirst for the Classics

Much like those in the United States, Australia's immigrants—hailing from England, Ireland, and elsewhere in Europe—shaped the evolution of its beerscape. They attempted to brew the styles they loved from back home, including pale ale, porter, and stout. A lack of key ingredients, a warm climate, and poor quality control meant that English varieties continued to be a regularly imported staple. Pale ales brewed in London and Burton upon Trent destined for India were also sent to Australia, a voyage that could take three months. Beer historian Martyn Cornell offers evidence that the term "India pale ale" (see page 70) was first used in Sydney, not England, in 1829; advertisements in the *Sydney Gazette and New South Wales Advertiser* offered "East India pale ale" for sale.

Though these styles originated far away, brewing on Australian soil was done locally. Diversity abounded, though not consistency. Paralleling a global trend that swept much of the world in the 1800s, Australia saw an increased popularity of all things pale—specifically pale ale and lager. When the 19th century drew to a close, Australia had around 300 breweries for a population of only four million.

Crafting Big Business

Now at 19.5 gallons (74 L) per capita, beer consumption in Australia has decreased steadily since the 1960s, a decline that has hit brewing conglomerates such as AB InBev (Carlton and United Breweries) and Kirin (Lion). This decrease in consumption hasn't diminished the country's thirst for craft beer, which accounts for 5 percent of the Australian beer market. An interesting trend unique to Australia's beer scene is the overall acceptance of "craft beer" made by macrobreweries. Though former craft breweries Little Creatures and James Squire are now owned by the Japanese-based beverage company Kirin, their products are still widely consumed by craft beer lovers.

Despite the growing enthusiasm for craft beer, hurdles to the movement's expansion remain in the form of taxation. The country's 300-plus breweries—up from 25 in 1988—have to deal with rather complicated alcohol taxes that make Australian beer some of the world's most expensive: The stronger the beer, the higher the taxes imposed on it, making boozy beer an expensive commodity. Lagers remain more popular (and cheaper) than most craft beer, but the nation's beer knowledge and interest continue to blossom.

Australia's beer drinkers provide an enthusiastic audience, so it's no surprise that craft beer output grew by 20 percent a year from 2011 to 2015. Innovation runs deep with Australia's craft brewers, who are producing a cornucopia of styles to feed the country's demand. The Australian industry's rapid growth will see it claiming an increasingly influential role on the world's craft beer stage.

Little Creatures Brewery in Fremantle, Western Australia, gets its name from the yeast used in the brewing process.

BEER GUIDE

WHERE BEER LOVERS GO

The faster the Australian craft beer scene grows, the more overwhelming a beer drinker's choices. To help quell any indecision, visit these beer destinations recommended by Australian brewers.

1 | Nomad Brewing Company

Sydney, New South Wales

The owner's roots are Italian, but this craft brewery is all Australian. Though the brewery is young (established in 2014), its résumé includes collaborations with U.S. breweries Jester King, Stone, and Cigar City. Its own line of beer includes such offerings as Jet Lag IPA and Choc-Wort Orange imperial stout.

2 | Lord Nelson Brewery

Sydney, New South Wales

Sydney's oldest continually licensed pub pays tribute to the past. Stepping inside is like stepping back in time, given its wooden plank floors, exposed beams, and tables made out of barrels—only the flat-screen TVs give away what decade it is. Enjoy a schooner of Three Sheets, a pale ale brewed on-site.

3 | Moon Dog

Melbourne, Victoria

These guys love brewing so much they used to live in their brewery—talk about taking your work home with you. The atmosphere is laid-back and the beer is superb, especially the Skunkworks, a cognac-barrel-aged double IPA. They have opened a new brewery two doors down to expand their brewing capacity.

4 | Hobart Brewing Company

Hobart, Tasmania

An American and a Tasmanian sat down for a beer in 2014 and came up with the idea for what is now one of Tasmania's finest breweries, producing beer made exclusively with Tasmanian ingredients. Visit Hobart's inviting taproom to try its beers by the fire pit. Pair Saint Christopher Cream Ale with food from one of the local food trucks that regularly stop at the brewery.

5 | Feral Brewing Company

Baskerville, Western Australia

Located just outside Perth, this brewery has won many awards for its "undomesticated" beer. Feral pushes the style envelope, producing lagers and ales that defy easy categorization. It was voted best Australian brewery in 2016, sweetening the rewards of making a trip to Australia's west coast.

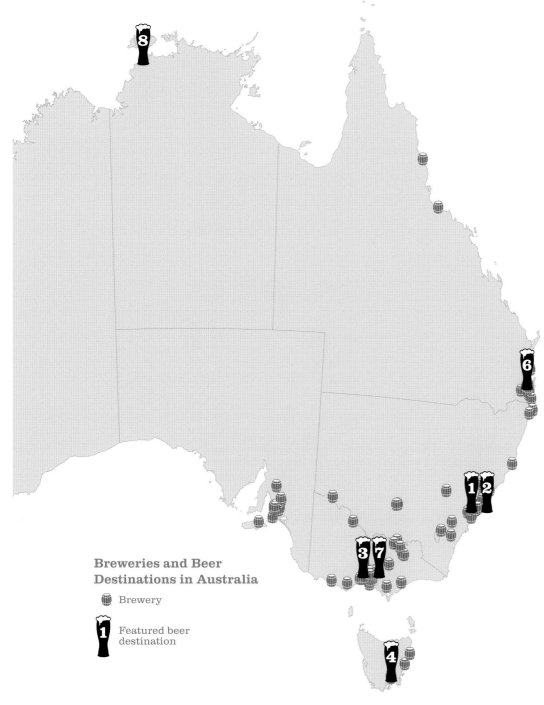

find and very much worth seeking out. It's a restaurant serving mouthwatering Asian cuisine alongside an impressively stocked beer bar. Boasting more than 200 beers, it patriotically promotes Australian beer as well as an extensive international selection. Take your time with the menu, which is dense enough to be mistaken for a novel.

8 | One Mile Brewing Company

Darwin, Northern Territory
This brewery got started when two homebrewing friends noted a lack of craft breweries in Darwin. One Mile, founded in 2012, produces five beers, including the 4:21 Kolsch, named after the Northern Territory's strangely specific quitting time. In brewing, timing is everything.

Breweries and Beer Destinations in Australia

🛢 Brewery

1 Featured beer destination

6 | Bacchus Brewing Company

Brisbane, Queensland
Few breweries in Australia make as many different types of beer as the Gold Coast's Bacchus Brewing. At last count, they had more than 120; with 15 taps and small brewing volumes, they need to keep things flowing. The brewery can make up to 12 different beers a day, and on average produces three new beers a week.

7 | Cookie

Melbourne, Victoria
Like many of Melbourne's culinary gems, this place is both hard to

Photos
2 *Lord Nelson Brewery is the oldest brewpub in Australia.* **5** *Feral Brewing Company offers a range of interesting beer styles.*
7 *Cookie, a restaurant in Melbourne, Victoria, has an extensive beer list that highlights local brands.*

MELBOURNE & ADELAIDE

BUSTLING BEER HUBS

TESTING THE WATERS Perched on Australia's wind-lashed southeastern coast, Melbourne is a city that takes food and drink seriously—including beer. The country's craft beer capital's recent claim to fame is that it has more craft breweries than tram stops. (Note: It has a *lot* of tram stops.)

One hundred years before Melbourne became the continent's craft beer mecca, one event laid the foundation

meet the brewer
Dean O'Callaghan

Imagine a warm day at the park with someone pedaling something akin to a small cart on a bicycle. Is it a new take on the old-fashioned ice cream man? Not quite. Meet Dean O'Callaghan, or "Deano," a mobile kombucha purveyor in Melbourne. Kombucha is a fermented beverage made of tea, sugar, and a symbiotic colony of bacteria and yeast (SCOBY)—a gelatinous mixture responsible for the drink's fermentation. Deano's business grew into the Good Brew Company, producing solar-powered kombucha along with local beer, cider, soft drinks, and SCOBY in one of the most environmentally friendly and sustainable breweries in Australia. This self-described "eco-fascist" now has a license and can often be found at parks and music festivals in Melbourne with his portable brewery, selling kombucha on-site. It isn't often that a brewer has a mission to "save this world one brew at a time."

for its modern beerscape: the rebuilding of the city's waterworks infrastructure in the late 19th century. Auguste de Bavay, a Belgian chemist who worked for the Victoria Parade brewery, declared his belief that the city's fireplugs (fire hydrants) were letting in germs and sewage, which led to the government laying new pipes, improving water quality and thus the city's beer. He also discovered an Australian wild yeast, *S. de Bavii*, and developed the first commercially used pure yeast. He eventually joined Foster's Brewery, which, by 1895, was selling its beer in more than 40 locales. Such success built brewing giants like the iconic Carlton and United Breweries (CUB), started in 1907.

The U.S. West Coast has had a strong influence on Melbourne's craft beer scene—in the form of hoppy beer and wild beer. Brewers say West Coast IPA is the most popular craft beer style in Melbourne, but its popularity is being challenged by wild ales, such as those from La Sirène. Regardless of which style proves most popular, brewers are increasingly turning to local ingredients—a move that produces interesting variations, offering adventurous beer lovers an ever changing array.

SPARKLING BASTION OF STYLE Founded on the banks of the River Torrens in 1836, Adelaide's proximity to the ocean made it South Australia's bustling port. Numerous industries developed around this burgeoning colony, including brewing. Adelaide's first brewery dates back to 1838. By the mid-1860s there were more than 30 in operation.

One such brewery was founded in the home of

Melbourne is one of the world's most livable cities, and home to two dozen craft breweries.

Thomas Cooper in 1862. It went on to become the now giant Coopers Brewery, which produces Australia's only native beer style: sparkling ale. In Australia's early years, its brewers struggled to reproduce the beers imported from Britain. But necessity is the mother of invention, so Coopers created sparkling ale, a light-colored, bottle-conditioned beer with high carbonation and fruity esters, to get Australians drinking local beer.

The demand for sparkling ale waned as lager became popular, but it remains a distinctly Australian style. Aussie barkeeps find creative ways to shift the sediment that settles at the bottom of a bottle of sparkling ale, turning the beer from clear to the desired haziness. Sometimes they pour the bottle's contents twice to mix it. Sometimes they pour most of the beer then swirl the last bit in the bottle before pouring it out. And sometimes they just roll the bottle along the bar, ensuring the beer is cloudy when it's poured into the glass.

MELBOURNE
Two Birds Golden Ale

Two Birds Brewing's Two Birds Golden Ale combines the melony Australian Summer hop variety with New Zealand's Motueka to create a unique aromatic signature for this easy-drinking session beer.

ABV 4.4% | **IBU** 20

Aroma Apricot, melon, and citrus, with light honey notes

Appearance Full antique gold with amber highlights and white foam

Flavor Dry and brisk, with light caramel notes and stone fruit

Mouthfeel Light-bodied and effervescent

Presentation British pint glass

Food Pairings Seafood, barbecue, goat cheese

ADELAIDE
Sparkling Ale

Australia's only recognized indigenous beer style, sparkling ale is a holdover from the early days of the country's period of colonization. It recalls the original British "Burton ale" but is paler and bottle-conditioned to a very high fizz, making it appear "sparkling."

ABV 4.8–5.8% | **IBU** 30–35

Aroma Lightly malty with notes of apple, pear, and grassy hops

Appearance Honey-colored and clear (if left undisturbed; hazier if the yeast is roused), with orange highlights

Flavor Dry yet biscuity, with an ironlike hop bite and lemon zest and apples into the finish

Mouthfeel Brisk and medium-bodied, with almost scouring carbonation

Presentation Tumbler or British pint glass

Food Pairings Thai and Chinese spicy dishes, shellfish, barbecue, traditional cheddar cheeses

Classic to Try Coopers Brewery Sparkling Ale

New Zealand has been blessed
with the right climate and soils
to grow grains and hops, feeding
its growing beer industry.

NEW ZEALAND

MOUNTAINS OF HOPS

When it comes to describing New Zealand's landscape, "dramatic" is an understatement. Located nearly 1,000 miles (1,600 km) east of Australia, across the turbulent Tasman Sea, this island country is home to beautiful extremes: snow-covered mountains, expansive glaciers, active volcanos, frost blue lakes, unique flora and fauna, and miles of pristine beaches and rocky shores. Its people, nicknamed Kiwis, have had a penchant for beer since the 1700s.

The Maori, who settled New Zealand around the 13th century, were not known to brew beer—at least there is no oral or archaeological evidence to prove it. It was 18th-century settlers from Britain who first introduced it. James Cook, a prominent British cartographer turned explorer began to map the island country in 1769, but he didn't brew New Zealand's first beer until 1773. By that time, beer had long been a staple on sea voyages. Cook erroneously believed that wort and malt prevented scurvy, a disease that plagued many a maritime explorer. The more likely preventive was the vitamin C–rich botanicals native to New Zealand that the brewers added during the brewing process—particularly the young sprucelike tips of the rimu tree and the leaves of a tea tree known as manuka.

Will Paddle for Beer

The first wave of European settlers to this wild land were whalers, sealers, traders, and missionaries. By the 1840s immigrants from Great Britain and Ireland had settled around the coast, bringing their brewing equipment with them. In 1835, English immigrant Joel Samuel Polack established New Zealand's first commercial brewery. In 1850, the Moutere Inn became the country's first pub, and it still operates today. The pubs in this young British colony, predominantly located in hotels like the Moutere, served mostly English-style beer, such as pale ale, porter,

AT A GLANCE
Featured Locations

🛢	Brewery
★	Capital
●	City
NORTH ISLAND	Physical feature
Tasman Sea	Water feature

The world's first triploid cultivars, or **seedless hops,** were developed in New Zealand in the 1970s.

and stout. Locals tell legends about Maori warriors, and even Maori chiefs, stopping by waterfront pubs like the Thistle Inn in Wellington for a quick drink before leaving again by way of a *waka* (canoe).

The Six O'Clock Swill

Between 1917 and 1967, what began as a temporary wartime measure became a standard way of life and wreaked havoc on New Zealand's drinking culture. Under pressure from temperance advocates, called wowsers, the government created a rule that forced public hotels to close their doors at 6 p.m. sharp. Promoted as a patriotic duty and aimed at increasing the workforce's efficiency, it actually led to the six o'clock swill—an hour-long drinking binge shared by working men for 50 years. The drink of choice for this evening binge was beer. NZ draught, to be exact—a native beer style amber or brown in color and malty sweet in taste. This Kiwi brown lager likely evolved from the British mild ale and was highly sessionable, making it a favorite with working-class men. Glasses were filled regularly at standing-room-only pubs, usually from a spigot-adapted plastic hose connected directly to a tank in the cellar or by way of refillable jugs. During these decades, women didn't drink with men—or even serve them drinks. Private bars catering to women did exist, and were normally upstairs from the male-dominated drinking establishments.

Beer was big business, which led to consolidation. The 1920s saw an upswing of mergers and brewery buyouts, and what had been 57 breweries in 1921 dwindled to a duopoly by 1976: Lager-dominated Dominion Breweries and Lion Nathan (now Lion) controlled nearly all the beer sold and consumed. When the 6 p.m. closing-time rule was lifted in 1967, the industry saw a precipitous decline

local flavor
Continuous Fermentation

Most beer is made in batches with a fixed amount of ingredients and for a fixed amount of time. In 1953, New Zealander Morton Coutts figured out a way to ensure that the brewing party never has to stop.

Coutts was an inventor from an early age. At 12, he built a working X-ray machine, and at 13 he became the first Kiwi to broadcast a shortwave radio signal. When he took over the family brewery at 15, he applied his penchant for invention to the business. Then Coutts discovered something revolutionary: how to brew beer continuously. The continuous fermentation process takes some fermented beer and

recycles yeast back to the wort of the next batch to be fermented—a process that can be repeated again and again. Continuous fermentation means that beer can be made constantly, with brewing times shortened from weeks to about 30 hours. It was all the rage in New Zealand, especially during the decades of the six o'clock swill. This system is ideal for making beer rapidly and consistently, but it works best when a brewery is producing only one style—changing styles means stopping fermentation to swap yeast strains. Many abandoned the process in the 1980s because of an increasing demand for more styles.

in beer sales. The decline continued as the decades went on, coinciding with an increasing popularity of wine and spirits. Consumption dropped from 48 gallons (181 L) per adult in 1973 to 17 gallons (63 L) in 2014.

Golding's Free Dive in Wellington has eclectic decorations to match its diverse selection of craft beers.

Shaking Things Up

These days, New Zealand has a lot more to offer than brown lager. Craft beer production started in 1981 with Mac's Gold, a lager from the country's first microbrewery near the hop-centered city of Nelson. Since then the craft beer revolution has gained momentum, with a growing number of breweries and brewpubs. Many have popped up around Nelson on the South Island and the city of Wellington on the North Island. Renowned for using unique hops, such as Motueka, Riwaka, and Nelson Sauvin, New Zealand brewers are creating Kiwi interpretations of classic beer styles, particularly pale ale, IPA, and other hoppy styles. The pungent aromas and flavors of New Zealand hops are new and novel to many, providing flavors unique to the land and climate of New Zealand.

Recent earthquakes such as the 7.1 magnitude temblor in Christchurch in 2010 cut off beer production in some regions, but not even natural catastrophe can keep New Zealand's beer scene down. There are more than 100 microbreweries and brewpubs providing an assortment of world-class beer.

BEER GUIDE

WHERE BEER LOVERS GO

New Zealand is a small country, but it boasts prolific beer scenes in places like Wellington. Try out these breweries and beer-related activities suggested by Kiwi brewers.

1 | Thistle Inn

Wellington

It's no small feat to be the oldest surviving tavern in New Zealand still operating in its original location. The site, which used to be beachfront property, is now several blocks away from the water, thanks to earthquakes and land reclamation. Enjoy a pint at the main bar or one of the unique dining experiences commemorating women's suffrage.

2 | Hashigo Zake

Wellington

If its popularity with locals isn't a good enough reason to check out this underground bar, then go for the beer selection—it represents the best of New Zealand and the world. Discuss the finer points of the craft with the local brewers who congregate here after a long day's work.

3 | Golding's Free Dive

Wellington

In the spirit of the American dive bar, this taproom has it all: science fiction memorabilia, taxidermied animals, dozens of artistically displayed snow skis, and a lot of strung lights. The

impressive list of tapped and bottled beer from New Zealand and abroad only makes this tucked-away bar more enjoyable.

4 | Shakespeare Hotel and Brewery

Auckland

In the play *Henry V,* Shakespeare wrote, "I would give all my fame for a pot of ale . . ." If you, too, wish for a pot of ale, pay a call at New Zealand's first brewpub. The distinctive red bricks set this hotel and brewpub apart from the towering skyscrapers of the central business district. Enjoy one of its many unfiltered, unpasteurized beers on tap.

5 | The Occasional Brewer

Wellington

Want to make beer instead of just drink it? With 12 styles and professional equipment, this is a place to make your homebrewing dreams come true. If you aren't sure what style to choose, don't worry—you can step up to the small bar and sample a range before you brew.

6 | Nelson Beer Trail

Nelson

This hot spot region for wine is also a hot spot for hops and boasts more than 10 breweries. Go on a tour of breweries and bars like the Totara Brewing Company—the country's only brewery located on a hop farm—and the Mussel Inn, where you can enjoy a pot of mussels with its popular historic beer based on an original recipe recorded by Captain James Cook.

7 | Garage Project

Wellington

This former automobile shop makes some of the most interesting and eclectic beer in

New Zealand. Go to the tasting room across the street to sample a few of the brewery's dozen or so available styles.

8 | Pomeroy's Old Brewery Inn

Christchurch

Housed in the historic Wards Brewery, this English-style pub is warm and inviting, and the beer on tap is some of New Zealand's finest. Owner Steve Pomeroy is gracious and entertaining; combine that with the pub's comfortable ambience and you'll see why this is the go-to place to enjoy a pint.

Photos

1 *The Thistle Inn opened in 1840 in Wellington.* **2** *Brewers come to relax at Wellington's Hashigo Zake beer bar.* **4** *The Shakespeare Hotel and Brewery serves up beer inspired by the famous bard.* **6** *Jane Dixon and her family run the Mussel Inn brewery in Onekaka.* **7** *The Garage Project creates some of the country's best brews.*

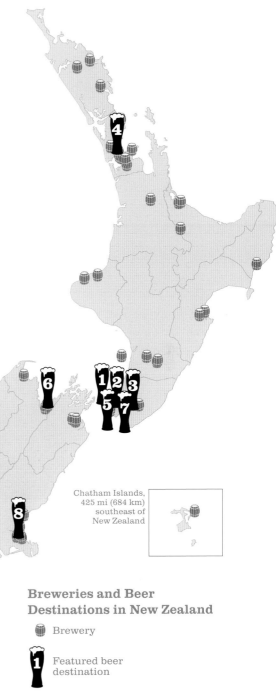

Chatham Islands, 425 mi (684 km) southeast of New Zealand

Breweries and Beer Destinations in New Zealand

🛢 Brewery

1 Featured beer destination

LOCAL BREWS

NELSON & WELLINGTON

CELEBRATING ALL THINGS BEER

HOP HEADS The North and South Islands both produce excellent beer, but which is home to the country's craft beer capital? Is it the Nelson region, located on the northern edge of the South Island? Or is it the rocky shores of Wellington, nestled 146 miles (235 km) across the Cook Strait on the North Island's southern side? Both have claims to the title, but Nelson has an agricultural edge: a perfect latitude and geography for cultivating hops. Family-run breweries, hotels, and taverns have grown up alongside the region's hop industry, resulting in its having the most breweries per capita in the country.

English and German settlers planted hops in the 1840s, but these didn't adapt well, so most hops were imported from Europe. Strained relations with Europe after World War II led to restrictions on hops importation, which led to the rise of a U.S. hop variety called California Cluster. When black root rot struck California's hops in the 1930s, the New Zealand Hop Research Committee worked to develop a fungus-resistant crop. It actually created three: First Choice,

New Zealand's oldest pub still operates in its original building.

Smooth Cone, and Calicross. Since then, New Zealand scientists and hop growers have cultivated new hops with distinctive, sought-after characteristics.

At the Hop Research Station in Riwaka, a small town 32 miles (52 km) northwest of Nelson, researchers have developed some of the brewing world's cult-classic hops. One is Nelson Sauvin, named after both Nelson and the Sauvignon Blanc wine grapes grown there. The hop and the grape have similar aromas and flavors: something akin to gooseberry, with hints of boozy, grapelike peach or passion fruit. Other all-star varieties include Rakau, a dual-purpose hop used for both bittering and aroma; Motueka, the Czech Saaz hybrid known for its flavors of lemon and lime zest; Wakatu, a German Hallertau hybrid with notes of citrus and fresh-cut flowers; and Riwaka, an aromatic hop with grapefruit characteristics.

DEVOTED TO CRAFT In the competition for the craft beer capital crown, Wellington wins out when it comes to the sheer number of breweries, brewpubs,

and beer bars, all of which reflect a local culture devoted to beer. One out of every three pints of New Zealand's craft beer is consumed in Wellington—that's a third of the country's beer drunk by around 10 percent of its population. But Wellington's craft beer devotion doesn't stop in its beer bars. Local restaurants and cafés treat their beer lists with the same appreciation as their wine lists, even if beer names like Sauvignon Bomb, Four Horsemen of the Hopocalypse, and Bouncing Czech are a bit tongue in cheek. Brewers here certainly have a sense of humor! It's easy to find a café bar where baristas are also bartenders, pulling double duty as they serve artisanal coffee and craft beer on tap. The city hosts the country's largest annual beer festival and it even boasts the Craft Beer College, where you can take either a short afternoon course on the basics of the burgeoning craft beer scene or more in-depth brewing classes using professional-grade equipment and high-quality ingredients under the careful instruction of Kiwi brewmasters.

local flavor
The Kiwi Pint

Defining a "pint" is a tricky thing. Historically, pint size is based on the size of a gallon, but there was a time when many different volumes were considered a gallon. In New Zealand, where beer is quite expensive, one of the most pressing reasons for this variation is cost. During World War II, the standard beer was 10 ounces (9.7 U.S. fl. oz.) and sold at a government-fixed price of sixpence. While most of New Zealand upped the price of beer to sevenpence in 1942, the increase didn't go into place on the west coast of the South Island until 1947, at which time west coast drinkers revolted, resulting in the Greymouth beer boycott. The boycott brought the price back to sixpence, but not for long. The 10-ounce was eventually replaced with the 7- and 12-ounce, and the cost of beer has increased steadily ever since.

 on tap with Garrett Oliver

NELSON
New Zealand Pilsner

Even before the modern craft beer movement took hold in New Zealand, brewers began using unique New Zealand hops like Nelson Sauvin and Motueka to create bold new flavors in otherwise traditional pilsners. New Zealanders also pioneered organic hop farming.

ABV 4.9–5.2% | **IBU** 22–30
Aroma Floral with a big overlay of citrus, gooseberry, and passion fruit notes
Appearance Full, clear gold with white foam
Flavor Crisp and direct, holding the malts dry while the hops bring fruit
Mouthfeel Dry and snappy yet softly textured
Presentation Pilsner glass
Food Pairings Great with hams, grilled seafood, and sushi—versatile
Craft to Try Emerson's Brewery New Zealand Pilsner

WELLINGTON
New Zealand IPA

Just as American brewers adapted the British IPA style to their own ingredients and tastes, so have the brewers of New Zealand adapted the American IPA to their own unique hops. Hops such as Nelson Sauvin have become mainstays of New Zealand brewing.

ABV 5.5–7% | **IBU** 50–70
Aroma Passion fruit and mangolike hop aromatics jumping out of the glass
Appearance Golden to amber and slightly hazy, with a small head
Flavor Sharply bitter but balanced, with mineral drive and big tropical fruitiness
Mouthfeel Medium-bodied, dry and flinty
Presentation Pint or Willi Becher glass
Food Pairings Spicy Thai cuisine, robust seafood, Tex-Mex, barbecue
Craft to Try 8 Wired HopWired New Zealand IPA

WHAT'S BREWING

in
OCEANIA

Fiji

This former British colony is the third most populous nation in Oceania, though only one-third of its 330 islands are inhabited. It has four breweries, which produce mainly lager (and mostly for tourists). In recent years, Carlton and United Breweries (AB InBev) and Coca-Cola have each purchased a brewery. Not bad for a country that needs to import ingredients to make beer.

65
12-oz beers (23 L)
Annual consumption per capita

170,400
U.S. barrels (200,000 hL)
Annual production

4.58
Fijian dollars (U.S. $2.20)
Average price of a 12-oz bottle

New Caledonia

This French overseas territory has two breweries, Brasserie le Froid and Grande Brasseries de Nouvelle-Calédonie, the latter of which is owned by Heineken. If pale lagers just won't suffice, there is a beer made with lychee fruit. Plan ahead, as beer is not for sale from noon until 9 p.m. Friday through Sunday, except at hotels and restaurants frequented by tourists.

25
12-oz beers (9 L)
Annual consumption per capita

85,200
U.S. barrels (100,000 hL)
Annual production

133.54
CFP (Comptoirs Français du Pacifique) francs (U.S. $1.19)
Average price of a 12-oz bottle

Zimbabwe's national beer shares the name of the Zambezi, a winding river that feeds the awe-inspiring Victoria Falls.

AFRICA

Papua New Guinea

The beer scene in Papua New Guinea is dominated by its lone brewery, South Pacific Brewery (owned by Heineken), which has won awards at the Monde Selection competition in Belgium and at the Australian International Beer Awards. If pale lager is not your thing, imported beer is also available in larger cities, and there's always the traditional high-alcohol homebrew, called *stim*.

51
12-oz beers (18 L)
Annual consumption per capita

600,000
U.S. barrels (700,000 hL)
Annual production

5.46
Papua New Guinean kina (U.S. $1.72)
Average price of a 12-oz bottle

Tahiti

The first brewery in Oceania outside Australia and New Zealand was founded in tropical Tahiti in 1914. Today, you can find two breweries and a surprising variety of beer styles beyond pale lager, including bière de Mars and bière de Nöel—not surprising given the country's French connection.

28
12-oz beers (10 L)
Annual consumption per capita

170,400
U.S. barrels (200,000 hL)
Annual production

409.59
CFP (Comptoirs Français du Pacifique) francs
(U.S. $3.65)
Average price of a 12-oz bottle

*Numbers were accurate at the time of printing.
They are averages, subject to change over time.*

Zulu beer such as *umqombothi*, which is made from sorghum, is traditionally brewed by women.

ANCIENT BEER ORIGINS

In Africa, contrasts abound: Arid deserts run up against expansive grasslands, and dense rain forests give way to fertile plains. This diverse land of extremes gave rise to modern humans (*Homo sapiens*)—and thus, in a way, it gave rise to beer. As humans migrated, they took grains like millet and barley with them. Grains were cultivated in order to make bread, but some scholars argue that it was people's desire for beer that drove the development of agriculture. From ancient Egyptian times—when it was an important healthy staple of a person's diet—to the modern day, beer has always been a way of life.

Drink of the Gods

Beer came to prominence with the rise of the ancient Egyptians, particularly from 3500 B.C. until Alexander the Great conquered Egypt in 332 B.C. The Egyptians believed that the art of brewing came directly from Osiris, the god of fertility and the afterlife. They actually learned it from the Sumerians, who lived in what is now Iraq. Everyone drank beer, as it was healthier than water and considered to be a food akin to bread. Temples had their own breweries; beer had its own goddess, Tenenet; and the laborers who built the pyramids at Giza were paid in beer rations. Ancient Egyptian hieroglyphics mention many kinds: "dark beer," "sweet beer," "friend's beer," and even "beer of truth," drunk by the gods who protected the shrine of Osiris.

Africa

███ Country in this chapter

Ancient Egyptians used barley to make their beer, but much of Africa brewed with sorghum, a native grass well adapted to the droughts and high temperatures that dominate most of the African continent. Wine took over when Alexander the Great conquered Egypt, and beer was suppressed by heavy taxation and regulation. Large-scale brewing went dormant in Egypt, but it lives on in the traditional brewing customs passed down through the generations.

Lasting Traditions

Traditional African homebrew is the omnipresent ambrosia for social occasions and religious rituals. Opaque and low in alcohol, most homebrews are foamy and consumed while they are still fermenting; if they sit too long, they will spoil in the heat.

Some African brewers strike a **match** over a vat of beer to check if it's ready. If the match goes out, the beer is done.

Indigenous beer is local by nature, its traditions passed down by the women who brew it. Brewers rely on local wild yeasts and bacteria to convert the sugars in grains to alcohol, creating beers that vary widely in taste and aroma. Indigenous beer is worth trying, but make sure to sample it from reputable sources, as some brewers adulterate the beer with poisonous compounds to expedite fermentation.

Sorghum is one of the oldest and most popular grains used to produce Africa's indigenous beer. It creates a slightly sour-tasting beer that is rich in calories and B vitamins. Sorghum beers are as varied as the names they are known by: *umqombothi* from South Africa, *doro* from Zimbabwe, *ikigage* from Rwanda, *merissa* from Sudan, and *tchoukoutou* from Benin.

Some traditional brews, such as *oshikundu* from Namibia and *oyokpo* from Nigeria, are made with millet, which adds a nutty flavor. Cassava root is used in the tropical regions, producing beer that is relatively sweet and light. In Ethiopia, a grass called teff is mixed with maize and *gesho*, a bittering agent, to create *tella*.

Indigenous beer is popular—some estimates suggest that Africans consume far more homebrew than they do commercial beer, though such an informal population is hard to poll—but most of the commercial beer on offer is European-style adjunct lager.

brewline
Historic Moments in Beer

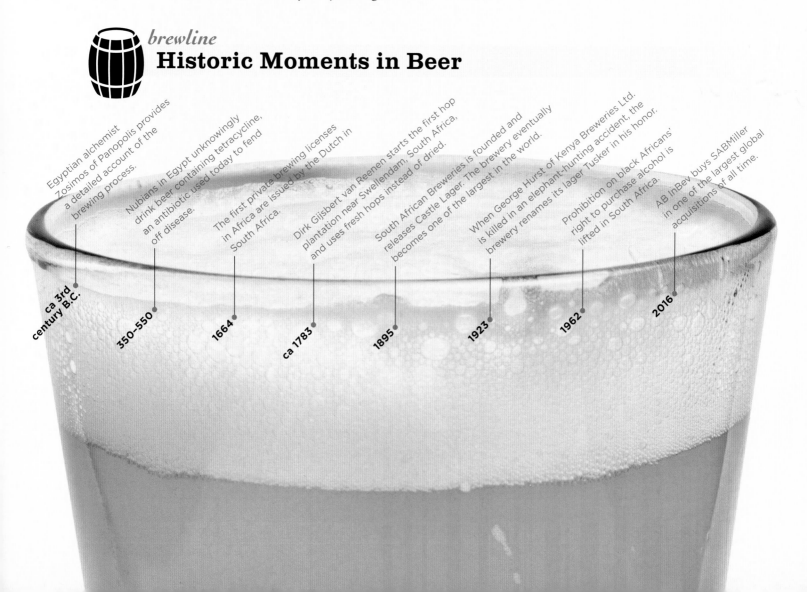

ca 3rd century B.C. Egyptian alchemist Zosimos of Panopolis provides a detailed account of the brewing process.

350–550 Nubians in Egypt unknowingly drink beer containing tetracycline, an antibiotic used today to fend off disease.

1664 The first private brewing licenses in Africa are issued by the Dutch in South Africa.

ca 1783 Dirk Gijsbert van Reenen starts the first hop plantation near Swellendam, South Africa, and uses fresh hops instead of dried.

1895 South African Breweries is founded and releases Castle Lager. The brewery eventually becomes one of the largest in the world.

1923 When George Hurst of Kenya Breweries Ltd. is killed in an elephant-hunting accident, the brewery renames its lager Tusker in his honor.

1962 Prohibition on black Africans' right to purchase alcohol is lifted in South Africa.

2016 AB InBev buys SABMiller in one of the largest global acquisitions of all time.

Africa's Best Beer Festivals

Clarens Craft Beer Festival | CLARENS | SOUTH AFRICA | Located just north of Lesotho, this beer festival features a curated list of craft breweries, ensuring the best South African craft beers are available for sampling. *February*

Africa Beer Festival | MASERU | LESOTHO | From breweries to traditional homebrewers, this festival celebrates African beer culture, culminating each evening with a huge bonfire and traditional dancing. *May*

Jo'burg Bierfest | JOHANNESBURG | SOUTH AFRICA | One of the highlights of this German-themed beer festival is a costume contest for the best dressed King Ludwig and Princess Therese of Bavaria. *September*

Oktoberfest Namibia | WINDHOEK | NAMIBIA | This festival requires that its beer follow the German purity law—barley, hops, water, and yeast are the only ingredients allowed. Attractions include log sawing and a keg-lifting competition. *October*

Beer festivals are growing in popularity across Africa.

Cape Town Festival of Beer | CAPE TOWN | SOUTH AFRICA | With more than 60 local and international breweries and serving 200 varieties of beer, this festival claims to be the largest in the Southern Hemisphere. *November*

Nairobi Art and Beer Festival | NAIROBI | KENYA | This festival offers 48 straight hours of music, arts, crafts, dancing, food, and local and international beers. Add another 48 hours to recover. *Month varies*

European Flavor

The beer the European colonialists introduced made a permanent impression on the continent. By the 1900s, the Dutch, English, and Germans all had established breweries in Africa—some are the oldest companies on the continent today. With the advent of refrigeration and a lot of ingenuity, South Africa saw the rise of South African Breweries (SAB)—now owned by AB InBev, the world's largest brewing conglomerate—and its mass-produced lagers.

Although many of these well-known brand-name lagers—Tusker in East Africa and Castle in South Africa, to name a couple—can be purchased cold in grocery stores and pubs, roadside kiosks remain popular. They sell warm lager alongside indigenous brews. Large breweries are now making beer with cassava and sorghum. They hope to entice Africa's homebrew drinkers by using local ingredients to bring some regional flavor into their offerings.

The African Lion bar, part of the SAB World of Beer museum in Johannesburg, feels like a time machine to the 19th century.

SOUTH AFRICA

A TALE OF TWO TRADITIONS

On the southern tip of the continent, South Africa is a land of dramatic variety. The country's narrow strip of coastal plains runs up against the vast grasslands of its high plateaus, combining into a landscape in which waterfalls crash and herds of animals roam. The extreme nature of the geography has found its way into South Africa's culture and politics, and has played an important role in shaping its two distinct, and sometimes contentious, beer traditions.

Well before Europeans established the first permanent settlement in 1652 at the Cape of Good Hope, the most southwestern point of the African continent, local women were brewing up sweetly soured sorghum beers like *umqombothi* for traditional rituals, meetings, and celebratory social gatherings. But then the Europeans came, bringing their preferences and beer ingredients with them.

Jan van Riebeeck brought beer to South Africa from the Netherlands when he arrived in Cape Town in 1652, and beer was being brewed there by 1658. The outpost was set up as a stopover for the ships of the Dutch East India Company, which had issued brewing licenses to colonials in 1664 to produce small quantities of beer, most of which was sold to sailors for their long sea voyages. Although the production of beer earned Cape Town the nickname "Tavern of the Seas," the Dutch East India Company's monopoly over imported ingredients and terms of sale stifled the beer industry. After the British took control in the early 1800s, new breweries sprang up, some of which consolidated and formed South African Breweries in 1895.

Taking Beer Underground

As the country's mining sector grew in the late 1890s, particularly with the gold rush around Johannesburg, so, too, did the demand for workers—a need that blacks rushed in to fill. But white mine owners worried that alcohol was curtailing

AT A GLANCE
Number of Craft
Breweries per Province

▨	Greater than 50
▨	26–50
▨	10–25
▨	Fewer than 10
GAUTENG	Province

All but one apartheid-run beer hall was burned or destroyed around the **1976** Soweto Uprising.

workers' productivity, and the Prohibition Act passed in 1897 made it illegal for blacks to consume it. Later, when the 1927 Liquor Act prohibited nonwhite South Africans from selling alcohol or entering licensed premises, mine bosses would often provide workers with their own beer, but on their own terms—giving it away as a reward for hard work. Despite the restrictions on alcohol, addiction was common; those who fell victim became known as *isidakwa,* Zulu for "drunkard."

Women brewers in black townships continued to brew beer despite years of temperance and racial discrimination. These "shebeen queens," named after the Irish word for places that illegally sell alcohol, brewed in secret during the apartheid years to provide men with an outlet to drink and as a source of income, independence, and power. Many of the women buried drums containing the illegal contraband underground to ferment. Networks of family members and neighbors would serve as lookouts whenever beer was dug up or reburied in these concealed drums, as the apartheid state made suspicion of homebrewing a key reason for raiding homes. When the apartheid government got in on the alcohol business after the Liquor Act was amended in 1962, many of the beer halls constructed in black townships were met with massive boycotts led by women who owned shebeens.

More than a decade after the fall of apartheid in 1994, an estimated 182,000 shebeens existed in South Africa. Today, they are the legal go-to place to buy alcohol, eat a meal, catch up on the latest local gossip, or watch a cricket match on TV.

local flavor
Umqombothi: The Original Craft Beer

Traditionally brewed in grass hut villages and drunk from a communal *calabash*, or bottle gourd, this is a low-alcohol, everyday beer, also consumed during social ceremonies, *imbizos* (group discussions), ancestral rituals, weddings, and funerals.

Umqombothi is traditionally made from maize and sorghum and brewed by women, usually the matriarchs of extended families, armed with secret traditions and recipes. While these vary from region to region, the beer is commonly made in a large-mouth drum by adding water and maize malt to a sorghum porridge, which is boiled, allowed to cool, and then left to stand for between three to five days. In some cases, the mixture is left exposed to the air and airborne yeast settles in. In other cases, yeast remaining from previous batches is added after cooling.

Before it's imbibed, a small amount is traditionally spit on the ground for the ancestors. Zulu tradition requires that women try the beer first to make sure it's safe before giving it to the men. Households that sell the beverage sometimes do so by the pail, which consumers bring with them much like a growler.

Most *Umqombothi* recipes are guarded family secrets.

Craft Versus Giant

While homebrewing has been going on for centuries in South Africa, the modern commercial beer scene is dominated by SAB, now AB InBev. It controls most of the domestic beer market and is part of the world's largest beer conglomerate. AB InBev is also a key producer of barley and hops, and hence controls their domestic distribution. The running joke in South Africa is that craft beer is any beer not brewed by AB InBev, but other global heavyweights such as Diageo and Heineken International have also entered the South African beer market.

A small craft beer scene is growing amid these titans, particularly in Johannesburg and the Western Cape. Mitchell's, the country's first modern craft brewery, opened in 1983 in the small coastal town of Knysna and soon enjoyed widespread popularity. Though it no longer counts as a craft brewery, Mitchell's is now the country's second largest brewery, proving that local, flavorful beer can be produced under brewery conditions.

While the craft market has recently been growing at roughly 30 percent a year, craft brewers are aware that they still face many obstacles. The craft brewery market share is small—around 2 percent—and it faces high start-up costs, low production, and a pricey end product. Some craft brewers obtain their ingredients, particularly barley, from AB InBev, forging a unique relationship between South Africa's small artisanal breweries and the largest brewing conglomerate in the world.

Beer is a popular addition to any *braai*, an outdoor cooking ritual that is now entrenched in South African culture.

BEER GUIDE

WHERE BEER LOVERS GO

South Africa is the continent's undisputed beermaking mecca. These local-brewer-picked destinations will help visitors choose from the country's many outstanding breweries.

1 | Market on Main

Johannesburg

This vibrant, bustling market in Maboneng is a great place for beer lovers to spend an afternoon. Check out the vendors preparing meals that range from traditional African dishes to Moroccan and Italian cuisine, and then enjoy a craft beer or two from resident craft brewery SMACK! Republic Brewing.

2 | Devil's Peak Brewing Company

Cape Town

This brewery takes its name from the towering icon of Devil's Peak, which gets its name from an urban legend about a pipe-smoking duel between a Dutch pirate and the devil. It uses local ingredients and educates beer drinkers on the various U.S., English, and Belgian beer styles it brews.

3 | Banana Jam Cafe

Cape Town

This Caribbean-themed pub offers more than 30 draft beers

Breweries and Beer Destinations in South Africa

🍺 Brewery

1 Featured beer destination

struggle of black South Africans adorn the walls and patio, offering up stories of their own.

5 | KwaZulu-Natal Beer Route

Eastern South Africa

This self-drive beer route is a treasure hunt for beer lovers—a chance to try some of the region's best craft beer while traveling through spectacular scenery. Spend a few days visiting breweries in Durban and the Valley of a Thousand Hills, then on to the Midlands and Zululand. Just make sure to have a designated driver in your group.

fully functioning nanobrewery called the Afro Caribbean Brewing Company. It makes unique craft beer styles, including its Coconut IPA and Bacon Chili Ale.

4 | Ubuntu Kraal Brewery

Soweto

This unassuming brewery is located in the Soweto township, not far from the Mandela House. Grab a pint of Soweto Gold and listen to the locals' stories. Photos, statues, and other museum pieces commemorating the

and 80 bottled beers. The kitchen can whip up just about anything patrons are in the mood for, from jerk chicken to goat curry to pizza. But the real gem is hidden away upstairs—a

Photos

1 Organic ingredients from *Exotically Divine Ital at Market on Main* complement any beer. **3** Banana Jam owner Greg Casey (right) and head brewer Shawn Duthie (left) visit with the authors. **4** Ubuntu Kraal Brewery carries on the Zulu tradition of female brewers. **5** The KwaZulu-Natal beer route starts at a picturesque beach.

LOCAL BREWS

CAPE TOWN & JOHANNESBURG

TINKERING WITH TRADITION

A CRAFT BREWING HUB With the Atlantic Ocean on one side and Table Mountain on the other, Cape Town has a picturesque setting that's home to more breweries than any other town in South Africa. Though the Western Cape is known globally for wines such as Chenin Blanc and Cabernet Sauvignon, Cape Town and its surrounding regions are becoming a hot spot for craft beer as well.

For Capetonians, living in South Africa's beer hub comes with certain perks. These include outstanding craft breweries like Jack Black's Brewing Company (named after the 1900s brewer, not the actor) and Devil's Peak Brewing Company, as well as taprooms like Beerhouse and Banana Jam Cafe that offer samples of the region's best brews. As the number of breweries increases, third-party companies such as Adventure Brew are starting to offer brewery tours for patrons to sample the region's varied beer offerings.

Yet despite its growth, the craft brewing industry is still quite small in South Africa. Since the nation's first craft brewery, Mitchell's, opened in the Western

Kitchener's Carvery Bar: a bustling pub in Johannesburg

Cape in 1983, craft beer has come to account for less than 2 percent (by volume) of all beers sold in South Africa. Craft breweries in the Western Cape region are working to increase their market share. And with more creative breweries entering the market, the future looks bright for a diverse and varied beer scene, which is expected to grow as much as 30 percent in the next few years.

FROM SHEBEENS TO TAPROOMS Johannesburg, called Jo'burg or Jozi by the locals, is steeped in a history of boom and bust, decay and renewal. Africa's first lager was brewed here in 1895 by South African Breweries. Castle lager was a hit with local miners, many of whom were living in squalid conditions in mine-owned compounds and hastily constructed housing in and around Johannesburg. SAB became the first industrial company listed on the Johannesburg Stock Exchange in 1897, followed by the London Stock Exchange a year later. Its recent sale to AB InBev included exclusive beer-selling rights for South Africa's cricket and football matches.

Nearby Soweto, a township developed for blacks under the oppressive apartheid system that has ramshackle narrow streets and shanties to this day, was home to many informal shebeens during apartheid. Illicit breweries and taverns kept the alcohol flowing in oppressed black communities and became meeting places and refuges for antiapartheid activists. The number of shebeens totaled around 4,000 in Soweto by 1989. Shebeens are now (mostly) legal, and the beverages made and imbibed within them include traditional beer styles as well as commercial beer.

The drinking scene has opened up since the fall of apartheid in 1994. Several up-and-coming breweries such as Oaks Brew House and Just Brewing make an assortment of traditional, European, and U.S. styles, while taprooms like Beerhouse Fourways and the Taphouse Pint Size Pub provide patrons with a wide selection of craft beers. Craft and traditional beer styles are crossing divides and are being embraced by a new generation of brewers and consumers.

meet the brewer
Nick Bush

What did Nick Bush, the head brewer of Drifter Brewing Company in Cape Town, do when he ran out of temperature-controlled space in which to store his beer? A scuba diver as well as a homebrewer, Bush found himself a cool place to stash it—about 100 feet (30 m) underwater. After he homebrewed a Belgian tripel, he decided the ocean would be the perfect place to stockpile his liquid gold. Bush does lament the effort it takes to retrieve the beer, but the treasure is worth diving for. Drifter's beer is influenced by African flavors, like its Stranded Coconut session ale made with Mozambican coconut.

on tap with Garrett Oliver

CAPE TOWN
Devil's Peak Brewing Company Vin de Saison

Devil's Peak Brewing Company takes advantage of the area's rich vineyard bounty by blending 20 percent Swartland Chenin Blanc grape must (juice) into a classic saison recipe to create a drink that rests on the border between wine and beer.

ABV 7.5% | **IBU** 20
Aroma Lemon, grape, white pepper, and oak, with a barnyard-like wild yeast character
Appearance Hazy pale orange with white foam
Flavor Dry and lightly acidic with bright lemon, honey, and grape notes
Mouthfeel Fine-bubbled and creamy
Presentation Tulip, Teku, or white wine glass
Food Pairings Fatty fish, pork, *braai* (traditional barbecue), aged goat cheeses.

JOHANNESBURG
Umqombothi

A porridge-like, funky sour beer that locals say is best drunk very fresh.

ABV Usually around 3% | **IBU** 0–5
Aroma Lactic and funky, with notes of yogurt, fruit, earth, and gasoline
Appearance Translucent to opaque, often with a pink hue
Flavor Yogurtlike, with earthy, fruity notes
Mouthfeel Flat to slightly sparkling, resembling a light porridge or yogurt drink
Presentation Traditionally drunk from a hollowed-out gourd, but today often packed in cardboard milk containers
Food Pairings Often consumed alone but sometimes with *braai* (barbecue), bunny chow (bread stuffed with spicy curry), or *bobotie* (meat stew)
Classic to Try Egoli Brewery Joburg Beer

While homebrewed beer dominates Tanzanian drinking culture, you can find draft and bottled beer at many local restaurants.

TANZANIA

HOMEGROWN BREWING

Tanzania's natural splendor attracts more than a million tourists each year, many of whom arrive thirsty. On offer are the country's widespread macrobrewery lagers, but the homebrewing tradition is also on full display in *mbege*, the country's indigenous banana beer.

Outside of mbege, the history of beer here is relatively young. The country has had various colonial rulers, including Portugal, the Arabs, Germany, and Great Britain. Typically only expats were permitted to consume alcohol, much of it imported from Europe. The country's first brewery, Tanganyika Breweries, was established in 1932, decades before the country gained independence in 1964. Kenya Breweries purchased it three years later, changing its name in 1936 to the one it bears today—East African Breweries Ltd. Local pride shows through in Tanzania's regional beers, especially those named after the country's most famous attractions: Kilimanjaro, Serengeti, Safari, and Ndovu ("elephant" in Swahili).

Primed for Growth

Beer is big business in modern-day Tanzania. Data shows that beer sales are an important source of tax revenue. In fact, Tanzania Breweries Limited is the country's single largest taxpayer. But a bigger story lies hidden from commercial view. The World Health Organization estimates that 90 percent of the beer consumed in Tanzania is part of an informal sector of the economy—it's not reported to the government, and thus no taxes are paid. Such data suggests that 90 percent of the beer consumed in Tanzania is not coming from large macrobreweries. Instead, it's coming from home kitchens producing local—and comparatively

AT A GLANCE
Featured Locations

- 🛢 Brewery
- ★ Capital
- ● City
- ✛ Peak
- *Zanzibar* Physical feature

inexpensive—homebrews like mbege. More than half of the population lives below the poverty line, and bottled beer is six times more expensive than homebrew. So though beer made at home varies widely from batch to batch, prompting health concerns, homebrew is the more cost-effective choice.

Even with so many people drinking homebrew, the country's demographics are ripe for an expanding beer market. Nearly half the population falls into the 15- to 45-year-old category—the age bracket most likely to spend money on beer. There are no craft breweries currently operating in Tanzania, and craft beer is priced too high to sell in sufficient quantities. Even so, population and income projections make Tanzania increasingly attractive to entrepreneurs who want to invest in the country's brewing future.

local flavor
Mbege: Banana Beer

Mbege, the popular indigenous beer from northeastern Tanzania, is traditionally brewed by the women of the Chagga people who live on the slopes of Mount Kilimanjaro. Brewers start by making *nyalu*, a porridge made from bananas that are peeled, boiled for hours, and then set aside to ferment spontaneously for several days. The banana mixture is strained, added into the *mso* (a wort made from malted finger millet), and set aside. The result is a thick, opaque, yellowish-brown beer with a 5 to 8 percent ABV, a sweetness from the bananas, and a sourness from the millet. Some find it more akin to wine than beer in taste.

The beer plays an important part in indigenous ceremonies, where protocol mandates that the eldest person present drinks first, as a sign of respect. Mbege is passed around at weddings, funerals, celebrations, and business meetings and drunk until it's time to refill. It also generates an important income stream in the informal sector of the economy, and can be found at local bars. Though the government has been cracking down on households that brew mbege, citing health reasons as well as lost tax revenues, this long-held brewing tradition helps define the local culture and remains popular with the older generations.

Banana beer is traditionally sipped through a hollow reed straw in many countries in Africa.

BEER GUIDE

WHERE BEER LOVERS GO

Tanzania's beer scene is small but growing. These recommendations from local brewers will make sure visitors don't miss its hidden gems.

1 | Ambassador Lounge and Executive Bar

Mwanza

On the ninth floor of a building with a panoramic view of Tanzania's second largest city, this bar offers a great selection of the country's beer. After a day of wildlife-viewing in Serengeti National Park, enjoy a Serengeti Premium Lager as the sun sets over Lake Victoria.

2 | George and Dragon

Dar es Salaam

This English pub is a favorite with locals and expats alike. Try a local beer or a wide selection of imported English ale while watching the latest football match taking place back in England.

3 | Taperia Wine and Tapas Bar

Zanzibar

Located in a former post office, this bar boasts one of the widest beer (and wine) lists on the island.

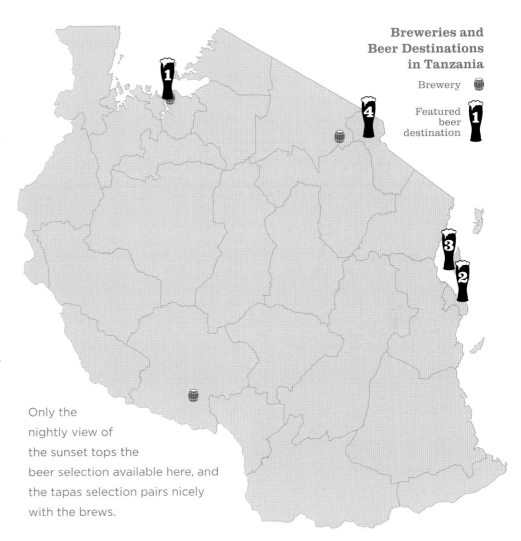

Breweries and Beer Destinations in Tanzania

Brewery 🛢

Featured beer destination 🍺1

Only the nightly view of the sunset tops the beer selection available here, and the tapas selection pairs nicely with the brews.

4 | Pub Alberto

Moshi

Those looking to enjoy a cold beer on the lower slopes of Mount Kilimanjaro should make sure to stop in this pub. It's a favorite with tourists and doubles as a nightclub as the evening wears on. It also has one of the largest varieties of beer available for miles around.

WHAT'S BREWING

in
AFRICA

Angola

France's Castel Group dominates the beer industry in the isolated coastal country of Angola. But traditional beer powers are facing challenges from a new player, the China Investment Fund, which has opened a $180 million brewery in the capital city of Luanda. Angola is seen as an up-and-coming beer market in Africa, so it's likely that new breweries will open soon.

175
12-oz beers (62 L)
Annual consumption per capita

9.4
million U.S. barrels (11 million hL)
Annual production

346.41
Angolan kwanzas (U.S. $2.09)
Average price of a 12-oz bottle

Democratic Republic of the Congo

Though the country is a former Belgian colony, Belgian beer is difficult to find. French- and Dutch-owned breweries are far more common, all producing ubiquitous lagers. The apparent lack of choice in terms of beer styles has not stopped the Congolese from drinking beer—they have the fourth highest beer consumption rate on the continent.

113
12-oz beers (40 L)
Annual consumption per capita

3.8
million U.S. barrels (4.5 million hL)
Annual production

1,603.24
Congolese francs (U.S. $1.16)
Average price of a 12-oz bottle

Namibia

German colonists brought beer production to the sand dunes and plains of Namibia. All abided by the Reinheitsgebot, the German beer purity law restricting beer's ingredients to barley, hops, and water (see page 53). Many of Namibia's brewers still follow the Reinheitsgebot today, by choice. Most craft beer in Namibia is exported to the larger market in South Africa.

293
12-oz beers (104 L)
Annual consumption per capita

2.1
million U.S. barrels (2.5 million hL)
Annual production

16.07
Namibian dollars (U.S. $1.21)
Average price of a 12-oz bottle

Gabon

Gabon, straddling the Equator and dense with beautiful rain forests, has some of the lowest beer prices in both the Northern and Southern Hemispheres. There is no tax levied on beer, and international beer is easy to import.

251
12-oz beers (89 L)
Annual consumption per capita

1.3
million U.S. barrels (1.5 million hL)
Annual production

462.62
Central African CFA
(Communauté Financière Africaine) francs
(U.S. $0.75)
Average price of a 12-oz bottle

Numbers were accurate at the time of printing.
They are averages, subject to change over time.

adjunct Any ingredient added to beer that isn't malted barley, hops, water, or yeast. Adjuncts may include grains such as maize (to lower the cost), fruit (to add flavor), and sugar (to increase the alcohol content).

alcohol by volume (ABV) The amount of alcohol (ethanol) in a given volume of a beverage, expressed as a percentage

ale One of the two major beer types, produced using top-fermenting yeast.

alpha acid The soft resin of the hop flower, which converts to iso-alpha acids during the boiling process and is responsible for a beer's bitterness

attenuation A measurement of how much sugar is converted into alcohol during fermentation, expressed as a percentage

barrel A unit of measurement. A U.S. barrel holds 31 U.S. gallons (1.17 hL) and the British barrel holds 36 imperial gallons (1.64 hL). Also, a wooden vessel used to ferment or age (condition) beer.

beer An alcoholic beverage made from fermented grains (malt)

bitterness The perceived bitter flavor of beer, imparted by the iso-alpha acids derived from hops. It's measured in International Bittering Units (IBUs).

blending The mixing of two or more batches of beer

body The perceived thickness or fullness (density or viscosity) of a given beer in the mouth

bottom fermentation A process in which fermentation occurs at or near the bottom of the fermentation vessel where yeast has settled

brewpub A restaurant that houses a brewery and sells more than 25 percent of its beer on-site

carbonation The effervescence from carbon dioxide introduced into beer, either naturally during the fermentation process or forced by the injection of a pressurized gas into a vessel or liquid

cask A container that holds beer. It's usually barrel-shaped and made of wood or stainless steel and aluminum.

cellaring Aging, storing, or maturing beer at a controlled temperature

cereal grain Any grass species that yields an edible grain. Examples include barley, wheat, millet, sorghum, oats, rye, and maize.

conditioning The brewing process after the primary fermentation stage in which yeast continues to break down unwanted fermentation by-products into desired esters alcohol. Conditioning can occur in bottles (bottle conditioning), casks, kegs, and in cold environments (cold conditioning).

craft brewery Small, independent breweries that experiment with a variety of adjuncts such as spices, fruits, and grains, and often produce several beer styles. The legal definition of a craft brewery varies from country to country, but the prime criteria have to do with production volume, ownership, and how much beer is sold on-site.

draft (draught) Beer drawn from a barrel, cask, or keg

fermentable sugars Sugars from wort that can be converted by yeast into ethanol alcohol and carbon dioxide in the brewing process

fermentation The process by which yeast and/or bacterium converts sugars into alcohol, gas, and acids

flocculation The clumping together of yeast once wort has been fermented. High-flocculating yeast is desirable, as it is easier to remove from beer.

grain bill The combination of grains used to brew a batch of beer. Base malts tend to provide fermentable sugars, whereas specialty malts contribute body, color, and flavor to beer.

gruit A mixture of herbs, spices, and fruits historically used for flavoring and bittering ale before hops were used extensively. Also, an ale made with the gruit mixture.

hop The conelike flower of the female hop plant that adds bitterness and aroma to beer

hoppiness Flavor, aroma, and bitterness from hops

hopping Adding hops to wort during the brewing process. Hopping at the beginning of the boil lends to bitterness, while hopping at the end of or after the boil adds flavor and aroma.

imperial A version of a beer style with a heightened ABV. Sometimes called double.

inoculation The introduction of yeast, bacteria, or other microbes into a medium that supports its growth

International Bittering Unit (IBU) A unit that measures the bitterness in a beer. IBUs measure the parts per million of isohumulone, the acid found in hops that adds bitterness to beer.

keg A cylindrical container made of aluminum, steel, or plastic used for storing, transporting, and serving beer under pressure. Sizes vary depending on the country of origin.

lager One of the two major beer types (ale is the other), produced using bottom-fermenting yeast

macrobrewery A large brewery, typically owned by a big beer conglomerate (for example, AB InBev), that brews beer on a large scale—often several million barrels annually

malt The dried, germinated seed from a grain like barley or wheat. Malting a grain develops enzymes required to convert the starch within it into sugars during the brewing process.

mash Malted grains that have been steeped in hot water to activate enzymes and convert the grains' starch into fermentable sugars

microbrewery As defined by the Brewers Association, a brewery that makes fewer than 15,000 U.S. barrels of beer a year, of which 75 percent or more is sold off-site, and that cannot be more than 25 percent owned by another company

mixed fermentation A process in which fermentation occurs as a result of multiple yeast strains and/or bacterium being added to the wort during brewing

mouthfeel Tactile sensations and texture perceived in the mouth. Mouthfeel can include a beer's body, carbonation, and aftertaste.

pint A common style of glass, usually with straight sides and a wide rim. Also a size of beer, which is 20 ounces (591 mL) for an imperial pint, 16 ounces (473 mL) for an American pint, and 15 to 20 ounces (443–591 mL) for an Australian pint.

prohibition Temperance movement, usually at the national scale, that makes the manufacturing, storage, possession, transportation, importation, and/or consumption of alcohol or alcoholic beverages illegal

real ale Beer that is unfiltered, unpasteurized, cask-conditioned, and served without forced carbonation

session/sessionable A beer with a low ABV that is easy to drink for prolonged "sessions" and balanced in flavor

sparging The process of running hot water through grains at the end of the mashing process to extract additional sugars from the grains

spontaneous fermentation A process in which fermentation occurs as a result of naturally occurring airborne yeast strains and bacteria entering the wort

terroir A French word meaning "earth" or "soil" defined by how environmental conditions—soil, precipitation, temperature, and sunshine levels—influence the ingredients grown in a place, and thus the taste and character of its food and drink

top fermentation A process in which fermentation occurs at or near the top of the fermentation vessel where the yeast is floating

wort The liquid extracted from the mash during brewing. It contains dissolved sugars that will be fermented into alcohol.

yeast A single-cell fungus that converts carbohydrates (sugars) into alcohol, carbon dioxide, and a number of compounds that add flavor and aroma to beer

MAPS

MAP ACKNOWLEDGMENTS

17, 18, 19, C. Monfreda, N. Ramankutty, and J. A. Foley, "Farming the Planet: 2. Geographic Distribution of Crop Areas, Yields, Physiological Types, and Net Primary Production in the Year 2000." *Global Biogeochemical Cycles* 22:1 (March 2008): 1–19; 21 Barth-Haas Group, *The Barth Report: Hops 2015/2016.* (Nuremberg: Joh. Barth & Sohn GmbH & Co KG, 2016); 22 World Health Organization Global Health Observatory data, who.int/gho/en; 147 Samuel A. Batzli, "Mapping United States Breweries 1612 to 2011" in *The Geography of Beer,* ed. Mark W. Patterson and Nancy Hoalst-Pullen (New York: Springer, 2014), 31–43; DOI: 10.1007/978-94-007-7787-3; 169 Matthew J. Bellamy, "The Canadian Brewing Industry's Response to Prohibition, 1874–1920." *Brewery History* 132 (2012): 2–17.

BOOKS

Alworth, Jeff. *The Beer Bible: The Essential Beer Lover's Guide.* Workman Publishing Company, 2015.

Bernstein, Joshua. *The Complete Beer Course: Boot Camp for Beer Geeks—From Novice to Expert in Twelve Tasting Classes.* Sterling Epicure, 2013.

Corne, Lucy, and Ryno Reyneke. *African Brew: Exploring the Craft of South African Beer.* Random House Struik, 2014.

Cornell, Martyn. *Amber, Gold and Black: The History of Britain's Great Beers.* History Press, 2010.

———. *Strange Tales of Ale.* Amberley Publishing Limited, 2015.

Hennessey, Jonathan, and Mike Smith. *The Comic Book Story of Beer: The World's Favorite Beverage From 7000 BC to Today's Craft Brewing Revolution.* Ten Speed Press, 2015.

Hornsey, Ian Spencer. *A History of Beer and Brewing.* Royal Society of Chemists, 2003.

Jackson, Michael. *The World Guide to Beer.* New Burlington Books, 1977.

Mosher, Randy. *Radical Brewing: Recipes, Tales and World-Altering Meditations in a Glass.* Brewers Publication, 2004.

Oliver, Garrett. *The Brewmaster's Table: Discovering the Pleasures of Real Beer With Real Food.* Harper Collins, 2010.

———. ed. *The Oxford Companion to Beer.* Oxford University Press, 2011.

Rail, Evan. *Why Beer Matters.* Kindle Single, 2010.

Webb, Tim, and Stephen Beaumont. *The World Atlas of Beer, Revised and Expanded: The Essential Guide to the Beers of the World.* Sterling Epicure, 2016.

WEBSITES

allaboutbeer.com An online magazine featuring news, reviews, and information about beer

beeradvocate.com An online magazine with interesting beer stories, a beer forum, and a beer rating section

beerconnoisseur.com An online magazine and blog with news and reviews on beer throughout the world

beervana.blogspot.com A blog featuring historical and contemporary pieces on all things beer

bjcp.org Beer Judge Certification Program site featuring a comprehensive guide to beer styles and the latest information on becoming a beer judge

brewersassociation.org Trade association site for all the latest information on the U.S. craft brewing industry

brewersofeurope.eu A website containing up-to-date statistics on beer in Europe

brewmistress.co.za The latest and most informative news and reviews on the South African beer culture

cicerone.org Provides information on becoming a cicerone, including the test and tasting requirements

craftbeer.com Reviews, interviews, and news stories on American craft beer

craftypint.com A website covering the Australian craft beer scene, complete with brewer interviews and the latest news

draftmag.com A website with news, beer reviews, and stories on beer

ratebeer.com A website dedicated to beer ratings submitted by beer lovers around the world

zythophile.co.uk A blog by Martyn Cornell featuring informative posts on beer

ACKNOWLEDGMENTS

THIS IS THE STORY OF BEER, told in both big, sweeping motions and with the finest level of detail. Regardless of the place, or time, or thousands of stories that were (or still need to be) told, this book would not be possible without the assistance of many important and special people.

A toast of gratitude goes to Brooklyn Brewery brewmaster Garrett Oliver for bringing his expertise and voice to this project, with his wonderful foreword and beer recommendations that pair well with our story. We are indebted for his help in getting the word out about this project, which has been our labor of love.

We are also indebted to National Geographic and the amazing individuals who worked tirelessly on this project: Robin Terry-Brown, our senior editor and biggest cheerleader, who was with us from start to finish; Barbara Payne, our project manager, who worked tirelessly (yet seemingly effortlessly) on directing this magnum opus; Kate Armstrong, our text editor, who helped bring the best and brightest tone and nuance to our writing; Bob Gray, our designer, and creative director Melissa Farris, who brought such beauty to the book's layout and cover; our photo editors Charles Kogod and Moira Haney, and photo director Susan Blair, whose attention to detail and beauty are evident throughout; and Mike McNey, our cartographer, who built such creative maps. Thank you to Michelle Cassidy for her help with captions, and to Justin Kavanagh for shepherding the book across the finish line. Thanks also to the National Geographic Expedition Council for their support of this project.

We would also like to thank Dr. Christopher Thornton, senior director of cultural heritage at the National Geographic Society, and Dr. Teresa Raczek, associate professor of anthropology at Kennesaw State University, who encouraged us to pursue this project in the first place. Inspiration has to come from somewhere, somehow, and that in and of itself can be quite interesting. Thanks to Tyler and John Hengs for being effervescent in their enthusiasm and accessible with logistical support. Much gratitude to Richard Stueven for giving us his brewery data to map.

After traveling more than 160,000 miles in a little over a year, we would be remiss not to thank the 400-plus brewers, owners, general managers, and other beer people we had the sincere privilege to meet along the way. You let us crash parties, talk politics, get sneak peeks, and drink straight from the fermentation tanks. You gave us recommendations on where to go next, whom to talk to, and even where to sleep (shout-out to Shoreline Brewery, New Holland Brewing Company, and Ulla and Fred at the Sundance Center). To all who create, package, store, sell, and drink beer—you make the beer culture what it is today. Thanks for telling us your stories.

Much gratitude to Tommy Tainsh from Trinity Brewhouse in Rhode Island for giving us the initial idea that morphed into the Beer It Forward program—giving a beer and getting one in return. Your idea defines our belief to act globally and drink locally. On that note, a big thanks to Roger Davis and the gang at Red Hare Brewing Company and Scott Hedeen at Burnt Hickory Brewery for being our biggest Beer It Forward contributors and allowing us to share your local brews worldwide. We are also grateful to Thomas Monti from Schoolhouse Beer and Brewing for his advice, suggestions, and beer.

Thanks to the various interpreters and new friends who helped us with many of these interviews and gave us an insider's look at the local beer scene: Sergio from Chile, Nicolás from Argentina, Dandarah from Brazil, and Huanbi, Jennifer, and Samuel from China.

NANCY HOALST-PULLEN, Ph.D
MARK W. PATTERSON, Ph.D

National Geographic Explorers Nancy Hoalst-Pullen and Mark W. Patterson are known as "the Beer Doctors." Hoalst-Pullen is a professor of geography and the director of the Geographic Information Science program at Kennesaw State University in Georgia. She earned her Ph.D. from the University of Colorado Boulder and has co-authored and co-edited several books, chapters, and articles on beer with Patterson. Patterson is a professor of geography at Kennesaw State University and earned his Ph.D. from the University of Arizona. He is an avid homebrewer and has published several books with Hoalst-Pullen, including *The Geography of Beer.* Together, they teach a university class called "The Geography of Beer, Wine, and Liquor," take students on beer-related study abroad trips, and host beer tastings aimed at educating people on the geography behind the beer.

GARRETT OLIVER
Brooklyn Brewery Brewmaster

Garrett Oliver is one of the world's foremost authorities on the subject of beer. He is the brewmaster at Brooklyn Brewery, editor in chief of *The Oxford Companion to Beer,* author of *The Brewmaster's Table,* and winner of the 2014 James Beard Award for Outstanding Wine, Beer, or Spirits Professional. Oliver has traveled the globe exploring exceptional beer and food pairings and has been a fearless innovator in the world of craft brewing. He's made beer with fresh sugarcane in Brazil, come up with new types of wheat beer in Germany, and invented the new culture of collaborative brewing. Over the past 25 years, Oliver has judged beer competitions such as the Great American Beer Festival and the Great British Beer Festival, and he has hosted more than 1,000 beer tastings, dinners, and cooking demonstrations in 16 countries.

ILLUSTRATIONS CREDITS

Front cover: (globe woodcut), Steven Noble; (label and star), Nimaxs/Shutterstock; (barley and hops), vso/Shutterstock. Spine: (bottle), iStock-Allaksel_7799. Back cover: (coasters), ullstein bild/Getty Images; (tap), iStock-bubaone; (wind rose), iStock-LongQuattro; (glass), iStock-Allaksel_7799; (bottle and opener), iStock-Ivan_Mogilevchik; 1, kokoroyuki/Getty Images; 2-3, Matthias Jung/Stern/laif/Redux Pictures; 4, Miquel Gonzalez/laif/Redux; 5, CactuSoup/Getty Images; 8, Courtesy Brooklyn Brewery; 9, Vitaliy Piltser Photography; 10, Scott Suchman; 11, Mark W. Patterson and Nancy Hoalst-Pullen; 14, Thinkstock/Getty Images; 15, julichka/Getty Images; 16, Danita Delimont/Getty Images; 17 (UP), Avalon_Studio/Getty Images; 17 (CTR), tuchkovo/Getty Images; 17 (LO), Avalon_Studio/Getty Images; 18 (A), anna1311/Getty Images; 18 (B), DustyPixel/Getty Images; 18 (C), AlasdairJames/Getty Images; 18 (D), kuarmungadd/Getty Images; 18 (E), IMAGEMORE Co., Ltd./Getty Images; 19, seregam/Getty Images; 20, Mark Stewart/Camera Press/Redux Pictures; 24-5, Abie McLaughlin; 25, ullstein bild/Getty Images; 26-7, MyLoupe/Getty Images; 28, Crouch/Getty Images; 30 (UP), ullstein bild/Getty Images; 30 (LO), Greg Dale/National Geographic Creative; 32, Photoevent/Getty Images; 33, Mark W. Patterson and Nancy Hoalst-Pullen; 34, Frederik Buyckx/The New York Times/Redux Pictures; 36, Merlin Meuris/Reporters/Redux Pictures; 36-7, Mattia Zoppellaro/contrasto/Redux Pictures; 38-9, indigolotos/Getty Images; 38, Hemis/Alamy Stock Photo; 39, Christoph Papsch/laif/Redux Pictures; 40 (A), Tony Briscoe/Getty Images; 40 (B), Tony Briscoe/Getty Images; 40 (C), Josef Hanus/Alamy Stock Photo; 40 (D), Floortje/Getty Images; 40 (E), Dorling Kindersley Ltd./Alamy Stock Photo; 40 (F), julichka/Getty Images; 40 (G), Dirk Olaf Wexel/StockFood; 40 (H), panossgeorgiou/Getty Images; 40 (I), tab62/Shutterstock; 42, Jock Fistick/The New York Times/Redux Pictures; 43, Arterra Picture Library/Alamy Stock Photo; 44, orpheus26/Getty Images; 46, Tyler Hengs; 47, Deleu/age fotostock; 48, Arterra Picture Library/Alamy Stock Photo; 49, Dave Bartruff/Getty Images; 50, Arpad Benedek/Getty Images; 52, Erol Gurian/laif/Redux Pictures; 54, indigolotos/Getty Images; 55, Jens Schwarz/laif/Redux Pictures; 56, ullstein bild/Getty Images; 58 (LE), Mark W. Patterson and Nancy

Hoalst-Pullen; 58 (CTR), Mark W. Patterson and Nancy Hoalst-Pullen; 58 (RT), Julie g Woodhouse/Alamy Stock Photo; 60, canadastock/Shutterstock; 61, Zoonar GmbH/Alamy Stock Photo; 63, Gordon Welters/laif/Redux Pictures; 64, Matteo Colombo/Getty Images; 66, © SIME/eStock Photo; 69, Bikeworldtravel/Shutterstock; 70–71, indigolotos/Getty Images; 70 (RT), FOR ALAN/Alamy Stock Photo; 71, Wikimedia Commons/Public Domain; 72, ullstein bild/Getty Images; 74 (LE), Bigred/Alamy Stock Photo; 74 (CTR UP), f4foto/Alamy Stock Photo; 74 (CTR LO), Billy Stock/Shutterstock; 74 (RT), John Sones/Getty Images; 75, Adrian Pingstone/Wikimedia Commons/Public Domain; 76, Craig Joiner/age fotostock; 77, FALKENSTEINFOTO/Alamy Stock Photo; 79, Jim Richardson/National Geographic Creative; 80, © SIME/eStock Photo; 82, ullstein bild/Getty Images; 83, CTK/Alamy Stock Photo; 84, Mark W. Patterson and Nancy Hoalst-Pullen; 85 (LE), Matt Cardy/Getty Images; 85 (CTR), Sergi Reboredo/VWPics/Redux Pictures; 85 (RT), Mark W. Patterson and Nancy Hoalst-Pullen; 86, Peter Forsberg/Alamy Stock Photo; 88, © Huber/SIME/eStock Photo; 90 (UP), ullstein bild/Getty Images; 90 (LO), Gilles Rolle/REA/Redux Pictures; 91, Stephane Remael/The New York Times/Redux Pictures; 92 (LE), iAlf/Getty Images; 92 (CTR), Joel Philippon/Courtesy Pico'Mousse; 92 (RT), Boris Stroujko/Shutterstock; 93, Courtesy Autour d'une Bière; 95, bbsferrari/Getty Images; 96, Design Pics Inc./Getty Images; 98, ullstein bild/Getty Images; 99, Christophe Boisvieux/Getty Images; 100 (LE), Joel Carillet/Getty Images; 100 (CTR), Barry Mason/Alamy Stock Photo; 100 (RT), Mark W. Patterson and Nancy Hoalst-Pullen; 101, genekrebs/Getty Images; 103, © SOPA/eStock Photo; 104, jenifoto/Getty Images; 106, ullstein bild/Getty Images; 107, Stefano G. Pavesi/Contrasto/Redux Pictures; 108 (LE), Onfokus/Getty Images; 108 (CTR), Xantana/Getty Images; 108 (RT), riccardo bianchi/age fotostock; 109, RossHelen/Getty Images; 110, ArtMarie/Getty Images; 112, Gerald Haenel/laif/Redux Pictures; 114, Imagno/Getty Images; 116, © SIME/eStock Photo; 118, Sven Nackstrand/Getty Images; 120, © SIME/eStock Photo; 122 (UP), ullstein bild/Getty Images; 122 (LO), Marco De Swart/EPA; 124, © SIME/eStock Photo; 126, Mark W. Patterson and Nancy Hoalst-Pullen; 128, © Huber/SIME/eStock Photo; 130, Fine Art Images/Getty Images; 132, Monica Gumm/laif/Redux Pictures; 134, ullstein bild/Getty Images; 136–7, Valentyn Volkov/Shutterstock; 138–9, Brian Jannsen/Alamy Stock Photo; 140, Everett Collection/age fotostock; 142, ullstein bild/Getty Images; 143, Mark W. Patterson and Nancy Hoalst-Pullen; 144, PLAINVIEW/Getty Images; 145, Boone Rodriguez/age fotostock; 146, Scott Suchman; 149, Cyrus McCrimmon/Getty Images; 150–51, indigolotos/Getty Images; 150, alexdrim/Shutterstock; 151, Mark W. Patterson and Nancy Hoalst-Pullen; 152–3, Andrea Johnson Photography; 153, Jamie Pham/Alamy Stock Photo; 154, Mark W. Patterson and Nancy Hoalst-Pullen; 156, sharply_done/Getty Images; 157, Sergei_Aleshin/Getty Images; 159 (UP), kjschoen/Getty Images; 159 (LO), Photo © Brewers Association; 160–61, Jodi Hilton/The New York Times/Redux Pictures; 162, Philip Kramer/Getty Images; 163 (UP), Mark W. Patterson and Nancy Hoalst-Pullen; 163 (LO), Mark W. Patterson and Nancy Hoalst-Pullen; 164, Randy Duchaine/Alamy Stock Photo; 165, Jaak Nilson/age fotostock; 166, Kate Russell/The New York Times/Redux Pictures; 167, tomwachs/Getty Images; 168, Songquan Deng/Shutterstock; 170, ullstein bild/Getty Images; 171, Mark W. Patterson and Nancy Hoalst-Pullen; 172, Andreas Hub/laif/Redux Pictures; 173, NielsVK3/Alamy Stock Photo; 175, ImagineGolf/Getty Images; 176, Lucas Vallecillos/age fotostock; 178 (UP), ullstein bild/Getty Images; 178 (LO), Eric Futran—Chefshots/Getty Images; 179, Kevin J. Miyazaki/Redux Pictures; 180 (LE), Christian Heeb/laif/Redux Pictures; 180 (RT), benedek/Getty Images; 181 (LE), visualspace/Getty Images; 181 (RT), Lucas Vallecillos/VWPics/Redux Pictures; 182, Courtesy Rob Kelly/Baja Brewing Company; 184, Anna RubaK/Shutterstock; 185 (UP), Givaga/Getty Images; 185 (LO), Olivier Le Queinec/Shutterstock; 186–7, Donatas Dabravolskas/Shutterstock; 188, Print Collector/Getty Images; 190 (UP), ullstein bild/Getty Images; 190 (LO), Jeremy Hudson/Getty Images; 191, Andres A Ruffo/Getty Images; 192, © SIME/eStock Photo; 194 (UP), ullstein bild/Getty Images; 194 (LO), eugenegurkov/Shutterstock; 195, Mark W. Patterson and Nancy Hoalst-Pullen; 196 (LE), Alex Joukowski/Getty Images; 196 (RT), Mark W. Patterson and Nancy Hoalst-Pullen; 197 (LE), Mark W. Patterson and Nancy Hoalst-Pullen; 197 (RT), Christian Goupi/age fotostock; 198, Yadid Levy/Anzenberger/Redux Pictures; 200, Heeb/laif/Redux Pictures; 202, ullstein bild/Getty Images; 203, Jon Hicks/Getty Images; 204 (LE), Mickael David/age fotostock; 204 (RT), Global_Pics/Getty Images; 206–207, Mark W. Patterson and Nancy Hoalst-Pullen; 208, Yadid Levy/Alamy Stock Photo; 210, Mark W. Patterson and Nancy Hoalst-Pullen; 212 (UP), Tegestology/Alamy Stock Photo; 212 (CTR LE), neil setchfield - objects/Alamy Stock Photo; 212 (CTR RT), neil setchfield - objects/Alamy Stock Photo; 212 (LO), claudiodivizia/Getty Images; 212–13, claudiodivizia/Getty Images; 213 (UP LE), Tegestology/Alamy Stock Photo; 213 (UP RT), claudiodivizia/Getty Images; 213 (LO LE), claudiodivizia/Getty Images; 213 (LO RT), Tegestology/Alamy Stock Photo; 214-5, © Weerapong Chaipuck/500px Prime; 216, akg-images; 218, ullstein bild/Getty Images; 219, Sim Chi Yin/The New York Times/Redux Pictures; 220, inhauscreative/Getty Images; 222, SeanPavonePhoto/Getty Images; 224 (UP), ullstein bild/Getty Images; 224 (LO), Mark Leong/Redux Pictures; 226 (UP), Mark W. Patterson and Nancy Hoalst-Pullen; 226 (LO), Daniel Case/Wikimedia Commons; 227, Mark W. Patterson and Nancy Hoalst-Pullen; 228, yongyuan/Getty Images; 229, Mark W. Patterson and Nancy Hoalst-Pullen; 230, jiratto/Getty Images; 232 (UP), ullstein bild/Getty Images; 232 (LO), Iain Masterton/Alamy Stock Photo; 233, © The Craftbeer Association and BeerFes®; 234 (LE), Bloomberg/Getty Images; 234 (CTR), JTB Media Creation, Inc./Alamy Stock Photo; 234 (RT), Trevor Mogg/Alamy Stock Photo; 235, Mark W. Patterson and Nancy Hoalst-Pullen; 237, fotoVoyager/Getty Images; 238, © SIME/eStock Photo; 240, Marco Bulgarelli/LUZphoto/Redux Pictures; 242, www.jethuynh.com/Getty Images; 244, TRV/imagerover.com/Alamy Stock Photo; 246 (LE), Nerthuz/Getty Images; 246 (RT), jimmyjamesbond/Getty Images; 247, Nerthuz/Getty Images; 248–9, Howard Kingsnorth/Getty Images; 250, State Library of Queensland/Public Domain; 252 (UP), ullstein bild/Getty Images; 252 (LO), Ralph Smith/Getty Images; 253, Courtesy GABS Beer, Cider and Food Fest; 254, Na Gen Imaging/Getty Images; 256, ullstein bild/Getty Images; 257, Travelscape Images/Alamy Stock Photo; 258 (LE), Mark W. Patterson and Nancy Hoalst-Pullen; 258 (RT), Jacqueline Jane van Grootel/Courtesy Feral Brewing Company; 259, Visions of Victoria; 261, © SIME/eStock Photo; 262, CSP_muha04/age fotostock; 264, ullstein bild/Getty Images; 265, Mark W. Patterson and Nancy Hoalst-Pullen; 266 (LE), Greg Balfour Evans/Alamy Stock Photo; 266 (CTR), Mark W. Patterson and Nancy Hoalst-Pullen; 266 (RT), ONEWORLD PICTURE/Alamy Stock Photo; 267 (LE), Tim Cuff/Alamy Stock Photo; 267 (RT), Mark W. Patterson and Nancy Hoalst-Pullen; 268, Tim Cuff/Alamy Stock Photo; 270 (LE), Sergiy Kuzmin/Shutterstock; 270 (RT), sumnersgraphicsinc/Getty Images; 271 (LE), Nitr/Shutterstock; 271 (RT), gresei/Shutterstock; 272–3, Dietmar Temps, Cologne/Getty Images; 274, Melville Chater/National Geographic Creative; 276 (UP), ullstein bild/Getty Images; 276 (LO), grandriver/Getty Images; 277, Brett Magill/joburgbrew.com; 278, Mark W. Patterson and Nancy Hoalst-Pullen; 280 (UP), ullstein bild/Getty Images; 280 (LO), Gallo Images/Getty Images; 281, Greatstock/Alamy Stock Photo; 282 (LE), Mark W. Patterson and Nancy Hoalst-Pullen; 282 (RT), Mark W. Patterson and Nancy Hoalst-Pullen; 283 (UP), Mark W. Patterson and Nancy Hoalst-Pullen; 283 (LO), wildacad/Getty Images; 284, Hemis/Alamy Stock Photo; 285, Mark W. Patterson and Nancy Hoalst-Pullen; 286, Steve Outram/Getty Images; 288, Blinkcatcher/age fotostock; 290–91, kyoshino/Getty Images.

Since 1888, the National Geographic Society has funded more than 12,000 research, exploration, and preservation projects around the world. National Geographic Partners distributes a portion of the funds it receives from your purchase to National Geographic Society to support programs including the conservation of animals and their habitats.

National Geographic Partners
1145 17th Street NW
Washington, DC 20036-4688 USA

Become a member of National Geographic and activate your benefits today at natgeo.com/jointoday.

For information about special discounts for bulk purchases, please contact National Geographic Books Special Sales: specialsales@natgeo.com

For rights or permissions inquiries, please contact National Geographic Books Subsidiary Rights: bookrights@natgeo.com

Library of Congress Cataloging-in-Publication Data
Names: Hoalst-Pullen, Nancy, author. | Patterson, Mark (Professor of geography), author. | National Geographic Society (U.S.), Issuing body.
Title: National Geographic atlas of beer : a globe-trotting journey through the world of beer / Nancy Hoalst-Pullen & Mark W. Patterson.
Other titles: Atlas of beer
Description: Washington, D.C. : National Geographic, [2017] | Includes bibliographical references and index.
Identifiers: LCCN 2017011583 | ISBN 9781426218330 (hardcover : alk. paper)
Subjects: LCSH: Beer--Guidebooks. | Breweries--Guidebooks.
Classification: LCC TP577 .H64 2017 | DDC 663/.42--dc23
LC record available at https://lccn.loc.gov/2017011583

Printed in Hong Kong

17/THK/1